D1320996

Spitfire Girl

Spitfire Girl

An Extraordinary Life in the Shadows of
War and a Century in the Making

DIANA MACKINTOSH
AND DOUGLAS THOMPSON

First published in 2020 by Ad Lib Publishers Ltd
15 Church Road
London, SW13 9HE

www.adlibpublishers.com

Text © 2020 Diana Mackintosh and Douglas Thompson

ISBN 978-1-913543-78-5

All rights reserved. No part of this publication may be reproduced in any form or by any means – electronic, mechanical, photocopying, recording, or otherwise – or stored in any retrieval system of any nature without prior written permission from the copyright holders. Diana Mackintosh and Douglas Thompson have asserted their moral rights to be identified as the authors of this work in accordance with the Copyright, Designs and Patents Act of 1988.

A CIP catalogue record for this book is available
from the British Library.

Every reasonable effort has been made to trace copyright-holders of material reproduced in this book, but if any have been inadvertently overlooked the publishers would be glad to hear from them.

Printed in the UK

10 9 8 7 6 5 4 3 2 1

For my boys, in order of appearance:
Ian, Cameron, Robert and Nicky

DIANA MACKINTOSH, at 101, remains as cool and collected as she was when using a Spitfire as a wartime taxi, and socialising with the Queen and the royalty of British cinema, Hollywood and theatreland.

DOUGLAS THOMPSON is the author of many non-fiction books covering an eclectic mix of subjects from major Hollywood biographies to revelatory bestsellers about remarkable people and events. An author, broadcaster and international journalist, he is a regular contributor to major newspapers and magazines worldwide. With Christine Keeler, he wrote her revealing memoir *The Truth at Last*. That instant bestseller was revised as *Secrets and Lies: The Trials of Christine Keeler* and the 2020 audio version recorded by actress Sophie Cookson who played Christine to critical acclaim in the successful BBC television series. His works, published in a dozen languages, include the television-based anthology *Hollywood People*, and a best-selling biography of Clint Eastwood. He collaborated with Michael Flatley on his *Sunday Times* bestseller *Lord of the Dance*. Douglas is a director of one of Britain's best-loved literary festivals, and he divides his time between a medieval Suffolk village and California, where he was based as a Fleet Street correspondent and columnist for more than twenty years.

www.dougiethompson.com

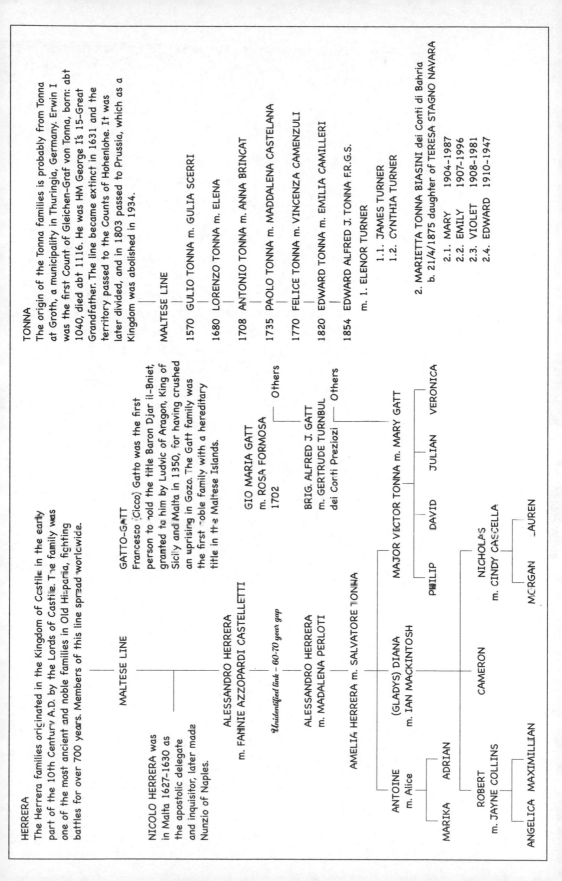

HERRERA

The Herrera families originated in the Kingdom of Castile in the early part of the 10th Century A.D. by the Lords of Castile. The family was one of the most ancient and noble families in Old Hispania, fighting battles for over 700 years. Members of this line spread worldwide.

MALTESE LINE

NICOLO HERRERA was in Malta 1627-1630 as the apostolic delegate and inquisitor, later made Nunzio of Naples.

ALESSANDRO HERRERA
m. FANNIE AZZOPARDI CASTELLETTI

Unidentified link – 60-70 year gap

ALESSANDRO HERRERA
m. MADALENA PERLOTI

AMELIA HERRERA m. SALVATORE TONNA

ANTOINE
m. Alice
— MARIKA
— ADRIAN

(GLADYS) DIANA
m. IAN MACKINTOSH

MAJOR VICTOR TONNA m. MARY GATT
— PHILIP
— DAVID
— JULIAN
— VERONICA

CAMERON
— ROBERT
  m. JAYNE COLLINS
  — ANGELICA
  — MAXIMILLIAN

NICHOLAS
m. CINDY CASCELLA
— MORGAN
— LAUREN

GATTO-GATT

Francesco (Cicco) Gatto was the first person to hold the title Baron Djar il-Bniet, granted to him by Ludvic of Aragon, King of Sicily and Malta in 1350, for having crushed an uprising in Gozo. The Gatt family was the first noble family with a hereditary title in the Maltese Islands.

GIO MARIA GATT
m. ROSA FORMOSA
1702
— Others

BRIG. ALFRED J. GATT
m. GERTRUDE TURNBUL
dei Corti Preziozi
— Others

TONNA

The origin of the Tonna families is probably from Tonna at Groth, a municipality in Thuringia, Germany. Erwin I was the first Count of Gleichen-Graf von Tonna, born: abt 1040, died abt 1116. He was HM George I's 15-Great Grandfather. The line became extinct in 1631 and the territory passed to the Counts of Hohenlohe. It was later divided, and in 1803 passed to Prussia, which as a Kingdom was abolished in 1934.

MALTESE LINE

1570 GULIO TONNA m. GULIA SCERRI

1680 LORENZO TONNA m. ELENA

1708 ANTONIO TONNA m. ANNA BRINCAT

1735 PAOLO TONNA m. MADDALENA CASTELANA

1770 FELICE TONNA m. VINCENZA CAMENZULI

1820 EDWARD TONNA m. EMILIA CAMILLERI

1854 EDWARD ALFRED J. TONNA F.R.G.S.
m. 1. ELENOR TURNER
  1.1. JAMES TURNER
  1.2. CYNTHIA TURNER

2. MARIETTA TONNA BIASINI dei Conti di Bahria
b. 21/4/1875 daughter of TERESA STAGNO NAVARA
  2.1. MARY   1904-1987
  2.2. EMILY   1907-1996
  2.3. VIOLET   1908-1981
  2.4. EDWARD   1910-1947

Map 5

St Paul's Bay

Takali

Citta Vecchia

Rabat

MALTA
Showing airfields in Spring 1941

0   1   2
Scale of Miles

Legend

Airfields

Flying-boat base

Flying-boat alighting area

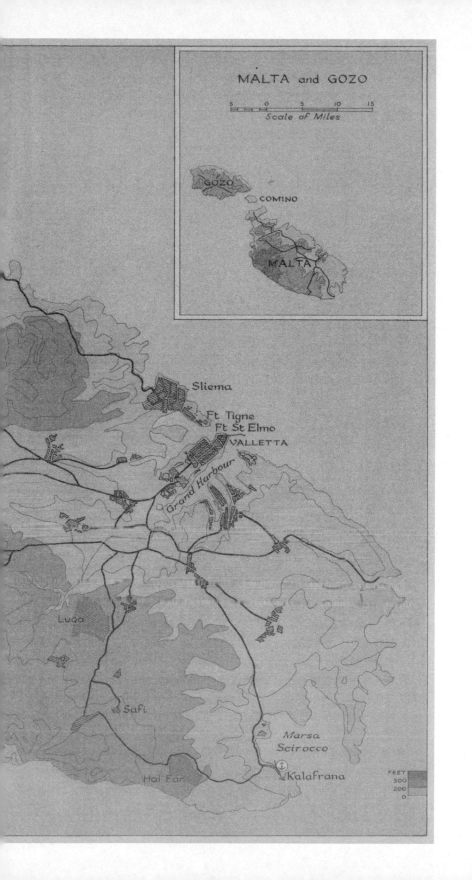

MALTA and GOZO

Scale of Miles

GOZO

COMINO

MALTA

Sliema

Ft Tigne
Ft St Elmo
VALLETTA

Grand Harbour

Luqa

Safi

Marsa
Scirocco

Kalafrana

Hal Far

FEET
500
200
0

CONTENTS

ACKNOWLEDGEMENTS

Before I attempt to thank all those who have been kind to me in life, which includes almost everyone mentioned in this book other than Hitler and Mussolini and that sort, I must offer a disclaimer. Although I was present at all the events reported on in my story, life around me has always been fast and furious; so certain facts and situations, such as exactly how close we all were in Malta to being bombed out of existence, the wartime heroics of the man I married, and the sometimes glamorous surroundings where I occasionally found myself, were just me getting on with life as it came to me. With the help of my sons, other members of family and friends and the patient ears of Douglas Thompson, I have been able to weave the long journey of my life together with the facts and statistics of the past into *Spitfire Girl* to give, with the gift of hindsight and a memory that's still in fair order, the context to my involvement with some extraordinary events.

So, my deepest thanks to everyone who has been a part of my life, my boys of course and all the members of my family in my native Malta, as well as in the United Kingdom. All the friends of my past and present who have been a part of my life, some who are still around like me, and others – just as important – who are waiting for us to catch them up later.

Diana Mackintosh, London, April 2020

Having kept a close eye on the progress of Diana's extraordinary journey, I realised that, rather like our mother, it is still going on and one story often reminds us of another. So, if there's enough material – and time – we might have to look at a Volume Two. Meanwhile, I have taken it upon myself to be the family 'editor', to ensure there is a plausible credence between a good story and exaggeration. A hundred years can play havoc with the truth. So if there are any complaints from anyone living or dead, you can blame me. But you may have to deal with Diana in either case.

Robert Mackintosh, 2020

LAST MAN STANDING

'I can be very stubborn.
They say that about Malta too.'
DIANA MACKINTOSH,
JANUARY 2019

The Great Siege of Malta in 1565 rather set the precedent.

It was a remarkable victory, with the Knights Hospitaller and their part-time army overcoming massive enemy forces on land and sea.

This siege, a confrontation of unspeakable brutality, was one of the bloodiest battles ever fought. Historically, it was a fight for the survival of Christianity. For the island of Malta, it was another struggle to hold on to their little piece of dirt and rock. But if vitally strategic Malta fell, the Muslim Ottoman Empire would swiftly dominate the entire Mediterranean. Even Rome was in peril.

Sultan Suleiman controlled the greatest fighting force in the world and had an armada of two hundred ships and an army of forty thousand troops when he launched his battle against the Knights. He planned to destroy Malta and the Knights of St John. Suleiman the Magnificent wanted world control.

On 18 May, all hell was unleashed with a Turkish artillery bombardment and, with unholy horror, the onslaught of wave after wave of screaming scimitar-wielding cavalry. Champion of Malta, Grand Master Jean Parisot de la Valette, vowed that the island would not be taken as long as one Christian lived there. It was close: six hundred knights, several thousand local peasants and mercenaries, and a couple of thousand Maltese irregulars defeated the larger and supposedly overwhelming enemy force. After more than thirty thousand Turks were killed, the Ottomans withdrew and the Knights celebrated victory on 8 September 1565.

The triumph of the Great Siege of Malta is an integral part of world military history. In the three years following, Grand Master de la Valette planned and built the great port and fortress city of Valletta. He died in 1568, a hunting accident of all things, and never saw his great project completed. He is buried in the city that has his name.

The Ottomans never returned in force.

Others did.

INTRODUCTION: THERE'S NOTHING LIKE A DAME

'All the world's a stage,
And all the men and women merely players,
They have their exits and their entrances,
And one man in his time plays many parts.'
WILLIAM SHAKESPEARE,
AS YOU LIKE IT, ACT II,
SCENE VII (FIRST PUBLISHED 1623)

Sir Cameron Mackintosh celebrated his seventieth birthday on 19 October 2016, two days after the day itself, and the cast of his latest triumph, *Half a Sixpence*, surprised him with a lively song-and-dance number at his own Noël Coward Theatre. There was much more flash-bang-wallop later that evening, when lavish tributes and partying began at an open-air party in central London. It was a grand affair, with much music, singing and dancing, as befitted a man also marking half a century in show business. He had centre stage; yet many were transfixed by one other enthusiastic celebrant. She was intent on enjoying herself. At one point, her dance partner, the singer Michael Ball, had to ask her to slow down her quick steps. Young dancers wondered who the guest was.

'Oh, that's Cameron's mother,' they were told. The answer resulted in disbelief and awe and mystified arithmetic.

Indeed, the indefatigable Diana Mackintosh was, as ever, intent on enjoying every last moment of the evening. When she returned from a holiday a few weeks earlier, she complained to me about her companions: 'All they wanted to do was eat and sleep.'

Which is more telling when you listen to her middle son, Robert Mackintosh, who explains: 'Diana doesn't like to travel with people more than sixty years old; she says they slow her down.'

And that is her only taboo. She won't slow down. Diana Mackintosh is all about the business of getting on with getting on. Her eyes pass over obstacles – in order to fix on opportunities. I have no precedent for her. Her home in St John's Wood, London, is elegant and tall, with several sets of stairs. When I first began visiting her there, I made the error of attempting to help with tea trays. It was made clear that she would most happily carry the tray, with full china tea service and gluten-free walnut cake, up and down the stairs herself. I'm now allowed to help, but only because she knows that I know she doesn't need it.

She has a fierce pride in being capable – and I don't believe it is simply to do with defying age, but a legacy of when being so was truly a matter of life and death. Diana came of age to the drone of sirens alerting the people of Malta to the arrival of relentless flights of belligerent German and Italian menace – the bombers she first imagined as a swarm of black flies, pests that stung and cursed her Mediterranean homeland. The three-year onslaught never took a day off; it was endless, but supplies were not. The hope of a shipment of high protein became an endless dream. The only time Diana wasn't hungry was when she slept, but that was intermittent, and the terrible hunger returned the instant the bombs woke the skies and all those beneath them. The explosions cracked and hurt the senses like punches in her empty stomach. Her story of that time, and she is now one of the few remaining who experienced it first-hand, makes you clearly understand why Malta was collectively awarded the George Cross, the highest British civilian honour for heroism. Of course, as she argues, no one was trying to be heroic. They became so by displaying remarkable hidden strength and, with their endurance, shifting the balance of the Second World War in the Mediterranean and North Africa.

As is her mission, Diana moved on from the events, the suffering the twentieth-century Great Siege of Malta inflicted on the island, and has never really spoken of the war in detail. The wartime British officer she would marry, Ian Mackintosh – badly shelled at Dunkirk and blown about by bombs in the Egyptian desert during Montgomery's rout of Rommel – was equally reticent about his extraordinary wartime experiences.

It was only after his death in 1996 that other combatants in those campaigns told his sons the stories of their father's bravery at Dunkirk and in the North African campaigns, one recounting how Ian Mackintosh had saved his life. In the aftermath of epic events, there are always the stories of individual endurance and triumph, tales that fortify us all.

Yet although Diana's war was quite an apprenticeship, it was only that – a dramatic start to an extraordinary, high-energy life.

In 2020, she retains about her the conjuring confidence of, appropriately, a Mary Poppins, always present at the right time, with the magic act or word to juggle if not absolutely solve the problem of the moment. She displays a nimble choreography with the difficult people and times in her life. As I said, she is fiercely independent, thriving, often driving her sons to distraction and herself to the shops, whizzing about London for lunch with friends, scuba diving and sailing, precise in dress, make-up and manner and hugely entertaining. She's one of those lucky people whom you can't ever imagine not being at their best. One agreeable attraction is that she projects a happy message; a healthy, full life we can envy and aspire to getting, perhaps, a sliver of. That, and her mischief, automatically enchants. She's special, but not because of her longevity, rather for the joyful manner in which she has scored a century, a feat perhaps explained by remarkable genetics, a Mediterranean outlook on life and lifestyle, and a charming bloody-mindedness to get on with life, no matter what.

Indeed, the formal message from the Queen has already found a private space in her hallway. They actually first met in Malta, where Diana was born, and the Queen spent 'some of the happiest days of my life' in the immediate post-war years, when Prince Philip was a naval lieutenant stationed on the island. They were young women with untold lifetimes ahead; yet, even then, Diana had an abundance of stories to tell. But there are so many more. It is a life of three acts: despite the ambushes and occasional elephants in the room, she organised her own stage direction with a vigorous sincerity that seems to leap out with a personality all of its own. She is great company, with a shrewd appreciation of the eccentricities of human nature. I believe her readers will find it instructive and joyful – as well as, at times, heartbreaking and moving – to spend time with her, and to be all the better for knowing her and her remarkable family.

Douglas Thompson, Lavenham, Suffolk, 2020

A NOTE FROM ROBERT MACKINTOSH

Being the middle brother gave me a particular perspective on family life that was certainly colourful. Cameron, at an early age, had already formed a strong and wilful character, as I recall when things didn't necessarily go according to his wishes – like lying down dead in the hallway to ensure sufficient notice was taken of his plight. However, he soon got bored as everyone simply walked around or over him. I think Cameron and our mother were very similar in temperament – as Sinatra sang it, 'My Way' or no way… To be fair, Diana had three boys to bring up, with a fourth in Dad, who tended to live a somewhat parallel life. I know it was a challenge.

With Cameron at boarding schools from the age of eleven and Nicky eight-and-a-half years younger than him, I observed, in my pre-teen years, the colourful combination of my parents' Mediterranean and Scottish blood, with a large helping of very loud Louis Armstrong – often played beyond human hearing. The household was certainly full of theatrics in temperament, if not actual theatre; but for us three boys it was a rehearsal for our lives ahead, in terms of our individual and joint love for food, music and, in one brother's case, the theatre.

While one could observe that Ian and Diana were an unlikely match of extremes, I truly believe that it gave us a wonderful balance and interest in the wider world. We were introduced to so much as a part of their vibrant daily lives, even though there were many turbulent times in the mix. At an age when the background of music was rock 'n' roll (daring to put Louis to one side!), Diana was definitely the 'rock' in our family life.

Like most families of our generation – an era without iPad or smartphone distractions – it was a time when you all sat together and a name, a remark, sparked off a 'Remember when…' or 'Whatever happened to so-and-so?' During the past twenty years, that has more often been about our dad, Ian ('Spike' to his music friends), who was quite a character – as well documented by fellow musicians and others. Our mother, Diana, started (probably from an occasional prod from all of us) to write down some of those moments in her long life with Dad, before and after, in no particular order and on various pieces of paper, which would then be tucked away in various drawers. This was also partly encouraged in case she (or we) began to forget them. When suddenly realising that her extraordinary age could no longer be hidden (by her), and the occasional 'innocent' defacing of the passport page displaying her true date of birth was now prevented by the new-style digital passport, we urged her to cease being coy about her real age, gather the notes she had hidden away and fill in the gaps. My good friend Douglas's 'A' list subjects probably seemed like far more daunting characters from which to extract the truth, but may now seem like a walk in the park in comparison to taking on the extraordinary life of Diana Mackintosh. Especially as, on her first encounter with her co-author Douglas, she immediately exclaimed (at ninety-seven years of age): 'Who would be interested in me? Anyway, I am looking at flights to Switzerland… I should be dead… How dare they charge such prices? Cameron's office will have to book it for me …'

Read on if you dare.

Robert Mackintosh, Somerset,
England, April 2020

PROLOGUE: GOOD KNIGHT

'Never in the field of human conflict has so much been owed by so many to so few.'
BRITISH PRIME MINISTER WINSTON CHURCHILL, 20 AUGUST 1940

Valletta, Malta, 2017

For the young Diana Mackintosh, he was a 'Galahad with a Spitfire and lovely long, blond hair'. To Winston Churchill and other leaders, he was the most valuable pilot in the RAF during the Second World War. Adrian 'Warby' Warburton is legendary for the daredevil starring role he played during the defence of Malta. Today, a reel of 6mm film, fragments of aircraft wreckage and a piece of his flying boot are on display at the Malta Aviation Museum; it is a celebration of the man and, tragically, all that is left – other than his exploits – to remember him by. A path of neat sandstone takes you to the three hangars comprising the museum on the site of the former RAF airfield at Ta' Qali village in the centre of the island. There are clusters of historic aircraft on display, variously being restored, preserved and in flying order.

Yet the story of Wing Commander Adrian Warburton pulls you dramatically back to earth. Diana Mackintosh has a photograph of her wartime self, a heyday Ava Gardner lookalike, relaxing on the beach with him. They dated: she was a good Catholic girl; he was a little too keen. They had fun, nevertheless – parties, dances, conversations. Yet, as so many wartime friendships would, he brought heartache. And Warburton's demise was all the more hurtful. He vanished. No one knew what had happened to him.

For Diana, like everyone else who knew Warburton, it was a nagging puzzle that was all the more irritating because believing the inevitable was going to hurt more. Better to be mystified. It took nearly six decades for the answer.

Warburton, who'd gone to school with other *Boy's Own* heroes, 'Dambuster' Guy Gibson and Douglas Bader, had reluctantly accepted a posting as the RAF Liaison Officer to the 7th Photographic Reconnaissance Group, at RAF Mount Farm, near Dorchester in Oxfordshire. He was posted on 1 April 1944.

The second-most highly decorated pilot of the Second World War, he did not regard liaison as a professional venture. Ten days after arriving at the base, he talked the commander, Lt Col. Elliott Roosevelt (son of American president Franklin D. Roosevelt), into allowing him to pilot one of the two Lockheed Lightning P-38 F-5B photo-reconnaissance planes that were to photograph targets in Germany. They took off on 12 April 1944, and flew together to a point about ninety miles north of Munich, before separating to carry out their respective missions: Warburton was to take pictures of a ball-bearing plant at Schweinfurt recently bombed by the Allies. The arrangement was that the Lightnings would rendezvous and escort each other to a USAAF airfield in Sardinia. Warburton was never seen again. Where had he flown to? The speculation ended in 2002, when his remains were found in the cockpit of his plane, buried 7ft into a field near Egling an der Paar, a Bavarian village about twenty-eight miles from Munich. The discovery was made on 12 August that year during the excavation of the site by German historian Anton Huber. He was following up a contemporary report of an Allied aircraft crashing there. At the time, a group of boys said they had witnessed an aircraft flying low and trailing smoke before flipping onto its back and driving into the ground.

The US Army helped Dr Huber find the site. There, he dug up an engine from the port wing and a plate that proved the aircraft was a Lightning. Other parts of the wrecked plane were found, including a bullet-hole-riddled propeller, along with scraps of blue-grey RAF uniform and bones that would eventually identify Warburton. As he was flying a USAAF plane with clear insignia, however, he was at first thought to be an American. He was buried in a grave marked 'unknown American Airman', but later his identity was confirmed and he was given a hero's funeral. On 14 May 2003, all of fifty-nine years after his disappearance over southern Germany, he was interred beside Commonwealth airmen who had been buried decades before. A Highland piper's lament played as members of the Queen's Colour Squadron of the RAF lowered his coffin into the ground at the British Military Cemetery at Durnbach, twenty miles south of Munich and protectively watched over by the Bavarian Alps. It was a short ceremony after such a long time.

There that day was Jack Vowles, a wartime NCO engineer who serviced Warburton's aircraft in Malta. The two men became friends. Mr Vowles recalled: 'Warby was never a swaggerer. He was driven by an absolute determination to get the job done. If he did a job badly – and that was extremely rare – he would refuel and go back straight away to do it again.' It was Mr Vowles, then aged eighty-three, who on 20 April 2004 presented the Malta Aviation Museum with the reel of film, standard for American cameras of the time; it is on show, with a piece of Warburton's flying boot and the Union Jack that draped the coffin during his funeral, in his memory.

Yet, as we discover from Diana Mackintosh, there is more to memory, to life, in wartime and peace, than what we think we know. So many untold stories to tell, explain and reveal. Did Warburton die for love?

Adrian Warburton was commissioned into the RAF in 1939, and the following year was posted to Malta, where he performed his greatest exploits flying Martin Maryland reconnaissance aircraft. In November 1940, he and his two crewmen carried out a near self-sacrificing sweep over the main Italian naval base at Taranto in preparation for a torpedo attack by Swordfish aircraft based on the carrier *Illustrious*. Warburton insisted on repeated perilous passes at about 50ft, so low that the Italians were unable to train their guns. He was all but on top of them – and proof of that was provided by a radio aerial from an Italian ship, found lodged in the Maryland's tail wheel. The intelligence he gathered ensured the success of the attack, allowing the Fleet Air Arm to sink the most important part of Mussolini's fleet. Still, like so many servicemen that Diana met, Warburton was a 'lost boy' when not at war.

Before he did high-risk battle in the Mediterranean skies, the pilot married Betty Westcott, the barmaid of a pub in Southsea, Portsmouth. She was seven years older than him and, by the time of his formal burial, ninety-one years old. She attended the ceremony and said afterwards: 'It was a wartime thing. He was incredibly young and I was simply bowled over by him. In a way we were never really married. We didn't live together, and I am not sure we even made love. Memories and dreams melt together at my age! He was a nice man, but too young.'

Instead, on Malta, Adrian Warburton romanced the unknowing Diana and, when gently rebuffed, went off and fell heatedly in love with

Christina Ratcliffe at the social bar of the Engineer Artificers' Club (ERA). She was well known in Malta from her entertainment group Christina Ratcliffe and the Whizz Bangs, who performed at clubs and pubs and dances. She died in 1988, sad, single and lovelorn, believing (as so many still do) that 'Warby' died while flying – escaping – to Malta to live with her. By serendipity, Diana Mackintosh was to 'meet' Christina Ratcliffe again through the power of the creative arts. It was fascinating to witness the encounter in April 2017, in Valletta.

ACT ONE: WARTIME

'It ain't over till the fat lady sings.'
(PROBABLY) TEXAS TECH SPORTS
INFORMATION DIRECTOR RALPH
CARPENTER, ALLUDING TO
RICHARD WAGNER'S
GÖTTERDÄMMERUNG (1876)

When the Second World War began, the three small islands in the central Mediterranean known as Malta were part of the British Commonwealth. Malta's geographical position was to be one of the most decisive factors of the war in the Mediterranean. Located 985 miles from the British base at Gibraltar and 820 miles from that at Alexandria, it lay astride Britain's sea lanes to Egypt and the Middle East and through the Suez Canal to India, Asia and Australia. From Malta's harbours the entire Mediterranean could be dominated by warships and submarines – and from its three airfields and seaplane HQ by fighters, bombers, torpedo and reconnaissance aircraft. It was a supreme prize.

1

FAMILY AT WAR

'I've always had a fondness for the story of Helen of Troy.'
DIANA MACKINTOSH, 2017

I took it personally when Benito Mussolini sent his high-flying assassins after me, for he played merry hell with my social life. With Hitler, it was another matter. His Stukas spraying mayhem and bullets from their horrid machine guns almost stitched me into the earth, certainly harassed me into ditches and totally ruined a favourite evening dress. The Führer made me very angry indeed. There were filthy marks all over my dress.

I joined all the other angry people of Malta in taking particular pleasure in doing all we could to spoil his plans.

We did this by surviving.

At times, during the longest siege in British history, it was a little tricky.

Yet, the outcome of great events in life can hinge on resolve. We had plenty of that, if very little else.

If I've learned anything in one hundred years on this earth, it's that I cannot abide being inconvenienced. When I am, I move swiftly on. Time is unforgiving and we must enjoy as many moments of it as we are given. I would never sit on top of some mountain spouting platitudes, and I've climbed a few! I'm not the preaching type; but if you pay attention, you can learn a lot. One early lesson for me is that what becomes familiar – bombs dropping all day, every day for three years can, remarkably, become commonplace – can make you feel dangerously secure and blasé.

If circumstances are so terrible, so awful, you think it can't get worse; and as your mind plays dreadful tricks, you are lured into a false sense of security. You have to fight it. It's the unfamiliar, the silences, that became terrifying. I learned to be always aware, to look around corners. The finger of death could appear without warning. Far greater odds than the Lottery!

It was needs must, and I had to learn that the hard way. In childhood, I never wanted for the comfort of food or clothing, the pleasure of a hot bath or shower, of sweet-smelling soap. When the loud-mouthed Mussolini joined in with Hitler on 10 June 1940, that signalled the start of the Siege of Malta. We had few defences; not enough ships for a regatta. The Axis horrors thought they could bomb us into submission, but Winston Churchill wouldn't give up on us. I like to think it was because we were his personal favourites, but Malta's strategic importance was possibly key. I was taught all that at school, for we had a long history of being invaded. What we all had to remember now was that sitting at the crossroads of the Mediterranean, we were in the middle of the whole wartime mess. Malta was the X mid-point where the supply route between Italy and the Axis armies in Libya crossed the Allied sea route between Gibraltar and Alexandria. Malta was, just by existing, a weapon in the desert war being fought in North Africa. If Malta survived, British forces could continue the fight to prevent Axis supplies from reaching North Africa. But we needed everything to be delivered to survive: people, food, fuel, ammunition, medical stores, aircraft and spares. Hitler and his brutes didn't want that – they wanted us to surrender – so they sent in the bombers, which arrived far more consistently than supplies. You could, and I did, set my watch by the Luftwaffe's schedule.

On Malta during the siege, there were always more bombs; in life, there are always more obstacles, handicaps and conflicts. You must face them, cope with them. I always have: don't look back, look forward, has been my policy. One which I am now about to break. For if you are going to tell a story, it is best to have a beginning, a middle (possibly a bit of a muddle in my case) and an ending. If you have a seat belt to hand, it's probably best to fasten it now. I've been a long time on my roller coaster and I've learned to rock with it when I've needed to; it's part of my heritage.

Family life the way my parents lived it was not for me. It left a big impression at the time and influenced the way I would be when I had my own family. I do not remember them making a simple, spontaneous gesture of true affection towards one another. Their bizarre marriage left me with two certainties: that human beings should not live together under false pretences and that children should not be exposed to such behaviour. Their lack of love worried me, as I grew to adolescence, and my own thoughts towards relationships troubled me even more. I had a typically religious upbringing in Catholic Malta. I did not lose my virginity until the day I married. I wanted to be certain of the man I would spend my life with; for me, there was no room for mistakes. Becoming a mother, a parent, taught me about putting my feelings aside. You don't own your children – you are there to help and encourage them, to keep them happy. It's all about unconditional love: you love them without expecting anything in return. What they give back is their choice. It is a wonderful thing to learn. My father, Salvatore Tonna, never did and I can't say I got on well with him; he was a serious man, a man for rules – for other people. I adored my mother, Amelia Herrera, whom everyone knew as 'Meme'. She was single-minded and feisty, a fighter – a quality that seems to have followed my family through history. The Herrera dynasty originated in Castile, which was a powerful kingdom on the Iberian Peninsula in the tenth century. It got its name because everyone lived in castles; they needed big stone walls for protection – they liked to fight: they were involved in battles for centuries. I think I got some of that in my blood!

More recently, at least in my terms, Nicolo Herrera arrived in Malta in 1627 as the Apostolic Delegate and Inquisitor, and from there the line ran down to my Spanish-born grandfather, Alessandro Herrera. He and my grandmother Madalena Perlotti were a love story. Her father was Italian, mother French, and they lived from time to time in Tunisia. It was there, in Tunis, that my grandparents met. There was some paternal conflict about their relationship – elements of *Romeo and Juliet* – but they were in love and their determination won out. They married and went on honeymoon to Malta where his father, also named Alessandro, had been the Spanish consul. *That* Alessandro Herrera was married to nobility – to Fannie Azzopardi Castelletti, whose family lived at the Auberge de Castille. The sensational building, proud Spanish Baroque architecture, is still standing opposite the cracked steps and wartime crumbled columns of the Royal Opera House in Valletta. It was built in 1574 as home for the Spanish and Portuguese langue of the Knights of St John. The stunning façade of the Auberge de Castille was created a couple of centuries later, the work of architect Andrea Belli, and has survived all.

I grew up around this grandeur, amid the town houses with their balconies that look out on the history. I love to be active, to be interested, and growing up there was always something to see or learn, often just around the corner. In Valletta, every street leads to the sea. I can't say it's like yesterday, but there's so much the same about Malta – the prizes granted by the geography of the place, the people, the smells and the atmosphere and attitude – that wandering or driving around can't help but bring the memories flooding back. I may not dwell on the past, but I've not forgotten it. There's still the heat and the sun and the dust from all that rock, the resilient creamy Maltese stone on which the Knights of St John built an island fortress.

Malta, with its unique position set like a crown jewel in the centre of the Mediterranean, a haven for sailing ships which couldn't cross oceans in one go, was a magnetic spot. From my schooldays, I can still recite in order the uninvited, pushy visitors: the Phoenicians, Carthaginians, Romans, Moors, Normans, Angevins, Castilians, Sicilians, Spanish, the Order of St John, the French and the British – who'd been in charge for a little more than a century when I arrived, just in time for tea, on 27 January 1919, with (most happily) the First World War all taken care of. By then, as part of the Empire, Malta was an important Royal Navy base and the Grand Harbour had been expanded and the dockyard built. And so had the pristine Royal Opera House, designed by Edward Barry, who had created the original in Covent Garden, London, and it became such a part of my early life. My maternal grandparents loved the place; they thought of themselves as founder members. They lived for the opera and the theatre – so much so that their house on Old Theatre Street in Valletta was opposite the Manoel Theatre (which remains one of the oldest working theatres in the world). Their home, a few minutes from Palace Square and the harbour at Sliema, then a summer resort, was always busy, happy and packed with people and hospitality. They were an extraordinary couple. They had twelve children: seven girls and five boys (two of the boys were stillbirths). Each child was named with an operatic link and some of them ended up with strange names, like 'Gioconda'. My mother, Amelia (her named character from Verdi's *Un ballo in maschera*), who was born on 1 June 1897, had coal-dark hair, which set off her fair skin and blue-grey eyes – deep, owl-like – like her mother. She was seventeen when she married my father, whom the family called 'Salvo', at the start of the First World War. He was twelve years older and very much a nineteenth-century man. It was a man's world and his word was what my older brother, Antoine, my younger brother, Victor, and I all had to be fluent in.

Our father took himself seriously and everything was done to maintain the status of the family. He dressed impeccably. His moustache was professionally trimmed, his hair carefully cut and treated with bergamot-scented hair tonic. His cigarettes were smoked through a holder. The pork-pie hat he favoured rather punctured his dignity; he put it on parade every Sunday when we all gathered at my grandparents' home on Old Theatre Street. My father was the owner of *The Odine*, which took visitors and business people on round trips between Malta and Tunis twice a week, Tuesdays and Saturdays. It was quite a magnificent ship, with thirty cabins and, below decks, room for freight and animal stock. It was always easy to spot in the harbour, shining in the sun that danced about the high sheen of brilliant white paint. Like everything else about my father, the image was important. He retained a 'family' suite on board. I went many times to Tunis and once, when I was about eight years old, visited French relatives of my grandmother's there. I was left to play on the beach, in the shallow waters at La Goulette – a place of ancient Spanish castles, a one-time stepping stone for the Ottoman Empire; but all I wanted to do was run around and splash about in the water. Suddenly, I fell into quicksand and felt myself being pulled in. An Arab vendor selling trinkets on the beach saw me struggling and rushed over with a rope to pull me out. I was in a dreadful mess, my apricot silk dress soaked and filthy. My face was covered in wet sand and I had to wipe around my eyes so I could see. I felt very sorry for myself. My brother Antoine found me and was walking with me back to the hotel when, through an open door, he saw a clothes dryer, an old-fashioned thing: you turned the handle and squeezed out the moisture and pressed the clothes simultaneously. He persuaded me to get 'pressed' in this dreadful machine; my dress got caught and Antoine flattened my arm as he turned the handle. My mother heard me screaming and rescued me. The machine had to be dismantled to free me.

I was the little girl lost and desperate for sympathy, but instead I got a whacking and was marched back to our hotel to be sterilised in the bath. My grandmother Madalena (my grandfather, who rather burst out of his waistcoats, called her 'Her' and she spoke to him as 'Him', which made for many confusing moments) was with us and she provided the comfort and hot chocolate. She was a woman of a different age, a mannered time, but even with her stately posture the kindness broke through. She had warm hands and eyes that matched. My grandparents displayed a stability that I recognised, even being so young. They died when I was ten years old, but they left me so much, a cornerstone to build on – which, of course, you don't realise in the moment, but soak in by osmosis. There is a correct way of doing things, a path to follow. On Malta, the hardships of history are always relevant, as much as the Catholic religion or the surrounding sea. It is strange how your world, the magic, works out: the relationship I had with my grandparents involved me going to the theatre or opera with them at least once a week. I would sit between them and watch and listen and be silent until the intervals. It was a grounding for me to become an accomplished musician, but nothing of the sort happened. I have always regretted my lack of musical talent, for my mother was an accomplished pianist and so were my aunts. For them, there were not the distractions that steal the time for music and such pastimes. My piano teacher Miss Calamatta, who had taught my mother, used to come to the house on my free days from school to give me lessons. She also acted as my dentist. I had a loose baby tooth and she tied a piece of string around it and the other end on the door handle. You know the rest, but I can still hear myself screaming the house down.

My parents had a spooky painting of a man above the piano in the drawing room and it used to terrify me, because I could feel the man's eyes following me about the room, drilling into my thoughts. I tried not to see the picture, but I couldn't keep from looking. My musical career was a nightmare. I put it on pause.

My brothers and I had a formal education, and when I was at boarding school I took up the piano again, and singing, but I wasn't much good at either. By some miracle, I passed my first exam with 'distinction' – my examiner had a crush on my music teacher. But my piano playing was something that even love could not conquer. I tried ballet lessons, but I was no Pavlova. What I did adore were languages. I had an ability to learn them. On Malta, the languages spoken were mixed and had become more so during the First World War. There was Maltese, spoken Latin, English, Spanish and a pidgin English. Italian was acknowledged by the majority, though, which made sense, as we were only fifty-eight miles from Sicily, and from there, a couple more nautical miles to the mainland. By the time I was growing up, Maltese had become the designated principal language but, of course, it was easy to hear and pick up so many others. I had an 'ear' and sometimes I heard too much. Much of it was my parents arguing. It was heartbreaking, so sad. After my grandparents died, my parents divorced. I don't think my mother wanted to separate while her parents were alive. They were so close and they so believed in being together forever. We lived with my father before boarding school, which was not ideal. He sailed with *The Odine* and that ship was his life. He adored it as much as a person and I'm told it is still in service, docked or working out of Tunis. If you care for something, it can survive. But for me, Tunis, like the piano, didn't leave me with happy memories, so I never returned to either.

I have never really talked much about my father to the boys. They just see him as someone who died when I was quite young – in fact I was twenty-four – before the end of the war. Once they were divorced, we were legally put under his care So, returning home from boarding school in the holidays, life with my father was quite dictatorial, without our mother to curb him. Probably because they were very alike in temperament, my father was naturally drawn towards our younger brother, Victor. Also, he was enamoured by Victor spending time with the Gatt family and particularly their daughter Mary, whom he probably thought would be a good catch for him, when he grew up. His elder son, Antoine, whom I was very fond of and had a much gentler character, was interested in a girl called Alice, who sang beautifully; but he frowned at their relationship, as her family were not up to the level of the Gatts. A terrible snob he was. They did eventually marry and were devoted to each other until they both died in their late nineties. Victor and Mary also married and were devoted to each other, but at the time, my father made it pretty clear who was his favourite. In his late teens, Antoine developed pneumonia and had to rest in his bedroom for a few weeks. The doctor visited and wondered why this tall boy, four years older than his brother was in the smallest room, as he said a large airy one would be better to recuperate. That room was occupied by Victor, who had simply taken the room he was given by his father. Anyway, I naturally became even more close to Antoine during that time, as I felt sorry for the way he was treated.

I was eight years old when my parents first separated (Antoine was ten and Victor six) – they simply got fed up arguing with each other – and in Malta in those days, the father, the one who had the money, automatically got custody of the children. I was sent to a convent school. My parents did get back together, though, but during the separation, we were looked after by a housekeeper, who was not a mother substitute; she was a useless creature. She also had this disgusting habit of playing our piano with bare feet – in the Maltese heat! My father saw nothing of this and only made us feel lucky that we had a housekeeper who was so talented. I was unhappy not to have my mother around for comfort, as my father kept strict control. I never found his better side to appeal to.

He was not in any way cruel or hurtful, but an old-fashioned man who liked order and routine, everything and everybody in their place at all times. It was an active life as I became a teenaged girl, with horse riding and skating, but we kept formal hours. It was a small island to grow up on and everyone took an interest in everyone else's business. Creating gossip was all but a mortal sin. My place at boarding school was to be a good Catholic girl. I wanted to be good – but have a good time too! I had many friends, including Connie Gatt – one of the youngest of the fourteen children of Brigadier Alfred Gatt, who had fought with the British forces in Gallipoli.

A magnificent soldier and a gentleman, he was always very kind to me and to my brother Victor, who married his daughter Mary. (The Gatts were, and are, an influential family: Francesco Gatto [Gatt] was the first person to hold the title Baron Djar il-Bniet, granted to him by Ludovic of Aragon, King of Sicily and Malta, in 1350. The Gatt family was the first family with a hereditary title in the Maltese islands.) Connie Gatt was much more modern and we liked to go to the movies. It was considered very chic to go after dinner to the 11 p.m. screening of a film. It was even more important that you had a handsome escort. In my early twenties, I knew a few of the midshipmen and I arranged for two of them to take Connie and me to the late evening film. We met at the Brigadier's house, but the boys never turned up. They left us all dressed up but with nowhere to go. Then, the Brigadier came in and said: 'Diana, you're still here …'

He was such an admirable man, one of four Maltese to be awarded the Military Cross 'for distinguished service in the field', but so kindly. I muttered something and was tearful: 'They didn't turn up.'

'Never mind.' He had just come back from the Governor's Palace and he was wearing his wonderful white helmet with the feathers, the magnificent plumes, and he looked at the two of us: 'Wipe your tears the two of you. We'll have something to eat here and then I'll take you to the 11 o'clock.'

And he did and we went in his official car and it was very, very grand; and I never dreamed that that would happen to me. I used to see the VIPs driving to the opera house. My grandmother's house on the Strada Reale ('Republic Street') was opposite the Opera House and I would watch in awe, never expecting to be part of such a party outing. I have no idea what the film was. Both Connie and I spent our time looking around to see who could see us. All I wanted was for everybody to see me coming in with this escort and looking very grown up. Of course, we were all to grow up very quickly.

When I was still a teenager, my father found me a place of work. With his social gadabouting and running the *Odine* line, his connections on Malta were excellent and he was friendly with the Strickland family, who were powerful in the same way as Beaverbrook (the newspaper dynasty) in Britain, and who owned *The Times of Malta* newspaper. My father believed in 'knowing the right people'. The Stricklands were certainly that, although my first close encounter with employer authority, with the formidable Mabel Strickland – very tall, very manly, with the hint of a moustache – was more terrifying than assuring.

Mabel Strickland was a remarkable character, a strong and, with reflection, positive influence on all who worked for her. She looked upon the family business as just that – a family. And we employees were all expected to know the family background: her mother was Lady Edeline Sackville-West, the daughter of the 7th Earl De La Warr from Knole in Kent, the home of one of England's largest historical palaces. Her cousin, the author Vita Sackville-West, was the matriarch of Sissinghurst and designed its marvellous gardens. Her mother died in 1918; her father, then Sir Gerald Strickland, married for a second time, to Margaret Hulton in 1926, and was made Lord Strickland of Sizergh, after his English estate, two years later. Lord Strickland, who had a British father and Maltese mother, went into politics both in Malta and Westminster, before becoming Prime Minister of Malta from 1927 to 1932. His second wife, Margaret, built the Hotel Phoenicia and set up St Edward's College, so they were hugely influential in the development of Malta; they established the newspaper group Allied Newspapers Ltd, publisher of *The Times of Malta* and *The Sunday Times of Malta*.

The deep-voiced Mabel Strickland – she spoke in a rumble of words that had a particular intimidating melody – became editor of *The Times of Malta* in 1935; being unmarried and always eager to help her father, whom she admired and adored, she turned the newspapers into an important part of Malta's political life. It was an achievement and a far-reaching one that only became clear to me in time: the Nationalist Party had dominated island politics, standing for everything Italian, as flaunted by their leader Enrico 'Nerik' Mizzi. Lord Strickland and his daughter were absolute Anglophiles – she showed me how to make tea 'the English way' – and committed to 'studied allegiance' to Britain. They were careful and clever; they spread English as a growing language by first promoting Maltese as the people's language, displacing Italian.

When I was ushered into Mabel's second-floor offices at Strickland House on St Paul's Street, only moments from the Grand Harbour, I was caught off guard and speechless. In that silence, Mabel guided me to sit down opposite her and we made our formal introductions. She looked so large. I am 5ft 2in tall and I thought I was in Lilliput. I was petrified. I had no work experience or idea what was going to happen, or what it was all about. Neither, astonishingly, had she. But she rumbled: 'Your father believes we can give you a future here.'

'Oh, that's nice.'

'Can you type?'

'No.'

'Have you done any secretarial work?'

'No.'

'Any journalism?'

'No.'

'Any writing of any sort?'

'No.'

'Oh. What about filing and general office work?'

'No.'

Our verbal tennis game went on as she stretched for more questions and I could only reply in the negative. I attempted a break: 'But my father thinks that I will pick up the work very quickly.'

Mabel Strickland's moustache all but curled. She had a look of astonishment on her face, but then kindness broke through. She patted me gently on the shoulder: 'Well, let's see what we can find for you.'

I had a job, but neither of us knew what it was.

Neither did we know that we'd have a ringside seat for one of the most important – and longest – stand-offs of the Second World War.

2

HELLO, SAILOR

'If you want to conquer fear, don't sit home and think about it.
Go out and get busy.'

DALE CARNEGIE, 1936

We also had a splendid vantage point to spot the arrival of the hunky young men of the Royal Navy, but I don't believe Mabel appreciated that as much as I did.

My offices at *The Times of Malta* were all but atop the Grand Harbour. The girls in the St Paul's Street Allied Newspapers building could identify the ships and we knew which officers were on which. In some cases, it was advance warning, for there were servicemen I learned to avoid if I could.

I found myself comfortable with the work. My typing soon got up to speed and much of my time was spent proofreading copy. As editor and boss, Mabel Strickland worked on a trust system and your responsibilities increased with your behaviour and skills. Of course, just by being around a newspaper office, I knew a lot more than most of my friends. Mabel was very political and deeply loyal to Malta and Britain. British officials and government ministers who visited the island would always make a courtesy call; the more senior would be entertained at the Strickland family home, the beautiful Villa Bologna in Attard in the centre of the island. She had what I suppose was a salon, where information was exchanged and motivations analysed. In my late teenaged years, I was surrounded by intrigue; the world was changing, but we had a narrow view. There was no television, no Internet, no mobile phones or news other than that which Mabel thought we should be reading. I couldn't just get the information on my iPad, as I do now.

In the offices there might be one telephone for a set of rooms and operations, but what we might think of as 'buzz' was very much by word of mouth. There were about a quarter of a million people living on Malta in the late 1930s, all but 5 per cent born and bred there. Everybody, it seemed, lived within four miles of the Grand Harbour, the bullseye in a maze of narrow streets, sacred and profane buildings, architectural marvels and monstrosities; a sort of structural catalogue of past civilisations, with its monasteries and convents, auberges, grand palaces, the enchanting white Malta stone buildings. It was never a village in size. But it was in the way we lived. I loved knowing everyone else's business. Italian state radio, the source so very close (the distance of London to Edinburgh), streamed easily into our ears, although not everyone had a wireless – ugly things in dull brown cabinets. You could always find the radio, if not reception. If you had short wave, you could tune into the crackle of the BBC from London.

What war gossip and rumour there was circulating in Valletta competed with news from London, which said Prime Minister Neville Chamberlain didn't think such an upsetting thing would happen. That was the news I wanted to hear and I believed it. I could carry on dancing. There were always dances at officers' clubs – this was the headquarters of the Royal Navy's Mediterranean Fleet. Having completed his training, my brother Antoine was working as a lawyer and an example of how diligent studying paid off. Victor always wanted to be in the army and in time he joined the Royal Malta Artillery. He was to be busy. As we all were. But in those early days at *The Times*, I'd happily catch the bus and get to work by 8 a.m. We started early so we could have a break in the heat of the day; it was a semi-siesta culture. Yet there was always work to do. Horribly, I found I liked to buy things, but never had enough cash.

There were always dances and dates and a need for a new dress. And shoes, of course – they were a necessity. What I truly needed was more paid work.

I saw how. Contributors of short stories to the newspaper were paid well, and according to the length of their stories – linage. I thought: 'I can do that.'

And I did. The most popular and lucrative were the weekend contributions, so I went to work. I began writing children's stories for *The Sunday Times of Malta*, using a pseudonym, and it was good money. Then I came up with a naughty scheme; I wonder now if they'll want the money back! When I was promoted to being assistant cashier, I suggested that this writer – me – was very good and we should pay her more. We did. I got five shillings a time for the articles. It encouraged my editorial output, but it became more difficult to get into the pages of the newspapers, as real stories began to oust the fantasy ones.

The carefree years all seemed to scream into each other, creating a traffic jam. I was always more intimidated by Mabel Strickland than Hitler – one-on-one, she'd have sorted him out; her voice boomed a little more than before, but her forthright and calm persona never changed. On 10 March 1939, Chamberlain was saying peace was more likely than ever, but then, on 15 March, came the news that Hitler had gone in and taken Czechoslovakia. We seemed to be so far away from it all.

We were putting out extra editions of the newspaper, and then – it was a Friday – the German troops went into Poland. That was 1 September, and two days later, 3 September 1939, we all huddled around a radio and heard Chamberlain announce: 'This morning, the British ambassador in Berlin handed the German government a final note, stating that unless we heard from them by 11 o'clock that they were prepared at once to withdraw their troops from Poland, a state of war would exist between us. I have to tell you now that no such undertaking has been received and that consequently this country is at war with Germany.'

Golly, I hadn't any idea what this meant.

For my family, for the people of Malta? For me?

We were all asking ourselves the same question and if it wasn't voiced, you could see it in people's eyes. It was wonderment.

Instantly, the Grand Harbour seemed to be empty of ships. Where once Britain's Mediterranean Fleet had proudly floated, there was now only the *Westgate* to protect the harbour. London had decided that we were so close to Italy, the Mediterranean Fleet should sail to the more protected waters of Alexandria in Egypt. It was extraordinary. Across the Grand Harbour were the 'Three Cities' – Vittoriosa, Cospicua and Senglea – the dockyards and Admiralty headquarters and the homes of nearly thirty thousand people, families whom some faceless person in a London office had decreed were indefensible. Whose side were they on?

Mabel Strickland and our newspaper were among the many demanding to know why we had seemingly been abandoned – and the answer was quick and diplomatic, if clearly nonsense: Malta could be defended just as adequately from Alexandria as from the Grand Harbour. We had the gunship HMS *Terror*, and it had the weaponry to live up to that name, but it was a veteran First World War seahorse. The word circulated: were we British or Italian? Who loved us? Just in case no one did, we set about getting our own Dad's Army, a Home Guard and Air Raid Precaution (ARP) organisation. Servicemen and police trained volunteers in how to administer first aid and how to prepare for air raids. The gas masks were terrible things. They were given out at schools and at police stations. The law was you had to carry them all the time. There was something like a soup-tin-sized bit on the front and you tied this over your nose and mouth.

The masks for babies were grand affairs and big enough to coddle them in. They had bellows, a pump with an anti-gas filter that you used to circulate filtered air for the infant. We had to go to talks about how to use the masks and there were lectures on Rediffusion, the island radio network, offering instruction on how to tape up windows to prevent glass imploding, shattering inwards. As part of the preparations, loudspeakers were set up at central points, usually in the market squares. There were training air-raid alerts, usually in the afternoon when the working day was almost over. The sirens gave me a prickly feeling. Even when I hear them today I get goosebumps. There were simulated attacks, and navy Swordfish planes would swoop over Valletta and the Grand Harbour, imitating bomb and gas drops. I had nightmares about gas attacks, about choking, drowning in fumes. When the alert sounded, shops would close and if you were in one you had to stay until the 'all-clear' sounded, which told you what became such a welcome phrase: 'Raider Passed'. It was clear, if you thought about it, that we civilians would be participants in whatever horror happened; not spectators from afar.

There was, in the high political ranks, a feeling that we were being forgotten and had better take care of ourselves. Mabel Strickland and *The Times of Malta* were campaigning to do battle and be protected; isolated or not, we would be prepared. I had to raise an eyebrow, though, at the bomb-proof air-raid shelters, which had wooden beams – matchsticks to the bombs hurtling towards us.

My father was unconcerned. Our house looked over Fort St Angelo and the rest of the Grand Harbour; it may have been a sensitive location but, for Salvatore Tonna, it was the 'right' address. Anyone, especially the German flight commanders, could see that. Our location was now even more fashionable. A bullseye.

Ineffective defence? Aerial bombing? In the beginning, I knew more about Scottish country dancing, the Dashing White Sergeant and the etiquette of the ballroom, than I did the rules of engagement. I think, had any of us known the half of it, we would have been terrified. Instead, we lived and danced on. No one, it seemed, had declared war on us. Yet, what the Americans called 'the phoney war' was just that. Mussolini was still not in the war, but London was convinced that the Italians would join at any moment. At the newspaper we heard stories of Maltese who were pro-Italian being taken into custody by British agents. Yet we all prayed that what seemed certain would not happen. I knew from my brother Victor that the Royal Malta Artillery was filling its ranks as fast as possible. And there were many more RAF pilots at the Friday and Saturday-night dances. There were Red Caps – British military police – patrolling the bars. It actually got so that all these preparations for war were quite fun, exciting, something out of the ordinary, for they became an everyday part of my routine.

So you had to wear a gas mask for an hour every other day. If it was first thing in the morning, it saved time on make-up! Some families left Valletta for the inner island villages but many, unconvinced that war would arrive, stayed. It was only slowly that I noticed that people were buying more food than they needed – I thought they were being greedy – and, at times, there were shortages of tinned provisions. It would have been a proper panic if people had known in May 1940 that Paul Reynaud, the French prime minister, had suggested that after the Battle of France, Mussolini might be kept happy and appeased with the correct concessions – which included me and the rest of Malta. Thankfully, Winston Churchill was now the boss and his war cabinet decreed no concessions, no giving Malta to these devils. Indeed, we were going to get what Mabel and our newspaper had been screaming for: protection.

But there was a snag.

The only aircraft on Malta were in packing crates.

An aircraft carrier had left behind the spare parts, comprising ten obsolete Gloster Sea Gladiator biplanes. If you believe in omens, this was it. As a Roman Catholic, the sure foundation of our religion is faith and hope and charity. Only three Gladiators took to the skies at any one time and that's what they were called: 'Faith' and 'Hope' and 'Charity'. It made us feel we had God on our side.

In time, the fighters, Malta's first air defence, didn't show much charity to the enemy. Still, with France having been badly knocked about in May and June 1940, and with the French Navy crippled, Italy had the confidence of supremacy in the air and at sea.

On 10 June, around lunchtime, my brother told me that Mussolini was going to treat us to one of his verbal tirades, a 6 p.m. broadcast over

Italian radio. Radios were on all afternoon and set to the Rome network. From 5 p.m. you could hear the crowds gathering in the Piazza Venezia and having a real fascist singalong, the favourite anthem 'Giovinezza, Giovinezza Primavera di Bellezza' preparing the way for Il Duce.

He was a master of the rant and we listened to every word. Benito Mussolini, silly man, went on and on:

Soldiers, sailors, and aviators! Black Shirts of the revolution and of the [Fascist] legions! Men and women of Italy, of the Empire, and of the kingdom of Albania! Pay heed!

An hour appointed by destiny has struck in the heavens of our fatherland. [Very lively cheers.] The declaration of war has already been delivered [cheers, very loud cries of 'War! War!'] to the ambassadors of Great Britain and France. We go to battle against the plutocratic and reactionary democracies of the west who, at every moment, have hindered the advance and have often endangered the very existence of the Italian people.

Recent historical events can be summarised in the following phrases: promises, threats, blackmail, and finally to crown the edifice, the ignoble siege by the fifty-two states of the League of Nations.

Our conscience is absolutely tranquil. [Applause.] With you the entire world is witness that Fascist Italy has done all that is humanly possible to avoid the torment which is throwing Europe into turmoil; but all was in vain. It would have sufficed to revise the treaties to bring them up-to-date with the changing needs of the life of nations and not consider them untouchable for eternity; it would have sufficed not to have begun the stupid policy of guarantees, which has shown itself particularly lethal for those who accepted them; it would have sufficed not to reject the proposal [for peace] that the Führer made on 6 October of last year after having finished the campaign in Poland.

But now all of that belongs to the past. If now today we have decided to face the risks and the sacrifices of a war, it is because the honour, the interests, the future firmly impose it, since a great people is truly such if it considers sacred its own duties and does not evade the supreme trials that determine the course of history.

We take up arms to resolve – after having resolved the problem of our land frontier – the problem of our maritime frontiers; we want to break the territorial chains which suffocate us in our own sea; since a people of forty-five million is not truly free if it does not have free access to the ocean.

This gigantic struggle is nothing other than a phase in the logical development of our revolution. It is the struggle of peoples that are poor but rich in workers against the exploiters who hold on ferociously to the monopoly of all the riches and all the gold of the earth. It is the struggle of the fertile and young people against the sterile people moving to the sunset. It is the struggle between two centuries and two ideas.

Now that the die are cast and our will has burned our ships behind us, I solemnly declare that Italy does not intend to drag into the conflict other peoples bordering her on land or on sea. Switzerland, Yugoslavia, Greece, Turkey, Egypt take note of these my words and it depends on them and only on them whether or not these words will be rigorously confirmed. Italians! In a memorable meeting, which took place in Berlin, I said that according to the laws of Fascist morality, when one has a friend, one marches with him to the end. ['Duce! Duce! Duce!'] This we have done with Germany, with its people, with its marvellous armed forces. On this eve of an event of century-wide scope, we direct our thought to His Majesty the King and Emperor [the multitudes break out in great cheers for the House of Savoy], who, as always, has understood the soul of the fatherland. And we salute with our voices the Führer, the head of great ally Germany. [The people cheer Hitler at length.] Proletarian and Fascist Italy stands up a third time, strong, proud, and united as never before. [The crowd cries with one single voice: 'Yes!']

The single order of the day is categorical and obligatory for all. It already spreads and fires hearts from the Alps to the Indian Ocean: Victory! [The people break out into raucous cheers.] And we will win, in order finally to give a long period of peace with justice to Italy, to Europe, and to the world. People of Italy! Rush to arms and show your tenacity, your courage, your valour!

People held their ears. Some cried openly. Many prayed. They said the Italians might drop propaganda leaflets on us, but never bombs.

And if there were bombs?

'*Gesu, Guzeppi, Marija, KItfghu l-bombi fil-hamrija.*' ('Jesus, Joseph, Mary, make the bombs drop on soil.')

But many were convinced the Italians would not attack us.

Sir Hannibal Scicluna, one of Malta's greatest historians and a cousin of my father, was entrusted with the safety of ecclesiastical art treasures before the bombs did indeed fall. One of the clergy leaders told him: '*Se gli aeroplani italiani arriveranno a Malta lanceranno fiori e baci di ciocolata.*' ('If Italian planes fly over Malta they will only drop flowers and chocolate sweets.') Clearly, Italy's efforts to infiltrate Maltese social circles and to promote fascist ideology had been effective.

My mother was, of all things, an Italian, of Italian ancestry, and that made Mussolini's decision to attack Malta all the more difficult for us to believe. We learned to read, write and speak Italian at school and our road signs were in Maltese and Italian, so an Italian attack seemed quite unbelievable. Many felt the same way. Opinion went one way and then another. People dismissed Mussolini's raving; Italians were cowardly and would never dare come near us. They were our friends, our brothers and sisters of the easy-going Mediterranean. They were simpatico.

Indeed, for the outside world, the acknowledged relaxed temperament of the people of Malta posed one big question about us. How would this quiet, docile, oranges-and-sunshine island react? Would it just roll over? On the balance sheet of what we had going for us and what we lacked, the statistics of war were stacked against us. If you could add up the pros and cons, the answer looked like the arithmetic of an apocalypse.

'*Gesu, Guzeppi, Marija, KItfghu l-bombi fil-hamrija*' may have been a chant, but it was a defiant one. Malta put its heart and belief into faith, hope and charity, in all their manifestations and strangely, for a Catholic people, into a Protestant gentleman and veteran army officer: Lieutenant General Sir William Dobbie. He was appointed as the island's Governor in the April before Mussolini started putting his bombs where his mouth was.

Governor Dobbie was a member of the Plymouth Brethren and his strong belief found sympathy with the faith of the islanders. He was an elderly man to a girl my age; a grandfather type, and that in itself was comforting. He was – yes, the right word is 'pleasant', of the old school; a man who had survived the Boer War and the First World War, who was sure of what the right thing was and his determination to do it; and was not easily intimidated.

Which was just as well, for many most certainly were. Almost every evening Dobbie, as Commander-in-Chief and Governor – and so in charge of the military and the welfare of the Maltese people – broadcast over the Rediffusion radio system. But it is his message to Malta's tiny garrison, the day after Mussolini declared war, that I remember most clearly. It was so calming. It was a wonderful performance, because in all the wide world it seemed that only he and Churchill thought we should battle on:

> The decision of His Majesty's government to fight until our enemies are defeated will be heard with the greatest satisfaction by all ranks of the Garrison of Malta. It may be that hard times lie ahead of us, but I know that however hard they may be, the courage and determination of all ranks will not falter, and that with God's help we will maintain the security of this fortress. I call on all officers and other ranks humbly to seek God's help, and then in reliance on Him to do their duty unflinchingly.

He was a morale booster. He easily transmitted his belief and, in the worst of days, reassured us that God was on our side. He was nicknamed 'Ironside', but that was tempered by his faith, which he displayed on the radio the day before the bombs began dropping like showers of confetti. He told us:

> I have absolute trust in the people of Malta in maintaining the utmost calm and trust in God, which is the greatest contribution civilians can make toward the common good and toward the defence of their island home. We have prayed for justice and peace. Mussolini, against the wishes of the Holy Father and the people of divided Italy, has decided upon war.
>
> Malta is ready for it, both in the matter of military defence and passive defence needs of the island provided the people, under the guidance of the passive defence organisations and their own common sense, maintain the disciplined action which their leaders in this grim struggle expect of them. We need all persons of goodwill to play their part and I know, full well, that the people of Malta will show themselves worthy of the trust reposed in them by the Empire. May God help each one of us to do our duty unstintingly and may He give us His help.

Around Valletta that evening, it felt refreshing to know where we stood; the uncertainty had vanished. Near the main police station on Kingsway the new era was clearly set out; crowds watched as Italians on the island were brought in for transfer to interment camps. People were singing the 'Marseillaise' and making patriotic noises. But the crowds soon melted away as people took refuge in their homes and cellars, the old railway tunnel and anywhere else that might shield them from destruction. Everyone seemed to have a bundle of something, babies or blankets, and often both. Many families were hiring taxis, taking buses, jumping on horse-drawn carts and getting out of the area, which we all knew was the prime target.

Yet just as many were staying put, convinced that Italy would never attack Malta. They were our friends. The Maltese are the most stubborn bunch, and I should know. I'm one of them.

I don't recall that schools were to close down or classes interrupted, unless by an air-raid alert. All was to be as normal. I carried my rosary. The churches were never busier. A silver lining for religion.

My mother, her concern etched on her thinner face, was with us at home. I was told to stay under the kitchen table! Nothing happened and I kept creeping out from underneath, only to be pushed back again. It was a long, silent night. I tell you something I didn't know then and I am so very thankful I did not. The Italian air force, the Regia Aeronautica, had over five thousand aircraft in Italy and North Africa. That was the enormity of what we were dealing with: the Italians had 975 bombers, 803 fighters and fighter-bombers. They also had 400 reconnaissance aircraft, 285 maritime reconnaissance aircraft, 80 transports and 400 fighter biplanes. The Savoia-Marchetti SM.79 (Hawk) carried 2,200lb of bombs, the servicemen called them S79s, with three engines and could also carry two torpedoes.

But it was the ones with bombs that came first. I'd watch them through my opera binoculars – slivers of sparkling aluminium that closed in on us, and by some magical metamorphosis turned into monsters of destruction.

By 6.30 a.m., that first day, after my uncomfortable hours with a couple of blankets beneath the kitchen table, the air-defence teams were on alert: the island radar had picked up the incoming Regia Aeronautica. At 6.50 a.m., the banshee wails of the air-raid warning sounded; it was the first of the three thousand air-raid alerts I would hear over the next three years, a howling call to attention that would never fade in my memory.

It all sounds so cold presented as facts, the terror of the time so long ago. But our first sight of the enemy was ten S79s flying towards Hal Far airfield and then another fifteen of them swooping in for Valletta – the dockyard, the two major harbours. Another bunch were swarming about the seaplane base at Kalafrana. All of them were guarded by squadrons of Macchi 200s, which were high-powered fighters armed with a pair of machine guns, nasty things that still haunt me. Like oversized hornets in summertime.

I know all this – the details, the dimensions of our would-be destroyers – because my brother Victor was with the Royal Malta Artillery, trying to shoot them out of the air on a daily basis. He was trained to knock out the most deadly first. The force of the artillery barrage that fogged the sky over the Grand Harbour surprised the Italians and frightened them. They'd expected an easy time with no operational RAF base on Malta. Still, one Gladiator – either 'Faith' or 'Hope' or 'Charity', that trinity of morale boosting – limped into the sky and flew against a contingent of some fifty S79s and their twenty-fighter escort.

It was the S79 pilots who blinked on that one.

Still, the swirling pillars of deep black smoke that began appearing everywhere you looked proved the Italians bombers had been effective, whatever jokes may have been made about their ardour. I learned to tell the difference between that black smoke from the bombs and the light brown clouds from the artillery, which seemed to steam into the sky instantly, like iced water on hot coals. To my ears, it was just noise, bombs and guns, a confusion. In time, I could identify an implosion from an explosion, an Italian warplane from a Luftwaffe fighter, and how to physically and mentally cope with an anonymous army attempting to wipe all of us on Malta from the face of the earth. The very land seemed in jeopardy, covered in dust from the bombarded buildings, ancient dust that had gathered undisturbed for centuries. The earth seemed to move like an ocean wave but without the water, an invisible gush of movement.

The pounding of the bombs would reverberate, roll through the rock of the island. Dust to dust, indeed. Yet, I can't say what I thought in those moments. It was always a race for shelter, for safety, and when I did survive an attack, there was this awful fear in the pit of my stomach about my mother and brothers and father. The girls at the office. I worried about trivial things: did Anna in the office have that lunchtime meeting with her naval officer? I never questioned if she was alive, had survived (which she did, to enjoy oodles of grandchildren). Survival was around 1 per cent good sense and 99 per cent chance, the blink of a moment could change everything when the shooting began. It was quite a start, though a characteristically Italian start, to the Siege of Malta: the Regia Aeronautica returned – after lunch.

The Italians spent the afternoon trying to scare us: another forty bombers, escorted by a dozen fighters, buzzed Valletta, destroying buildings and killing several office workers. The intent was to knock our morale. But if anything, it boosted it. Maltese are like its rock foundation – uncompromisingly hard.

People ran into the street shouting 'Bastards! Bastards!' The shouts were as effective as me throwing a brick at a tank, but it was all people had, and it made them feel better; so that was the start of our war.

On that first day, the Regia Aeronautica offloaded 140 bombs. One of the first drops of high explosives hit the target of Fort St Elmo, a star fort and prime defence point for my brother Victor's Royal Malta Artillery. The 'cannon-ball proof' Fort St Elmo defended Malta in the Great Siege of 1565, looming, at attention, on the Sciberras Peninsula and dividing the Grand Harbour and Marsamxett Harbour. It was a rallying symbol and the enemy knew it. They plastered Fort St Elmo with bombs.

In that first attack, six of Victor's fellow artillerymen were killed, including Philip Busuttil, a fresh-faced lad known as 'the boy soldier'. He is named, along with Carmel Cordina, Michael Angelo Saliba, Richard Micallef, Joseph Galea and Paul Debono, on a memorial plinth on the fortified platform, the Cavalier, at Fort St Elmo. It's a simple tribute:

These Six Men Were The First Soldiers Who Died In Malta In The Second Great War. They Were Killed In Action Whilst On Duty Exactly On This Spot At 7.45 AM On The 11 June, 1940.

Philip Busuttil was younger than me, only sixteen years old. In that long day, so many had to grow up. The bombers targeted the airfields at Luqa, Ta' Qali (aka Ta Kali) and Ħal Far. The last of these was the base for the island air 'defence', the recently crated Gloster Sea Gladiators, which comprised the Ħal Far Fighter Flight – as haphazard a unit as it sounds.

The pilots, young boys who were learning to fly and some commercial pilots, had no experience of fighter operations. But that Gladiator pilot who was never identified, shy of being set on a pedestal, flew into the explosive unknown and stared down the S79s – and they retreated, at least for those moments, from our airspace.

Governor Dobbie could have invoked David and Goliath.

We all needed to beat the odds.

A miracle would be nice.

3

STORMY WEATHER

'One after another all the other great sieges were eclipsed –
England and Odessa, Sebastopol and Tobruk. Malta
became the most bombed place on earth.'
ALAN MOOREHEAD, *THE DESERT WAR* (1944)

I'm not in any way certain that we truly understood the enormity of
what was happening. How do you explain war if you've never been in it?
Those who'd survived the First World War were now too busy fighting
this one to have the time to instruct us.

When the shelling began, I didn't know what to expect and neither
did any of my family or friends. But I soon learned that any outrage was
possible. It was remarkable that so much courage came from so much
fear. The Italians had three-engine bombers that came in very low; they
had flying dots above them – fighter planes. The aircraft, the bits of blue
in the sky, the anti-aircraft guns booming and sending up innocent
looking white puffs of smoke intent on destruction, not decoration. It
was fascinating to watch them, like sparkling stars, and often it was only
the insistent wail of the bombers diving in to attack that made me tear
my eyes away. You forgot for a moment that they were trying to kill you.
You were cemented in the moment like a stone statue, cast down like a
pillar of salt.

I was young enough to find it a mixture of excitement and, at times,
terror. The gravity of it all only truly hit home when those close to me
were bombed from their homes, or they – or their nearest and dearest
– were killed or maimed. Injuries were reported as injuries, but for
someone losing a leg or an arm, sometimes one of each, sometimes all
their limbs, injury seemed such a weak word.

My father was never going to be intimidated by the Italians, but the
war gave him an opportunity to move to an even better address: the high-

society location of Tower Road in Sliema, three or four miles (depending on your driving) north from Valletta and situated parallel to the Sliema Front promenade. By the nature of our new address, our building faced out to the open Mediterranean Sea.

My father saw it all as advantages:

It was a wonderful house.

My goodness, what a magnificent view.

You could see the bombers and fighters coming at you. Front row seats!

Of course, we were a particular attraction for the enemy, for also on Tower Road was Sliema Point Battery, alternatively known as Fort Sliema or the Searchlight Battery. It was, of course, an artillery battery – my goodness, it was known as *Il-Fortizza*, The Fortress. Clearly, an installation the bombers wanted to knock the hell out of. But my father didn't care about being close to such a fanfare of a target. He obviously believed they wouldn't dare shoot at anyone of such grand social position.

The rent was tiny, peppercorn small, for no one wanted to live there, directly in the firing line. Indeed, many homes stood empty, despite the rock-bottom rents asked for them. My father insisted that the Italian air force couldn't hit a barn door. They hit the house two doors up from us. They demolished it and a few along the street, too. That, for my father, was not a problem. The houses were not rented; no one was hurt.

And, yes, it was a wonderful area, 'very English'.

Indeed, you could easily go swimming, which we did. We improvised, stole the safe time we could; we learned to work around the Italian bombing raids. If you went to the cinema, a ninety-minute film could go on for hours with the bomb-alert intermissions.

Undertakers were on twenty-four-hour alert, but life, and death, went on. I don't think of it as bravado, for we didn't have much choice. Precautions were being taken. All those who could shoot or do something like that to protect us were doing it. My job, and that of those like me, was to keep the system going.

My son Cameron says I won the war, for I kept the troops happy. Not that happy, I must add! Malta was full of the navy; the harbour seemed to be carpeted in grey. It was covered with warships and, grandly, HMS *Glorious*, the aircraft carrier. As I worked at the newspaper and the ships were coming in, so many boyfriends – boyfriends galore – knew where I worked. One day, four ships came in together and all my friends accumulated in the lobby waiting to make a date with me.

Mabel Strickland appeared and, although she wore a smile on her face, barked: 'This is not a naval rendezvous centre. This is a very important newspaper. Boyfriends? No!'

Mabel believed all efforts should be concentrated on the battle for Malta to survive. We had to get on with everyday life, and everybody had to do a job and work towards that. It was us, the people, who were all-important in winning this war.

Back in the office, she gave me the rest of that rocket. But she forgave me. Of course, it didn't keep the Royal Navy – or any of the Services – off the premises. They were a determined bunch. All the girls attended dances and flirted and went on dates and had romances – innocent and, of course, some not so innocent. The servicemen were always proposing marriage to settle their nerves. They also proposed other not-so-lifelong opportunities, but a rejection rarely offended. In the heat of the circumstances, it was understandable. We were like cats on a hot tin roof. I never drank much, but alcohol remained in good supply and there was a party feel at times, although the atmosphere could sometimes become maudlin, especially when someone didn't return from duty.

My romantic encounters were very much dictated by my strict Catholic upbringing; home discipline was run like a parade ground. I wouldn't dare get up from the table without permission. When I went to dances, I kept to my father's curfew, to be home at a certain time. We celebrated that first 1940 war Christmas fully believing it would all be over long before the next.

We still had birthday parties for, extraordinary as it was, we wanted to live as though we weren't on borrowed time. Life went on. Slowly and with difficulty. You could get on a bus for a twenty-minute trip and that journey could take two or three or four or more hours, depending on how often we had to take shelter along the way from the bombs. That problem never stopped us getting on the bus in the first place. And so it was with the dances. We would get dressed in our finery, in long dresses, and attend functions and dances and parties with the servicemen. We were young; we thought we could still have a happy time, no matter what; it was looked on as part of the war effort. You had to steal a moment, a smile, or just say a nice word to someone. The RAF pilots in particular had no idea if they were coming back from the next flight. I'd watch them flying over the house and I'd say: 'See you at the party.' When we saw them, we always tried to make them feel they would be coming back, but, of course, a lot of them did not turn up again for a dance. The dance evenings were quite formal. I'd have a card and would dance with any number of people. It was cheek-to-cheek music, although with my height it was more cheek to chest. But I always had an escort to and from the dance. I wore elegant, old-fashioned dresses; it was part of the fantasy, part of the escape from what was really happening to us.

Despite our apparent acceptance of the circumstances, life was on the edge for everyone on Malta. And for those trying to protect us – such as Adrian Warburton, who was my rather colourful introduction to the world of RAF heroes.

When I first met him, he had done so much; he had killed and escaped death himself many times. He was born in Middlesbrough and was only a year older than me, but had been so daring. We were kindred souls. His father, Geoffrey, was a submarine commander and Adrian was christened aboard his submarine in the Grand Harbour. By the time he returned to Malta, he was a tall, wiry man in baggy, grey flannel trousers, with a flop of blond hair, huge confidence – he was twenty when he joined the RAF in 1939 – and a reputation as a brilliant, if eccentric flyer. He was also hugely attractive and he knew it. Adrian was a romantic. But even as an unsophisticated young girl, I also sensed a troubled soul. I can picture him standing in front of me today. The officers used to wear a formal uniform, but not him.

'Ties, I don't like them,' he'd say, 'too tight around the neck.'

He wore a silk cravat. He never wanted to be confined. Maybe he inherited claustrophobia from his submariner father. He dressed with an abandon, like a character Errol Flynn – who was the reckless film idol of the moment – might play: all devil-may-care, a wicked smile and into battle. That said, he was, until he thought he might get lucky, charming and proper with me. I'd been to boarding school and as a naval officer's son he'd been sent to one too: St Edward's School, Oxford. The wartime heroes Douglas Bader and 'Dambuster' Guy Gibson went there as well, but when the war started they were proven airworthy. Adrian could just about fly a plane, but always admitted take-offs and landings were difficult for him. I suggested those were two essentials, but was dismissed for heresy. Yet his bravery, when he got into the air, was unquestionable and the results he brought back from his photographic reconnaissance missions compensated. Most people, especially those who didn't know him, called him 'Warby', but for me he was always Adrian.

He talked about his missions, but dismissively and never in detail. His view was that we were in a skirmish, while back home they were fighting for survival in the Battle of Britain. One time, he was struck by a bullet, but it was already spent. It knocked him out, but that was all. The luck, he said, 'of a good boy'. Of course, our departing words were always 'See you at the party' and although he was flying off to danger, there was also a good chance I'd be blown away by a bomb before he returned – but it never felt that way.

I was very, very fond of Adrian, but not *that* fond. I wasn't going to hop into bed with him and he knew it. I was very popular with the pilots, but as I was a very strictly brought-up Catholic girl, these 'romances' were chaste. Taking things any further was never a consideration for me; what was important was my upbringing and the teaching I'd received. I was popular, but not too popular. I have a photograph of me on the beach with Adrian and you can see why he was such a romantic figure, a Biggles-type of character, a *Boy's Own* hero with long blond hair and really startling blue eyes. He was very keen to make more of it, but Malta is a very Catholic country and it didn't occur to me to have affairs. I just didn't dare.

I'd spent a lot of time with Adrian. We got on well, we clicked, but I knew I was getting the push when he said to me: 'You should find someone more worthy of you.' It was no big emotional break-up and we remained good friends although, explicitly, without the wartime benefits so many of the flyers expected. We'd see each other at the officers' club dances and we'd talk. He had opinions on everything, but when he was on the ground it was all about living and not risking his life in the air. He had that pride of youth, of being good at what he did and cocking a snook at authority. Like so many of them, he never thought for a moment that he'd be hurt or killed; all fear had been packed away down inside his unpolished flying boots. You see, it is the familiarity of the horror that breeds such nonchalance, such madness.

You could see the physical toll in the eyes of everyone, but especially those at the front line, the dry look of the eyes from the dust and the sleeplessness. Yet, Adrian would brush a hand through his wavy hair and shake away any hint of despondency. He was super copy for *The Times of Malta*, for all newspapers, and the stories about him in the Service clubs would become grander and grander. At *The Times* we had to check them for accuracy and, mad as some of his exploits appeared, the 'brass' confirmed the majority of them – although not those concerning bootlegged booze!

Most everybody was in awe of him or a little bit in love with him. An RAF Spitfire pilot, Group Captain Duncan Smith, found his way into the newspaper talking about Adrian: 'I was his escort on many a mission. I remember a particular raid when I was assigned to fly his escort plane. We took off and headed for the area that he was going to take pictures of. When we got there, the target was covered in flak. Warby said: "Wait here, I'll be back" in a very calm voice. Some enemy fighters approached and started a dogfight with me. A few seconds later I heard: "Hurry up, I'm not going to wait for you all day." He didn't treat a bomber like a bomber; he treated all planes like fighters.'

He was a one-off, a maverick, but a delightful one. He was so good at getting photographs of the enemy forces, of gathering intelligence to plot attacks, that he was ordered not to engage the enemy even if he encountered them. He shot down nine anyway.

But he'd never talk about it. Every mission was like an adventure. His plane was knocked about by so much flak while he was photographing installations over Bizerte in Tunisia, that he had to fly off and landed in France, near Beaune in Burgundy. The French accused him of being a German spy and locked him up. It took three days for him to establish his identity. Then he talked himself into getting a French fighter and flew the 985 miles to Gibraltar. There, he swapped his plane for a Spitfire and took off, with a stop to collect his cameras and some wine at Beaune, for Malta. He encountered and shot down a German fighter en route. I was told by one of his friends that when he did arrive back at base he said: 'Sorry I'm late.'

Yet, for all the marvellous exploits, the biggest story was his invaluable contribution to the success of the Battle of Taranto, at the heel of Italy. In January 1941, he was awarded the Distinguished Flying Cross for it. The citation in *The London Gazette* read: 'This officer has carried out numerous long distance reconnaissance flights and has taken part in night air combats. In October, 1940, he destroyed an aircraft, and again, early in December, he shot down an enemy bomber in flames. Flying Officer Warburton has at all times displayed a fine sense of devotion to duty.' It was the start of many honours and it was wonderful, for we all needed heroes so much. I'd always been looked after by a strong family and I found strength by being part of the struggle to survive. Adrian was a talisman.

Young as I was, as we both were, I began to appreciate the eccentricities of human nature through him. He wasn't a big drinker and would sip Horse's Neck, his weak mix of brandy and ginger ale, so he never became overemotional. He was very much the loner, that type of independent boarding schoolboy, and he needed someone who would complement his nature. In time, he became heavily involved with Christina Ratcliffe, who found herself stuck in Malta when Mussolini declared war.

Christina was a music hall singer and dancer. She formed the ensemble Christina Ratcliffe and the Whizz Bangs and performed cabarets in the servicemen's clubs. When you bought a ticket, it was with the guarantee that if the show was bombed out there would be a refund. Christina was a worker: with the RAF as a telephonist and later as a plotter at the underground war headquarters in Valletta. Like so many on Malta, she had learned to love life even more, to celebrate it, because of the constant threat of it being snuffed out. Christina was vivacious, outgoing and just what Adrian needed. He knew I wasn't the type to hop into bed with him and that's why he went out with Christina. She did hop into bed with him. She provided the comfort I wasn't prepared to give. For them, it was a wartime romance that seemed to go on forever.

I'm convinced he was taking time, going AWOL, to visit Christina in Malta when he vanished; the two of them had become so much part of Malta and the story of our survival. Sadly, she both did and didn't survive. When Adrian – who'd vanished before and always returned – never came back, Christina was never herself again. They talk of 'injury' in war, but she of course was one of those they don't add into the statistics. She never enjoyed another relationship, remained on Malta and died alone, penniless and unhappy in 1988.

I tried so hard not to take the men or life too seriously, because you never knew when it was going to end for you or someone you cared for. It's easy to think like that but feelings do overwhelm you, as they did for Christina. I learned – we all do – that it's never possible to ignore or discard true beats of the heart. I did feel romantic about a couple of the boys, but it was never serious. Oh, yes, I'd say I'd get engaged to them or be 'a steady girlfriend', but that was part of the flirting, part of the game.

Adrian wasn't a 'romance', but he was a joy, a flirty, stereotypical, big smiling pilot with that irreverent bravado that entered the room with so many of the servicemen. That's how he kept his demons in check. We all sheltered from death in some way – in the catacombs, in caves picked out in the rocks, in basements, and inside our heads and hearts. We all wanted to escape the death and damage, which fell unceasingly from the skies. Often the injuries appeared more harrowing than death itself. It was everywhere to see and it was graphic.

It was also about to get much, much worse. Hitler's flying gunmen were on the way and they had me directly in their sights. As the weeks turned into days before Christmas 1940, there were more dances and receptions and bombing raids. If the air alerts screamed, and some days they wailed all day, you took shelter at designated areas. For me, it was like being in an echo chamber. I felt the whole island shake with the bombs.

Rather than get distressed, it was better to be distracted, to help young children or comfort mothers whose children were not with them – and, worse, if their brothers and husbands were at sea in the Mediterranean.

Everything on and beneath the sea was a target and the enemy were gathering. As an early 'present' for Malta, Hitler had moved around two hundred planes – the German Fliegerkorps X, or Tenth Air Corps – from Norway to Sicily to provide firepower for the Afrika Korps in Libya. This bunch, with big bombers, torpedo bombers and the dive-bombing Stukas, were superb instruments of destruction – and now the islanders' new next-door neighbours.

The Navy was getting hit with bombs just as we were, and the sailors were living on land in makeshift accommodation, sometimes temporary shelters improvised on the rocks. Sliema was a ghost town, as were areas like Msida, and there were many empty homes. The naval commanders believed their men were safer spread around there. It was war economics: if they had all been in one place, a solitary hit could destroy a total command. So, we had Royal Navy submarine officers staying close to our house, and the knowledge they were nearby gave us a sense of security. Tower Road was busier and the numbers growing in Sliema offered support. The Mediterranean around us was closely mined and the British submarines had to operate with a caution they despised, for almost all the enemy convoys of armoury, men and supplies were sailing across the water to Tripoli.

Those convoys carrying men and supplies arrived in Tripoli at almost the same time – St Valentine's Day, 14 February 1941 – as Lieutenant General Erwin Rommel. Now, there's a man I would still like to offer up a good Maltese curse to. He was about to have a good eighteen months. We were to get the biggest bashing of all time. We were bombed a dozen times in a day. We had no proper shelters when it all began, so if any of us were at home my mother still used to make us go under the kitchen table for protection. Trying to say it wasn't much use was pointless. It made her feel better that she had done something to protect us. And we were lucky. Until the Luftwaffe arrived to teach us what the agony of war was really all about.

Mussolini's failure to kill us all gave the Führer one of his hissy fits. He was after me again! Mad as a snake, Hitler ordered German forces to head in our direction, with firepower that would bring misery to the whole Mediterranean, especially Malta. Most Italians would have preferred lunch to war with their neighbour. The Italian pilots were dismissed as cowards and incompetents, the bombers flying too high and off target, the fighter pilots equally as ineffective. Looked at in a kinder way, this reflected the Italians' unwillingness to attack people they regarded as friends, even allies, than any lack of skill or bravery; the Italians were not ruthless like their Axis partners.

On Christmas Day 1941, an Italian pilot flew over Ta Kali airfield and dropped a package: inside was a hand-drawn card with the inscription 'Happy Christmas to the Gentlemen of the Royal Air Force at Ta Kali from the Gentlemen of the Regia Aeronautica, Sicily.' There were also many reports of Italians dropping bombs in the open sea and firing their guns into the air. Adrian Warburton told one story of a Spitfire pilot being chased by an Italian fighter. No matter what he did, the Italian stuck on his tail and the RAF pilot could not understand why he wasn't being blasted by bullets. Eventually, the Italian pulled up alongside, waved, fired his guns into the air, and disappeared back to Sicily.

Their partners in crime were never, ever like that. The German fighters were determined and deadly. They flew down into the opposition and seemed oblivious to the shells being fired at them. The Germans were wicked with their Stukas, the Junkers Ju 87 dive-bomber, and would scream down and machine-gun people walking around. I was terrified of it; the whining noise of it went through your head. The planes howled like werewolves as they dived and then the rat-a-tat-tat of the guns. We'd look up in the skies and the pilot's eyes seemed to be marking you out, singling you out, like that portrait in my childhood piano room. It was all the fears of being brutalised, tortured, raped and killed. The Nazi pilots stalked you for a particular, and often deadly, pleasure. It always seemed that way to me. It was not just war on a nation, it was personal. That's what made me mad. By making me frightened, they made it very personal. The thought of the Germans coming onto the island, of invading us, which we all believed could happen the next day or even in the next couple of hours, made me shake. All the time you had to gather such thoughts and pack them away somewhere else in your head and get on with your life.

Yet it was hard to forget, for every day, every moment, you could glance in the sky and there might be three hundred planes at a time, big clouds of them. Everyone wanted to be in command of our tiny island. Our existence was so crucial to the war in the Mediterranean that the Axis powers were determined to have us. Strangely, the telephones stopped. The Italian navy cut the underwater cables that connected us to Gibraltar and abroad and there was only wireless contact. Even though we rarely used a phone, it made you feel even more isolated. 'You'll all have to shout louder,' ordered Mabel Strickland.

I never missed a day's work. *The Times of Malta* won a reputation for objective reporting and prided itself on being published every day, no matter what. Working there gave me a very scary picture of what punishment was being hurled at us on a daily basis. Yet even when the latest round of bombs were dropped, it was just a matter of time before they'd begin again. We were only fifty-eight miles from Sicily and the fighter planes and bombers were flying from there to attack us from the moment Italy entered the war. By the middle of 1942, we were attracting more bombs than anywhere else on the planet. It sounds trite now – a badge of honour, perhaps? But it was hell.

Always, or it seemed that way, there were black clouds of attacking aircraft stacked over us and smoke from burning buildings billowing up around them. It was as if the garden was covered in black flies that eclipsed the sun. After raids, rescue workers had to fight to get survivors from collapsed buildings. People seemed tragically mangled with masonry and there was always that dust, that choking dust, which 'crept' under your skin. It felt as though you could never wash it off. Another shower was never enough. There were the smells too, the sewers, the rot of bodies buried but not found. Body parts, legs rather than arms, pointed from the rubble. Sometimes wet sheets would be thrown around the room if tear gas dropped on the streets, but for all the rehearsals and lessons with gas masks there were never any full-scale gas attacks in that long, long time.

The house in Sliema was still home. My father would smoke his cigarette on the front porch and watch the action in the skies, the dogfights and the black smoke – shrouded fanfare of the destruction all around. Like he was at his own personal cinema.

He was such a snob. A terrible, terrible snob – happy to take the risks simply to live in the right part of town. He would not be intimidated by the attacks and refused to leave our house and take shelter. He'd watch incoming attacks from our doorway for simply ages. One night, the

Germans came over with incendiary bombs and dropped them as they machine-gunned the house.

My father was wearing his tobacco-coloured pork pie hat and a bullet from one of the Messerschmitt Bf 109s – we knew them all by sound and sight – went through the crown of the hat and hit the wall. He put his finger through the hole in his hat, shook it around a bit, put it back on his head, and announced that maybe it was best if we didn't stay in our house that night.

He wasn't frightened for himself, but the house was ablaze. I could see all our things burning, our clothes and furniture, and the flames shooting through the upstairs windows. Possessions were being burned away, but it was not worth sobbing about. Calmly, as a unit, we walked away from the house and the flames enveloping it, away from so much that we treasured.

By then, being alive was enough.

I supposed that's all we thought of; it was on my mind so much that sometimes when the alerts sounded, they made no impression; the screech of the fighters in the air, the spectacular wail of the bombs dropping to the ground, were daily sounds. People were homeless, starving and frightened, and, strangely, it was when the bombardments ended, replaced by a foreboding silence, that the truly terrifying goosebumps began.

In the witching hours, Malta was a silent island of darkness. I always felt that we could have heard a pin drop, so desperate were we to know what the Devil was going to send us next.

My father was proud and still refused to take any nonsense from the Germans. His vanity wouldn't allow that. We moved to a flat in a block with a basement shelter.

Naval officers from the submarine base occupied the other cheap apartments nearby so, childishly, I felt protected and took some comfort in our new quarters. The rent was modest but the location was one of Sliema's most illustrious. And, of course, our apartment had a grand view and faced the sea – again, directly in the firing line of now both the Regia Aeronautica and the Luftwaffe.

Who, I imagined, could see the whites of my eyes.

4

DAY AT THE OPERA

'The Winds were hush'd, the Waves in ranks were cast,
As awfully as when God's People past:
Those, yet uncertain on whose Sails to blow,
These, where the wealth of Nations ought to flow.'
JOHN DRYDEN, *ANNUS MIRABILIS* (1666)

They said 1666 was bad, the Year of the Beast, but I believe Satan also made a date in his diary for 1942.

For all of us on Malta it seemed like the end of time.

Which had endless ramifications.

All my close and near relatives were in the firing line. My friends were involved in defending Malta; some were in love.

My best friend Tessa's sister, Bella – a beautiful girl who'd gone to school with me (we'd had dance lessons together) – was twenty-one and had married a Royal Navy officer. He was just a young boy, but now also a worried husband and father. With the tremendous and so real horrific dangers and hardships of 1942, he arranged for her and their baby boy, a cute little thing called Andrew, usually bundled in a blue blanket with a cross like the St Andrew's flag, to fly on a transport aircraft to Gibraltar and then on to join him in England. It wasn't easy to get permission to leave Malta, so we were delighted she could go. By accident, not enemy attack, the plane crashed and broke up on impact. Bella's beautiful baby was thrown out of the aircraft to his death. Bella and several others were rescued but died on the way to hospital. It was a brutal lesson, for it seemed no one could escape the horror of Malta; even the innocent could not survive.

I was young and conscientious and at the same time aware how little I could personally do to defend my family, my people on my island, my friends. That was a torment, the fear of what might happen to us all. It was often a close thing. Or a tragedy, as befell Bella and her new family. War is not a time for love but, of course, it is the perfect place for it. You want the comfort and security of another person. One of my brother Victor's jobs was to seek permission for his men to marry. Or not. Often he and the commanding officer would try to talk the young men out of so big a step in their lives. Victor managed to save one or two of them by persuading them that a civil marriage would have tied them for life. So not to act impulsively.

One besotted boy, George, wasn't having any of this fluff. Victor got all dressed up and found the lad's intended. She was a Romanian artist and he explained that her boyfriend had a small job in the Malta dockyard and he had to look after his mother and sister. It was also very likely that with the shortage of houses, they would have to live with his mother. It was a great sacrifice she was making for love. The girl started crying and then wrote a letter to George, saying she'd changed her mind. He, in turn, moped and said he would never eat again. He turned up for his rations two hours later. It wasn't something anyone wanted to miss. Most of us were starving all the time. Sleep, when you accomplished that miracle, helped. Many have tried to explain how it felt to be on Malta during the Great Siege, but it's like me trying to describe the emotions of the Siege of 1565 when Suleiman the Magnificent was flashing his scimitars at us. That was a bloody affair. Our one was savage too, and dirty: the smell of cordite in your hair, the dust all about you, making you cough and dig a finger in your ears; the smell of distress and death; the sudden movements on the ground when gouts of flame spat out. Noise was not a friend: sound signalled trouble, a falling building, a dying cry, a rumbling empty stomach.

Bombs we had plenty of, and in three months in the spring of 1942 there were over eight hundred air-aid alerts. During April, nearly seven thousand tons of bombs were dropped on Malta. The invasion of the German and Italian armies was expected at any moment. And we were hungry. There were, of course, plenty of miracles, but none of that five-loaves-and-water-into-wine kind. We were essential to the Allies' strategy in the Mediterranean and we lived and coped with the bombs, horrid as they were; but for a time it appeared that we'd be starved into surrender. It seemed as though ships attempting to bring oil and food to us would not get through and there would be no more food. All supplies – the powdered nonsense we were so grateful for, the loaf of bread we made last a week for the family – would not be there. There would be nothing to eat, to live on.

We had to queue for our ration when it was available, and it was so little, I don't know how we stayed alive: a small piece of bread only a couple of inches long. When I got my piece, I would crumble it in my mouth with my tongue and suck on a tiny portion at a time. I know that's where the expression 'suck the life out of it' came from; it was like doing just that.

I'm not very tall, so there's not a lot of me, but I was always very hungry. We were surrounded by water, but cut off from it: the fishermen couldn't go out because of the submarines beneath them and the fighter planes above them. People tried to grow crops and there was a little fruit, but the milk was often powdered, as goats had been slaughtered for meat.

My father would still go into restaurants and, because of his grand manner, be treated with some lavish offering. He liked to believe his 'connections' kept him in fine and ample cuisine, but his badly fitting suits, narrower waistline and pinched cheeks belied that fantasy. Like almost everyone, he was suffering from lack of nutrition, and his grandeur couldn't disguise that. People were shrinking, but because everyone was, it wasn't so evident or so shocking.

He used one particular restaurant in Sliema and one day was happy to find rabbit on the menu. Pointing to it, 'Please, if you can do such a thing,' he said as he smacked his lips. It wasn't grilled Bugs Bunny that arrived, though. What sat on his plate was rather obviously Mr Rat. But, as my father said later, it was a big rat. They obviously had a better source of food than we did.

Throughout the bombing, not a single cat or dog was ever visible on the island. I was certain they had been cooked in the small restaurants. I never let my cat, Mitch, out. Better, I reasoned, to be bombed into infinity than deep-fried or grilled. In those months the bread ration was dropped to one-and-one-half ounces per head, per day. There was one pint of goat's milk for each family. There were coupons for everything. The one distinctively difficult item to get was fuel – oil – for paraffin was so essential to the war effort. There was a queue for most things. If one formed, you joined it. It didn't matter what the queue was for, you lined up instantly. There was never any question it would be essential for yourself or the family.

During the siege, the overwhelming emotions were fear and gratitude.

Our food was dehydrated: eggs, potatoes, onions, fruit, and cabbages and green beans. Most of the sacks of dried foods were held in protected storage in houses, garages, offices, requisitioned by the authorities. People got to know the loading and unloading schedules and would turn up with pans and brushes to sweep up any precious droppings. Often sacks had more holes in them than they should have. A pencil could do that. An extra handful of food, dried or not, was something to celebrate. How your body and taste buds adapt to the circumstances! The mind can make a feast of so little, but all around Malta you could see the suffering from lack of nourishment, the dwindling body fat, the strawberry-red eyes, the slower walk, the slumped shoulders, the fading muscles – people didn't have the energy to stand up straight. Now I understood that when they spoke of nations being 'bowed' by events, this was an illustration of it.

I could suffer my hunger pangs knowing that there would be something in the day even if it was faux bread. There was nothing to spread on it – butter and margarine were fond dreams, jam a silly thought; nothing at all to disguise the taste, which was sour like a very old, rotten lemon. The bakers used whatever they could: bran, interesting dust, sometimes potato, which made it go 'off' but never so much as to stop me eating it. All the time my mother said she had sufficient to eat. We told her she must have nourishment, must eat:

'No, I don't need it. I'll say when I'm hungry.'

She simply wanted us to have her rations but I insisted: 'There is no way we will do that.'

She'd complain: 'I'm not hungry.'

I forced her: 'You eat or we won't.' She did.

My mother never wanted to leave the house or the apartments 'in case they're bombed' – her reasoning being that if she was there she could save our belongings. We had to fight against this all the time. My brother Victor was a regular soldier, a soldier's soldier, and he was very strong. He saw a lot of war. My brother Antoine was a lawyer, tough in his way, and he married Alice Falzom, who had a wonderful operatic voice. I can't explain it, but when life is dominated by one giant horror – the war – then you reach out for distraction. I found it hearing my sister-in-law sing. She was mesmerising. When Tito Gobbi was establishing himself as one of the great operatic baritones, he always wanted to sing with Alice if he performed in Malta. He'd announce: 'I want to sing with Signora Tonna!' And he did. Alice was a true talent with a natural voice and they sang together at the Opera House. I still have a later review, from *The Times of Malta*, dated 20 September 1946, when Alice played Violetta in

La Traviata and the critic praised her 'remarkably pleasing' performance. Tito Gobbi was enchanted by her.

So, of course, was Antoine. My brothers were both strong-minded. And there was me. I looked after myself and I was home, protective of my mother. She was my friend as well as my mother. She was younger than many of my friends' mothers; we could talk and she guided me through the scares and the sadness.

In those weeks and months, children crying for want of food was common in the streets. Babies had low survival rates and older people were simply dying off through lack of nutrients or infection and disease, which spread in the heat and dust because of the deteriorating hygiene and the basic lack of clean running water. 'Victory' kitchens were set up to provide cooked meals. The menu was erratic: tinned sardines, 'goat meat' stew, macaroni, vegetable soups, beaten egg powder with tomato bits and 'leftovers du jour'– given an exotic name, *balbuljata* – or 'UFOs' (unidentified frying objects).

It wasn't first come, first served. You had to get your coupons from the official 'Victory Kitchen' by presenting a ration book to prove you were entitled to the rationed items. It cost sixpence for a coupon, which got you one portion. The number of portions were, in turn, rationed and set by the size of a family.

If reservoirs were bombed, the shortage of water became acute. Dysentery and dehydration killed. Goat meat meant no goat milk. It helped children and the elderly eat, but deprived them of pasteurised milk. Powdered milk, and precious little of it, was all there was.

Clothing was limited too, especially shoes, as every day involved a walk though streets jagged with debris; leather was in short supply, sometimes boiled for thin soup-style sustenance, and was acquired when possible on the coupon system.

But food. Everyone craved food. I dreamed about tinned peaches, the fruit itself and especially the sweet syrup. Rubbish bins were rarely seen standing upright; they'd been upended and foraged through for scraps to eat. A pot of gold left on the street would stay around longer than a breadcrumb.

In 1942, on Malta, the chances were you'd be shelled or starved to death. There'd be no guaranteed last cigarette, either – they were rationed. There was no magic protection against this other-worldly evil; you couldn't chew garlic, if there was any, for protection, or wave crosses, or conjure up an invisibility shield. Food supplies were at their lowest levels. The flour mills were directly hit and the power station was repeatedly put out of action. We were close to the necessity of surrender and there was even a code name for that: Harvest Date. No one wanted to surrender, but equally no one wanted to die. For the majority, though, there was not much choice, as they were never going to submit. It was hard to be brave. The Grand Harbour looked like a maritime junkyard, with only the remains of battleships visible, the scattered debris of defiance.

The topsy-turvy look of the airfields, like a painting you don't know which way to hang, showed they'd been bombed by a determined enemy. Life mattered and it depended on where a bomb dropped, or if a convoy of ships carrying food managed to get through the hellfire of the Mediterranean. Alan Moorehead, an Australian journalist who spent much of the war at the front line in North Africa for London's *Daily Express*, spelled it out in his superb book *The Desert War*. He caught the immensity of the onslaught:

> The greatest of battles for supply fell upon Malta. This was now turned into a hell. Malta was a base for British submarines and aircraft preying on Axis lines of supply to Libya. In the spring of 1942, the Axis decided to obliterate that base and they wanted to starve it as well. Right through the spring they turned such blitz upon Malta as no other island or city had seen in the war. It was a siege of annihilation. One after another all the great sieges were eclipsed – England and Odessa, Sebastopol and Tobruk. Malta became the most bombed place on earth.

During one raid we were in a shelter for forty-eight hours. Every emotion that could happen in human life was enacted in front of my eyes. The tremendous courage of some, the sad and terrible fear of others. I was sitting on a rock watching water drip from the cave walls and imagining it was sweet lemonade – but it was hard work to smile, put on a brave face. I felt I was in a never-ending, claustrophobic corridor travelling through an echo chamber as the bombs seemed to be bouncing about, exploding and doing the trick all over again, the thunderclaps of them going back and forward. It was as if the gods were having a noisy party. The walls and the ground trembled with the explosions.

Babies cried; older children got sullen and angry with boredom and fear; the women suffered in distress and grandeur; and the men tried to appear stoical; not all of them succeeded. It was as if we'd already left the world: strange, I even shuddered when the siren wailed a straight note meaning 'Raider Passed'.

They weren't gone for long.

I had plenty of near misses. We all did. The bombing was carefully choreographed.

The constant daily raids, anywhere from four or five to a dozen a day, brought formations of up to a hundred enemy planes at a time. They had the immensity of an aerial cavalry charge, with customised firepower: incendiary and big explosive bombs for the airfields; delayed-action bombs for artillery installations and defence bases; a 'happy pack' of bombs linked together for concentrated destruction; anti-personnel bombs supposedly targeted at troops but dropping like leaves – leaves without trees – anywhere and everywhere; deep-penetration bombs for shipping and the dockyards; and parachute mines intended for the sea, but which so often landed on land.

Or nearly in my lap, as it happened.

One afternoon, the Germans were having a real go at us. I was at a car showroom in the centre of Valletta, a big glass building that had been commandeered as military offices. One of my young officers was based there. There was plenty of glass so that passers-by could see the cars for sale, but now in the narrow street it was an extreme hazard. I was on the top floor when a raid suddenly began. We had no time to get out of the building.

Captain Stokes-Roberts, who liked to be in charge of me, decided I would be safer in a large safe. He was one of those many officers, from all the Services, whose first social call in Malta was to visit us at *The Times* building and attempt to make a dance date. This time there was no request. He didn't ask me anything but simply looked around, rushed over, grabbed me and, turning me about, pushed me in the safe and shut the door. This all happened in seconds. Siren alert, whining of bombs, grabbed and then shoved. I hadn't time to be frightened stuck in this black space, my nose pressed against the safe-deposit boxes.

It was pandemonium outside my bomb shelter; walls were crumbling and I didn't know what to expect when the door opened. It was the usual, scrambled walls and masonry, but all sprinkled with jags and slivers of glass, sparkling like a Christmas tree. There was dust and destruction – and across the street in the window of an ice-cream factory was another present from the Luftwaffe.

A parachute mine was hanging in the window.

This big bomb was menacing and floating there, but like a garden swing, moving ever so gently back and forth. Next to it was a huge cardboard cut-out affair of an overflowing ice-cream cone advertising all the flavours and combinations of sweet delights on offer, with an image of a chocolate and vanilla attraction.

I don't know what annoyed me most, the ticking bomb or the false advertising – for none of us had seen an ice cream for months and months.

My hero, Stokes-Roberts, was more practical and set about evacuating the building and those around us. The parachute mine was so close and all the time moving about on its rope, which I suppose could have snapped at any time. If it had gone off, we'd have all gone off into space – including the safe and me inside it.

There were scores of injuries: the shattered glass had done lots of damage stabbing into faces and through clothing, sharp little arrows that bloodied and blinded everyone it touched. I didn't know until I got home that our flat in Sliema had taken a direct hit in that raid. We had flat number eight, so we were quite high up and when I got there the building was a shell, with bits of floors and walls slanting this way and that. I saw my clothes hanging from what had once been our ceiling; the clothes rail had been blasted into it. I could hear Mitch, my cat, squealing, yelling his head off, but he was alive – hidden under a chest of drawers – and I managed to save him. He was the only one at home when the bomb hit the flats, and lucky to have those nine lives that Easter Sunday, 1942. The next day, Monday, 6 April, there were a dozen bombing raids. It was getting so intense, so familiar; there was the threat of not taking enough care, but I found the hunger kept my senses alert, the mind aware. Which, as it turned out, was the only blessing of starvation. And being scared. I suppose I was always scared, but you just forgot to be scared when you were rushing around trying to stay alive. With the apartment destroyed we were evacuated to Rabat in the north of Malta, home to the catacombs and, more importantly for my father, to the island's aristocracy.

My cousin Frank La Ferla was at a college nearby in the old capital Mdina with his best friend, Edward de Bono (yes, the brain-training pioneer who later came up with the concept of 'lateral thinking'). Frank's father was an engineer and, at their family house on the main street in Rabat, had masons excavate a specially designed shelter in the rock, using picks and shovels, below the garden of the house. The family kept beds and cooking facilities there. When the bombs were dropping, some people stayed there for days and days. And the bombs were dropping. All the time. It was a terrible time and I still don't know how we survived, dodging death at every moment.

I'd got off a bus from work and I was heading somewhere when the sirens blared in the middle of Valletta. I hadn't time to get to a shelter. I wasn't particularly worried, it was just another bomb.

But 7 April 1942 was not just another day on Malta.

It was a day we set some unwanted records, including the two thousandth bombing raid against us, the day when what was left of centuries of heritage was finally destroyed.

The day when hell all but swallowed up Malta.

The Royal Opera House in Valletta, Edward Barry's architectural enchantment, was easily one of the most beautiful buildings in the city; a glorious venue for many of the visiting opera singers of the time. One moment I was walking across the road from it and the next I was thrown on my back by a bomb blast. I came close to being bombed to destruction along with the Opera House. I was blown off my feet as squealing Luftwaffe bombers took out much of Valletta's principal Strada Reale, including the corner that, quite majestically, the Opera House had graced for eighty years. As the air cleared, all I could see was a heap of stones and a grotesque pile of twisted metal.

On Hermann Göring's direct order, to inflict even deeper pain into the heart of any morale Malta still harboured, his prized Luftwaffe had scored a direct hit on the Royal Opera House, with devastating consequences for the building. I was stunned and stumbling around in the smoke and dust along with a crowd of others who'd been knocked over but only shaken about. As we dusted ourselves off, all that remained of the Opera House were the terraces and parts of the columns, which were crumbling in front of me. Pieces of masonry fell off as I watched; the roof wasn't there, only a spaghetti of girders twisted about and pointing to the black of wartime in the sky. The back of the Opera House from the colonnade seemed to be intact, but a huge pile of weathered, creamy white stone and rubble was all that was left of the portico and the auditorium I had sat in so often with my grandparents.

I could feel the heat as the Opera House burned and shrugged itself off and into the ground. It was deflating to see such a magnificent building in ruins, smouldering, just debris in a wanton act of war. It was simply more evidence of the wickedness of it all. And the sound and sight of it. The fires grabbed anything flammable, gripped it for but a moment, and then with a horrible whoosh, sent the flames rocketing into the sky. My eyes were locked on the flames, which were crimson and gold and hypnotic.

I watched as the fires found masonry normally resistant to burning, but even that dense matter could not withstand the gnawing heat and flames which danced up again towards the sky in a ghastly celebration. That damage was symbolic, though, not a direct part of the human tragedy, of the loss of precious lives. I learned too well about that. There could be no other subject: we were fluent in the ugly language of the war. Yet curse them as we did, the bombing wouldn't stop. I would wonder silly thoughts, such as: when did the aircrew go to the bathroom, if they were always up there dropping bombs on us? When did they eat? Sleep? Maybe they never did, for the bombs certainly did not.

The demolition of the Opera House was only part of the heaviest bombing in one day we experienced. A radio broadcast that evening reported:

Valletta is a stricken city … all the beautiful old palaces are bombed, all the churches have been ruined, blitzed … hundreds of houses are no more … nearly all shops destroyed … the streets are impassable, stones and dust everywhere … stones are piled high in the streets, often twenty feet high.

Many of Valletta's ancient palaces have been badly hit: the Auberge de France is in ruins, the Governor's Palace and the Market severely damaged.

The Auberge d'Aragon and the Auberge d'Italie received direct hits. The King George V Hospital in Floriana is destroyed.

It is estimated that 70 per cent of buildings in Valletta and Floriana have now been destroyed or damaged.

Later, there was more radio news:

Today, Malta experienced the heaviest attack yet made from the air – and it was directed at the civilian population. The 280 tons of high explosives dropped on the tiny peninsula of Valletta this afternoon were not stray bombs intended for Grand Harbour. Luftwaffe operations reports reveal a deliberate intention to bomb Valletta itself, with targets including the Governor's Palace and several residential quarters in the city.

The enemy employed heavy high explosives for maximum destruction: Berlin radio claimed that many one-ton bombs were used in the raid.

Disregarding the danger to civilians, the bombing was an apparent attempt to destroy the heart of Malta's government. The Governor and Commander in Chief has now decided to evacuate the administration inland.

There wasn't much space for optimism with all that. But many of us had escaped, including Mabel Strickland – and she played it very much against the odds. Mabel worked endlessly and even the bombs could not drive her out of her office. However, her angels were with her on 7 April 1942, and she was persuaded – I don't know by whom, but my salutations to them – to go down into the shelters. Soon after, her office was blown to bits. The impact bomb landed on it as though it was a bullseye. This direct hit destroyed sixteen rooms, but the printing press was saved. The next morning, leading by example, she was back at work, although sitting a little farther down the hall. The office she'd had yesterday no longer had a front wall. Or much else. It didn't slow her down in any way.

Her reputation for tenacity was paramount among the Royal Navy. Admiral Cunningham, the Commander-in-Chief, Mediterranean Fleet, growled to his adjutant when the telephone rang at 6 a.m.: 'It's more war or it's Mabel.' The thing is, Mabel was committed, and by that I mean committed by her nature to do everything to help Malta and her people survive, and for Britain, the Allies, to win the war. It was people like her that made survival possible when, for such a long time, that didn't appear an option.

What a dreadful time it was. But the closeness of my family, the remarkable camaraderie of so many people who simply would not give up – the defiant defenders like Mabel Strickland – took us through it. I will truly never know how that was managed, for it was the darkest of days, as the official battle log shows. What the timeline doesn't reflect is the incidents of individual suffering when lives were ended or ruined forever.

Civilians shied away from prime target areas, Grand Harbour or Marsamxett, the airfields at Luqa, Ħal Far, and Ta' Qali. It was deemed safe to be in Gozo as there were no military installations, no anchorage for shipping and, so, no reason for bombing raids. Many of our friends had moved there to stay out of range. Families with young children were encouraged to be there.

Some of them became what they cruelly call collateral damage, a misfortune of war. Two Luftwaffe planes were flying over Gozo, chased by RAF Spitfires, and to lighten their load, the German pilots jettisoned two 2,000lb bombs to give themselves more lift and speed. There was a whistling sound, one bomb landed in a field, the other in the Tax-Xelina village square near the school. Children died and so did those parents who had dropped them off and were buying bread in the bakery. There were bodies laid out on wooden doors with sackcloth 'pillows', and injuries ranging from lost limbs to shrapnel cuts. That was simply 'an incident' on that particular day.

The Axis air forces attacked incessantly — and that's the correct word, for it was every hour of the day that bombs dropped — with wave after wave of bombers in an onslaught more intensive and prolonged than the Battle of Britain. Families had burrowed into the caves, the catacombs of Malta, and made their homes there. They had taken with them furniture that hadn't gone in a blast or fire; they'd turned all manner of areas in the rock into shanty towns for shelter as the towns and villages were being reduced to rubble. The Italians were making plans to occupy our island and expecting the garrison and people to surrender. We'd been starved and bombed to death — what else were they to suppose?

The Luftwaffe pilots did not know where to drop their bombs, so great was the havoc seen from the air. What more could they find to destroy?

But the clouds of enemy planes kept sweeping in, with the blue of the sky only slightly visible behind the grey mass of aircraft. On those days the sun had Hitler's hat on.

They say statistics lie, but I can assure you that they're correct with regard to those concerning the bombs dropped on Malta that year. I felt many of them directly. During the entire siege, the statistics later given showed that the Italians flew 35,724 missions against us and the Luftwaffe 37,432, but the German devastation was achieved in a wickedly short space of time: in 1942 alone, the Luftwaffe completed 31,391 attacks on us. Do the maths — the months in the year, the days in the week, the hours in the day. The storms of bombers and the diabolical Stukas — 31,391 attacks.

After just that one horrendous day of 7 April 1942, it felt as though someone should give us a medal.

King George VI did.

It just took a little time for it to be delivered.

There was quite something of a war on.

5

ESCAPE

'Malta is the unsinkable aircraft carrier.'
WINSTON CHURCHILL, 1942

When Malta was presented with the George Cross, I had a new admirer, the dashing Wing Commander Arthur Donaldson. He was a gentleman and devoted to me. I still have the affectionate letters he wrote, kept safely in a neat blue box. Several of the letters were written while he was convalescing after being wounded in battle. He did like to fly right at the enemy bombers, ignoring the protective Messerschmitts swarming around.

He became my regular escort to the dances we adored as a way to forget our reality. They were, as I noted, a fantasy: the officers' club events were formal affairs, with gowns or at least home-made 'creations' from whatever material was available, and everyone made an effort. I literally put on a brave face with my make-up. I was lucky with my hair; it was long and thick and dark. Arthur and others would compare me to Ava Gardner so I felt quite the 5ft 2in movie star.

He was twenty-eight years old, one of a trio of brothers who were all fighter plots. Teddy and John were also squadron leaders, and between them had a mantelpiece of flying and bravery honours and medals.

Arthur, of course, was my favourite.

He saved my life.

He'd had what he called 'a good war' before he was posted to Malta. When the war began he was an RAF flying instructor and subsequently joined Douglas Bader's 242 Squadron flying Hurricanes. He took command of 263 Squadron and led many successful attacks on occupied French targets, including Querqueville Airfield. He wasn't so lucky in a June 1942 mission against Morlaix Airfield: his fighter was blasted by flak

75

and holed in three places. The shell fragments crashed into the cockpit and ripped his flying helmet open.

He was knocked unconscious, as the plane wobbled about in the air. He woke up, looked down, and there was the English Channel. Goodness knows how (the doctors told him it was impossible), he stayed alert and made it safely to Cornwall. Six weeks later he flew off HMS *Furious* to Malta leading a group of replacement Spitfires. When I met him he was Wing Commander (Flying) at Ta' Qali; by then we were taking the fight to the enemy and Arthur took part in the first offensive sweep over Sicily, scoring heavily against German and Italian aeroplanes. He was quite the 'ace' but so good natured and without the swagger of so many flyers. I understood the need for bravado, the swagger, but I preferred men without it. Although Arthur had met my father, and been round for tea, I was still on his strict curfew. Arthur wrote to my father telling of his intention to take me out, to 'date' me, but the curfew stayed in place. He also wrote to me all the time, letters when he could, telegrams most of the time. He always signed the letters with an added code, 'Up and Down', which was his way of saying he loved me.

Love was a popular currency during the Great Siege. I don't know how many times I was engaged or where the rings are, but they're around, somewhere. It was part of life and I'd see a pilot or a naval officer and announce: 'See you tomorrow.'

'Perhaps' was always the answer.

Perhaps. I met submarine officers who said they could never go into battle in the sky, deal with the enemy in the air, endure the fear-inducing vertigo of such combat. In turn, pilots swore to me they could never endure the claustrophobia of being under the sea. Still, up there, down there, on the sea, on the ground, they'd soon get you, the Germans. They were determined, with the relentless bombing and indiscriminate human target practice. I was upset for these young men – most of them were nineteen or twenty years old – who clung to a future which, perhaps, they might have. I felt sorry for them but was careful with my sorrow. Arthur was more assured. He'd been married and wrote to explain to my father that his wife had been emotionally ill and was now in a special hospital, adding that they were separated.

In fact, Arthur did bring a sense of security. I'd been to a dance at the Sliema Servicemen's Club and I left early on his arm. The Messerschmitt pilots, the cruel, wicked men in the cockpits of those 109 fighters, always targeted anyone they spotted in the open. Which was just where Arthur and I were as we wandered home.

He heard the Bf 109, the whine of an engine, before I did. He knew what was happening. 'Get down, get down,' he yelled at me and gave me a less than gentle shove onto the ground. There was no time for courtesy.

I was face down, but naturally I wanted to see what was going on. I was trying to turn my body around when from far off the first tracers of bullets began hitting the ground to the left of us. Turning, I could see the German pilot in his cockpit as the plane swooped towards us. He seemed to have a frozen face, a fixed grimace. Then, suddenly, that went blank as Arthur landed with a bump on top of me, trying to cover my body. He was willing to sacrifice himself to protect me.

The Messerschmitt roared low over us, strafing the road with gunfire, bullets spitting at us. The bullets danced, up and down and spinning back into the sky, it was like being in a hailstorm. The would-be assassins splattered bullets all around us, but didn't hit their targets. I couldn't scream, I couldn't make a sound, for Arthur was all but smothering me. We'd nearly been victims of kill-time tactics: fly in low, machine-gun anyone you see and escape. We were lucky, if you don't count the mess to my dress. For the German pilots it was just a bit of fun but Arthur the gentleman didn't think much of it; combat was one thing, scalp-hunting quite something else. I never saw him so angry. Not frightened – angry. I wasn't frightened either after I got over the shock. The attack was one of those things and it seemed the norm to accept it back then. Now, I feel it reflects simply the devilish do or-die lives we were trapped in.

Arthur shared his attitude to danger with all the other pilots I met. If the bullet had your name on it, that was it. Otherwise, you just had to get on with it; Malta was being blasted into the ground and you had to have a positive attitude, even if in the moment you were absolutely petrified. Life for so many of them was as good as the level of their pink gin.

The pilots were superstitious, like sportsmen before a big match or event. Arthur Donaldson came from quite a distinguished family: his father was a judge, and together he and his brothers had chests of medals (three DSOs, two AFCs and a DFC and Bar). Arthur wore a signet ring with the family crest. He was very proud of it. He asked me to keep it safe for him between missions, but he always wore it when he flew into action. Through him I was involved in the inside story on an extraordinary event, when the George Cross arrived in Malta. The award was announced on Wednesday, 15 April 1942 – at last some good news to punctuate the usual air attacks and more delayed convoys from Gibraltar and Alexandria. The George Cross was instituted by George VI as the highest honour to be awarded to civilians – equivalent to the Victoria Cross, which was reserved for Britain's Armed Forces.

We were told in detail, in recognition of all that we'd suffered and endured, of how that day the King had read through the latest dispatches on the war in the Mediterranean and then taken a sheet of Buckingham Palace letterhead and written a message to us: 'To honour her brave people, I award the George Cross to the Island Fortress of Malta to bear witness to a heroism and devotion that will long be famous in history.'

The King was genuinely moved by what had happened to us. I was particularly pleased that he associated himself with the artillery, which my brother Victor was involved with. King George VI wrote: 'I have been watching with admiration the stout-hearted resistance of all in Malta – service personnel and civilians alike – to the fierce and constant air attacks of the enemy in recent weeks. In the active defence of the island the RAF have been ably supported by the Royal Malta Artillery, and it therefore gives me special pleasure, in recognition of their skill and resolution, to assume the Colonelcy-in-chief of the regiment.'

Malta's Governor, Sir William Dobbie, replied: 'The people and garrison of Malta are deeply touched by Your Majesty's kind thought for them in conferring on the Fortress of Malta this signal honour. It has greatly encouraged everyone, and all are determined that by God's help Malta will not weaken but will endure until victory is won.'

Two days later, Governor Dobbie spoke over the crackling Rediffusion system: 'I am quite sure that everyone in Malta felt the thrill of real pleasure when they learnt of this high honour His Majesty the King has been pleased to bestow on this Island Fortress. I do not recall an instance when an honour of this kind has been conferred by a British Sovereign on a community. The safety and well-being of this Fortress rest under God on four supports: these are the three Services and the civil population.'

Arthur and his Spitfires were a more practical contribution, but the pride I felt in us not being forgotten and, indeed, saluted, something all of us gloried in, still exists. Mabel Strickland was beside herself. The Strickland House newspapers *Il-Berqa*, *The Times of Malta* and *The Sunday Times of Malta* gave huge coverage to the King's award, as did the outside world. Mabel had better contacts, though, and she secured a scoop, a front-page 'fudge', with a Stop Press item: the idea to award the honour to the island had been the King's own idea. Mabel plastered 'MALTA G.C.' on the leader page and wrote the editorial:

> The outstanding importance in the achievement of victory of maintaining civilian life on the front line of battle and of the civilians' magnificent response to the ordeal imposed on them by a ruthless enemy. Malta in her entirety, with the help of God, has withstood the test and the King has set his seal on the pages of history. His Majesty's act brings immense consolation to all in Malta and floods the humblest among us with joyous pride in having lived and strived through Malta's greatest hour.

The following day, 18 April, the George Cross was added to *The Times* masthead. A day later, our sister newspaper, the *Sunday Times*, boasted the George Cross and Mabel's new editorial, which included the line 'His Majesty the King has singled Malta out for fame and by his act has placed her at the top of the Empire and given her a place in the annals of history that will have a great bearing upon our future.'

I knew Mabel had been doing more than editorialising in print, however – she'd been preaching to Winston Churchill and the other war leaders too, about her lack of confidence in Governor Sir William Dobbie. She believed him a good man, but one who was about to give up, to surrender. And he may have if supplies had run out and the people began starving. Mabel, being Mabel, didn't care about any of that. Everyone should go down with the ship. I think she probably had the majority opinion. I never knew the intricacies of the in-fighting, but there was much going on behind the scenes involving Lord Mountbatten, Churchill and those protecting Malta. I do know that Governor Dobbie was tired and weary of carrying such a burden, but it was only reluctantly that Churchill replaced him with Lord Gort, who (we were constantly reminded) had won the Victoria Cross for extreme valour during the First World War. Lord Gort was a commanding figure and boosted morale. It seems strange now for me to see him through the ages for then, to the young me, he seemed so terribly ancient. Yet, that itself was a comfort, just as spotting him touring the streets was a tonic. He aggressively improved ways and facilities to fight back but for him, as for Governor Dobbie, everything depended on convoys getting to us with vital supplies, from bullets to powdered milk. And the bombs kept dropping. In those few spring weeks of 1942, the Luftwaffe imposed the most intense bombardment of the war on us. I had to wonder why they wanted to bash the life out of us if Malta was such a crucial element of war in the Mediterranean; there would be nothing left.

We had to queue for everything – including drinking water, as pipes for distribution and pumping were smashed up by the bombing. The new phrase was 'endurance and fortitude', which meant 'Don't use too much water'. I was wearing my mother's good curtains, which had been designed into a dress. My father's shoes had soles of rubber from car tyres; his pork pie hat, still with its bullet hole, was all that fitted him properly. Everything on four legs had been killed and those existing on two legs were awaiting their turn. Even if you had meat, though, there was no fuel to cook it with. Wood fires were fed by furniture, and antique wood, collectible pieces, burned best. We had no need for heat – the climate brought that and with it dehydration, which, of course, there was not much water to combat. Desperation spins like a wheel. In time, you couldn't even find a chair to sit and watch it.

Lord Gort – as the new man in charge, with Brigadier Gatt as his ADC – was fine but, as always, we needed miracles. I was still shaken up by the bomb that devastated the Opera House when two days later the Luftwaffe dropped three bombs on the church at Mosta near the Ta' Qali airfield. The area was very close to the fighter-plane base, so aerial bombardment was a matter of daily endurance, but these three bombs hit the top of the church, the Rotunda at Mosta, the third largest dome in Europe. Two of the impact bombs bounced off the Rotunda without exploding. Still, there's always one. The third, a huge affair, like an overfed torpedo, pierced the dome and continued on into the church. It was 4.45 p.m. and around three hundred people were inside, waiting for Mass. Above them was an unexploded bomb. The Royal Engineers made it safe and dumped it offshore. Luck? Oh, much more than that.

It's easy to see why it was declared a miracle. For me, as for so many of us, the next months were packed with miracles – depending on the definition.

The who, what and whatever of that is for infinite debate. All I know is that Spitfires and Messerschmitts were playing dodgems in the skies above us all day and every day.

Two attempts to relieve Malta failed when supply ships were bombed in the Grand Harbour and newly arrived planes, mostly Spitfires, were destroyed in enemy raids. It was like watching your long-awaited meal being snatched away from the table, just as you sat down to eat. It was a race against the clock but, despite the scarcity of food and ongoing health problems because of it, the people's attitude was strong. My mother was concerned all the time – but for us, not for herself. Like so many, she seemed to want to assume the burden of concern and fear from her loved ones. I'd still run under a table if she told me to.

The George Cross award strengthened our determination, but more significantly the determination of the soldiers, sailors and airmen who were daily targets in this worst of wartime periods for the Allies. At every turn, Hitler seemed to be winning. The Luftwaffe were instructed to clear the way for the Italian convoys supplying Rommel's Afrika Korps and it seemed nothing would stop them.

We had the George Cross award – if not the medal – but military resources and food rations were all but finished. Soup was thinly coloured water. If someone offered rabbit, it was certainly rat or cat. Fuel was restricted to military operations and ammunition was running out: the planes were attacking but the anti-aircraft guns were only allocated so many rounds to fire a day.

But we had my Arthur and his Spitfires, and hope that some fuel would arrive to allow the Spitfires to fly. We prayed… a lot.

Someone was listening.

It was not until the Santa Marija Convoy arrived (on the Feast of the Assumption, 15 August 1942) with food, arms and ammunition and all the other necessary paraphernalia of warfare that a brake was applied to the high-speed horror of all those long preceding months. It was even thought possible to arrange a formal presentation of the George Cross to Malta on 13 September 1942, in the Palace Square, Valletta. It was most appropriate, for that convoy, 'Operation Pedestal', is still commemorated in Malta as 'a gift from Heaven' and to the memory of all the lives lost trying so hard to get supplies to us. Only five of the fourteen merchant ships reached the Grand Harbour. It was a massacre of men.

The eventual safe arrival of the *Ohio*, with its ample cargo of food, general provisions, oil and desperately needed aviation fuel was, strategically, a triumph. It saved our lives. If it hadn't been for the *Ohio*, we would never have survived. Seventy-five years later, I am sitting on the same wall in front of our house, overlooking a now tranquil harbour opposite the Three Cities and recall a very different, breathtaking scene. For everyone on the island of Malta, our lives were in the hands of that ship.

It was bombed all the way. It came limping in like a neglected old dog. Along with the other four vessels it had made it past minefields, submarine squads, German E-boats, Italian motor torpedo boats and the swarms of fighters and bombers in the sky. More than five hundred Royal Navy and Merchant Navy sailors and airmen were killed – but not in vain. Once again, we could fight back. Spitfires sped off into the skies from the decks of the aircraft carrier HMS *Furious* to make merry hell for the enemy shipping. Submarines returned for underwater devilry. We also had supplies – not much, but the threat of starvation and imminent surrender was gone. But not the bravado of the fighting men, as you will learn. The ceremony to present the George Cross was as solemn and dignified as circumstances allowed. My brother Victor's regiment, the Royal Malta Artillery, accompanied by the King's Own Malta Regiment band, mounted a guard of honour after marching down Republic Street. The Regent Cinema, where I saw *Robin Hood* with Errol Flynn and Olivia de Havilland, and the Casino Maltese, where my father gambled, were piled in the street, their ruins levelled and stacked.

Everyone who could be was on parade. Lord Gort and the Chief Justice, Sir George Borg, were given an ovation as the former handed the box containing the George Cross and the letter from the King to the Chief Justice. Governor Gort proclaimed: 'By the command of the King, I now present to the People of Malta and its Dependencies the decoration His Majesty has awarded to them in recognition of the gallant service which they have already rendered in the struggle for freedom.'

The Royal Malta Artillery band was at full volume and the crowds were all around; everyone was desperate to see the George Cross. The party on the top table included the Archbishop of Malta, HH the Lieutenant Governor, the Vice Admiral Malta, the GOC, the Air Officer Commanding, the Bishop of Gozo, the Bishop of Tralles in Asia and many, many other important officials. Oh, decorum, decorum. We may have been physically shrunken through lack of food, but the people of Malta were bursting with pride that day.

My Arthur Donaldson was ordered to command three Spitfires on a low-level pass. It was to be textbook stuff, a display of the omnipotent RAF. Arthur's good friend was the Canadian pilot George Frederick 'Screwball' Beurling. He was a maverick, had crashed-landed a couple of times and survived, and his Spitfire kept getting riddled with bullets.

He was lovely, but he was only nineteen, possibly twenty, I think, and quite mad. He liked to get within a couple of hundred yards of enemy fighters. I called him 'Buzz', but his other nickname arguably fitted his antics much better. It was certainly 'Screwball' Beurling who was selected as part of the George Cross fly-past. Arthur told the story his way: 'They came roaring down the street wing-tip to wing-tip, almost grazing the walls on either side. As the leader, Beurling's task was difficult, but it was child's play compared to that of the senior officers who were defying death by inches. Screwball, however, decided to give the spectators an additional thrill and, to the amazement of everyone, most of all the wing commanders, who were congratulating themselves on the success of the venture, he calmly turned his plane over – and flew along the remainder of the street upside down!'

I thought it was appropriate following the twenty-six months of hell we had endured. The ultimate defiance.

It was only a distraction; the war was not over. Supplies had arrived, but how long would they last? Would we ever get more? People were now admitting that the thought of starving to death was their greatest fear. If you hugged someone in a greeting, you could feel their ribs. There was heartfelt relief when rations were raised ever so slightly; the bread allowance for men aged sixteen to sixty was a little more, and for the rest of us, cheese, fats and sugar were available. The snag was that without more convoys arriving, the food would run out by December (1942).

Even then, however, a battle that would mean so much in my life was being won in the North African desert. The Desert Rats, General Montgomery's Eighth Army, had begun their offensive against Rommel at El Alamein. After a bloodthirsty week as October became November that year, the Afrika Korps were in retreat. My nemesis, Erwin Rommel, the wily Desert Fox, had had his tail bitten off.

This, of course, helped Malta. We were still being bombed, but although deadly, the air raids were not so intense or frequent. And we were fighting back with our own attacks being masterminded from Malta.

Of course, Arthur Donaldson was hugely involved in this. I had been recruited from *The Times* as a civilian assistant/secretary in the offices of the Admiral of the Fleet, Andrew Browne Cunningham, known to us and many of his command as ABC. He was then Commander-in-Chief of the Mediterranean Fleet as well as First Sea Lord. Admiral Cunningham controlled the defence of the Mediterranean supply lines through Alexandria, Gibraltar and Malta. Arthur's squadron and the others had around two hundred Spitfires. There were also Mosquito fighter-bombers, Wellington medium-range bombers, Beaufort torpedo bombers and the vampire Beaufighters, which hunted in the night.

Arthur Donaldson was attacking the enemy day and night. I was very fond of Arthur, but I always felt he was too old for me; possibly not in years, but in attitude. Of course, he'd had to grow up fast, but I think his background, his own upbringing, had settled him in certain ways. As with everything at that time, the war wrote our story. Even with the horror going on around me, I refused to let it spoil my social life. After one mission I got a call saying Arthur had been in a huge dogfight and been hit and taken into the British military hospital. The doctor said he wasn't willing to be operated on until I was present. I had to go to the hospital and let Arthur see me before the operation went ahead.

His hand was tight on the throttle when a Messerschmitt blasted bullets through his aircraft, taking off two of his fingers. His 'lucky' signet ring was attached to one of them. He was shot in the feet and there was a bullet hole in his helmet, but it wasn't his time to die.

He never lost control of his Spitfire and got it down, but on a barbed-wire fence. He was covered in blood and shrapnel and cut by the fence. It was a very 'Steve McQueen in *The Great Escape*' moment.

His hand became gangrenous and his commanding officer insisted on sending him back to Britain for treatment. He wanted me to go with him but, although I liked him, the 'age gap' seemed too great. It was hard to look in his eyes, his sad, brown eyes. He took a £1 note and tore it in half.

He looked at me steadily and said to write a message on my half.

What to say? I liked Arthur, I was fond of Arthur. Might I have grown to love Arthur? It was something I paused to consider.

When I had to think about it, I knew that I was being true to myself when I offered a romantic gesture, a sort of we'll meet again, saying that after the war we'd get together. He accepted that I couldn't leave Malta, but if the passion and deep feelings had been there I would have. I knew I'd know, as it were, when I met a matching soul. Kismet. I'd seen enough sparks fly.

We wrote our words pledging to meet again and join up the two halves of the pound note and ourselves. And we did keep in touch, with affectionate cables and letters. And we did meet again.

But that was only after another bump in his road home. He was being flown out of Malta as a wounded stretcher case when the B-24 he was in crashed into the sea off Gibraltar. It was the cursed flight on which my friend Bella and her baby son died. But Arthur lived through it. In one of his letters to me he said he knew the plane was going to crash. He'd flown that way so many times and he knew the plane was too low.

Bella and her baby had died; my friends Tessa and Rosemary and I were a tiny, close group, but we were never really the same again. It affected us deeply. We'd been that little trio of girls who got on, knew each other's secrets, and would fight to help each other. Outwardly, Tessa's life went on, but she was not the girl I'd known before.

Arthur, however, never changed. He was one of three survivors. I thought he was like Mitch, my cat: he had the feline luck, the nine lives. He was in hospital again for many, many weeks before being moved to RAF Ibsley Fighter Station in Hampshire in March 1943. He wrote to me all the time, as persistent in love as he was in war. I believe I kept him happier during the conflict but, like Mabel Strickland, he was one of the committed. Arthur had faith that he was doing the right thing, for God and country. It is truly a gift to have certainty in war, but not so much in other times and moments. Arthur was still with me. But Bella and her baby had died. It wasn't possible to think straight. Life? Death? Who knows what tomorrow brings?

Happiness is an Aladdin's cave of compromises.

6

SWORD OF HONOUR

'Survival [...] is an infinite capacity for suspicion.'
JOHN LE CARRÉ, *TINKER TAILOR*
SOLDIER SPY (1974)

With my new job, I learned what a perilous predicament we were in. It was hard to disguise the truth so evident on the streets, but official statements and proclamations attempted to mitigate how awful it was.

Through the paperwork I saw in Admiral Cunningham's office, where I was now working, I clearly understood our desperate situation. We had supplies for the moment and Spitfires to defend us if they had fuel to fly. The air-raid sirens were like a deathly prelude, preparing us for the final act. We had suffered the worst months of the war by May 1942, but Malta survived as the prize of the Mediterranean. It was the 'must have' for the Axis and the Allies. I could see the tension stretching like a rubber band on the faces of Admiral Cunningham's commanders and advisers. I'd walk around carefully. I feared if I made a sudden noise they would snap.

Hitler was preparing to invade us and we were preparing to prevent it. We had the will but did we have the way?

In the middle of this entered the mild-mannered and misled boy Carmelo Borg Pisani. I'll always think of him as the 'boy' I knew around Valletta. He was an art student and seemed a nice lad, but he was shy. Even with all the tragedy that plagued my early years, what happened with Borg Pisani still haunts me. Only God can say the last words in cases like these.

He lived in Senglea, one of the three cities around the Grand Harbour, but he studied at the Umberto Primo art lyceum in Valletta. Before the war, Borg Pisani had won a scholarship to study at the Accademia di Belle Arti (the Academy of Fine Arts) in Rome. It was a huge honour; our great Maltese twentieth-century artist Emvin Cremona was there at the same time, but whereas he went on to be an heroic figure, his fellow student became despised. Borg Pisani believed Malta's heritage was suffering ruin through British rule. He thought, or was taught to think, that Malta should align with Italy and restore its Latin pride. His instinct was to join the army but he was turned down, rejected for his extremely poor eyesight. He was one Italian fighter with an excuse for not being able to hit a barn door. Tragically, with a great helping of naivety, he became a secret agent. Borg Pisani, with his milk-bottle-thick spectacles, was not cut out for that.

The Italian military intelligence (Servizio Informazioni Militare) were involved in planning the Italo-German invasion of Malta, codenamed Operation Herkules, and assigned Borg Pisani, by then in his mid-twenties, to assess the strength of our defences. On the evening of 17 May 1942, escorted by a torpedo boat, Borg Pisani left Portopalo in Sicily, for Malta, in a high-speed motorboat heading for the north-west of the island. The myopic man miraculously landed at the Dingli Cliffs in Ras id-Dawwara, which he knew from playing there as child. He transferred all his rations to a cave, which he also knew well from his youth. He was, in a way, captured by the weather. Storms and a rough sea swept away his rations and equipment and he would have gone too, had he not been rescued by a British patrol boat. He was taken to a military hospital, where he met the duty doctor Captain Tommy Warrington, a friend from his school days in Senglea. Warrington recognised him immediately.

This sorry episode and surrounding events has always been encompassed by confusion. It was all cloak-and-dagger stuff. Was there more to this story? That was certainly the insider talk in the inner war offices. Captain Warrington gave the boy hot drinks and food. In return, Borg Pisani happily told him everything about his mission. He had acted, he said, because he was frightened for his family, owing to the constant bombing, and wanted to see them. The patchwork transcript of this includes the following details:

> My nerves couldn't stand it. I thought of ways and means to get here, joined the Battaglione di Sbarco, then volunteered to do espionage work in Malta [...] Had about two-and-a-half months' training for the job [...] Having been shown a map of Malta marked with gun positions and defence posts, it was decided I should land in a small bay. I left in a rubber dinghy and had four haversacks. They contained twenty-two days' ration, water, medicine, bread which never goes stale,

concentrated fruit, transmitter and code written on celluloid group of letters, twelve grenades and an automatic revolver.

Captain Warrington, who remembered this man as a shy boy, was dismayed. Senglea, their home town, with its dockyards, had been the most bombed area of Malta. Borg Pisani had told him that he had sailed to the island out of worry for his family. But he was also admitting that he had offered to spy on Malta to help defeat his countrymen. Wasn't that treason? What was he sent to find out? Borg Pisani replied: 'What times the ghost ship comes into harbour [HMS *Welshman*, which brought supplies during the night and left harbour before dawn]. What are the military objectives in Gozo, the food situation and the morale of the troops and the population?' Crucially, he also admitted: 'I am willing to do anything to stop the constant bombings of the island by helping them conquer it.' It was the first of many interrogations over the following weeks, as charges were compiled against him.

Borg Pisani's arrest dominated much of our conversation. Were there other spies that we knew as friends? It made me look at people differently. My bosses just wanted it dealt with, and an example made of the perpetrator, and that meant one thing: execution.

Strange, that even with all the death and destruction, this was a horrifying thing, the premeditated disposal of a boy I knew. You parcel up the horror, put it in the attic.

The trial was held in camera and even the location of the court weighed against Borg Pisani. It was at the Lija Primary School. The courts had moved there from the Archbishop's Seminary in Floriana, after it was hit during an Italian air raid, having been transferred there from the Valletta Court House, which was destroyed in another Italian bombardment. Wartime had suspended the jury system, so three judges – Sir George Borg, president of the Court of Appeal, Professor Edgar Ganado and Dr William Harding – heard the first evidence on 12 November 1942. Borg Pisani was accused of having taken part in a conspiracy against the King and the Government.

He was charged with having landed in Malta on 'a spying mission with the aim of collecting information meant to help the enemy in their plans for the invasion of the island'. The defence did all that was legally possible, but their client had supplied all the conclusive evidence against himself and the result was inevitable. It was something to which all us islanders were connected; however you viewed the case, there was tragedy which, like cruelty, moves about like a searchlight, like the German pilots picking out random people and machine-gunning them. Cruelty roams about, without conscience, from one spot to another, spotlighting victims. Certainty is a blessing and a curse.

One thing was certain: Borg Pisani was going to die.

On 19 November, the court found him guilty on all counts and sentenced him to death by hanging.

The court, a British war tribunal, was justified in applying the law, and the execution took place nine days later. Many said good riddance and celebrated, but others argued that he died for his belief. For those whose ideal was to see Malta annexed to Italy he was a hero. But you can see why those who endured sufferings and hardships inflicted by the incessant bombardments couldn't (and still cannot) help but damn him as a traitor. War is ugly and very cruel, and the other side of the coin in this case was that all the Maltese with attachments to Rome thought they were doing their duty to shorten the war. Borg Pisani was one of them and decided to do what he believed in. The people of Malta condemned him as an Italian spy, when Italy was bombing his own country, and who can blame them? Who can judge any of it?

Complicating the matter even more was the suspicion that Borg Pisani had been set up by the Italians. It had all the hallmarks: the story of a young Maltese being executed by his own people might work internationally as profitable propaganda for the Axis. If that was the aim, however, it failed.

For me, the case lingers still, though. So many died in the Great Siege but it is, of course, the individual cases I remember. The pilots who never landed again, the sailors who never returned, the names that vanished from the dance cards These were people I knew and cared for. I believe these wartime experiences prepared me to deal with life and death for the rest of my life. If someone dies suddenly, it's easier emotionally to see it as an inconvenience, for it cuts the impact of the tragedy. It's happened, it's past, what's next? It worked during the bombardment; possibly it's the only way, at all times, to keep sane in such a capricious world. It gets me into arguments with myself when I get particularly passionate or annoyed about things which, in this context, are really not worth raising my blood pressure for – although it gets the blood whizzing around, which my doctor tells me is useful.

Death remained a daily possibility: we were nowhere near out of the firing line. We hoped for more hope. We needed it, indeed, for now it was a race either to succeed or surrender. Operation Pedestal had bought time but, as I knew, the next deadline was 3 December 1942. After that, no more food – at all.

No one escapes when there is nothing; rich or poor, it does not matter. The despicable black market criminals are impotent too. You can't barter your wits' end. There was little flour or other staples such as potatoes. Almost every animal on the islands had been eaten (Mitch, under lock and key, and a few other cats were exceptions) and fuel and ammunition were at the head of the queue. At times, it appeared the choice might be cannibalism or Hitler. I think most people would rather have eaten their own hearts out than succumb to the Nazis. That November, the war in North Africa was going our way: Tobruk was taken and the Desert Rats were marching on Benghazi. With the Axis planes distracted, a convoy – at great risk – was sent to us from Alexandria with supplies. Four ships arrived safely before the end of the month. And with two days to go before the 3 December deadline, there was more on the way from Egypt. When it arrived on 6 December, the gratitude was overwhelming, even if the smiles were weak through lack of nutrition and downright weariness. When I looked at the crowds cheering the arrival of the convoy, some people appeared translucent. Stoicism is suffering too.

Towards the end of that so-terrible 1942, daily life had become comparatively more amiable for me, but we were still living with the screech of bombs and the firecracker-like sequences of explosions. The cigarette smoke was more pungent – less straw, more tobacco in the mix – and there was gin and some whisky, brought in by pilots and sailors; yet fuel and food were still short in supply. For some, the extra food was too much. They couldn't eat it because their stomachs had shrunk.

I'm still amazed I ended up so healthy, for along with everything else there was so much disease, including tuberculosis and dysentery, and there were regular outbreaks of polio. A huge assortment of ways to die. There was no danger of gluttony, but I had to learn to eat again; we all did. Through the naval offices I knew about the extent of the supplies, but it was carefully portioned out.

There was no rash Christmas jollity – like good food, a fond memory – and it was February 1943 before rations were increased. I thought I must be getting old, for all the pilots looked so much younger, so many pimply boys risking their lives. Bombing raids were frequent, but I noticed that the planes were now in little groups, maybe a formation of five where before it had been fifty. And they had to be nippy, for the Spitfires would instantly be up and after them. So bombs were dropped in a panic and could and did land anywhere. There was no distinction about 'targets', although there never had been, really. The island and everyone on it had always been the target. We could watch ferocious dogfights above us as the pilots jousted, but you had to be careful for, like stair rods of rain, the dogfight debris – spent cartridges, bits of bullets and aircraft fragments – hammered down from the sky. My language skills saw me on call much of the time, and with my job as a secretary for the navy, I got an intimate view of the people's determination to preserve their homeland, which had been turned into a garrison, like a Foreign Legion outpost. The war commanders were there to do a job, but the civilians were just as dedicated. Now there were more commanders than ever. Malta, the place everybody had tried to avoid being posted to, was becoming popular: it was a bridgehead to the Allied victory and the frenzied activity in the offices of ABC Cunningham told me we were on the move. The background to this was the success against Rommel in North Africa, the Russians retaliating in Stalingrad, and supplies reaching us.

The tipping point was the Allied invasion of Sicily, from where so much of our early misery had arrived. For the landings in Sicily on 10 July 1943, all the Allied commanders, including Supreme Commander General Dwight D. Eisenhower, were in Malta. The airfields, which only weeks earlier had looked like derelict scrapyards, boasted over thirty British squadrons and over five hundred aircraft, while three American squadrons flew seventy-five Spitfires from Gozo.

Finally, the Maltese mouse was roaring.

Our offices were working non-stop, supplying information to Winston Churchill and the commanders who were overseeing what was the larger picture, as it were. If Italy was manoeuvred out and, as Admiral Cunningham hoped, 'turned against Hitler', it would be a tremendous coup. We were due some luck. It took a little time arriving.

First came the Luftwaffe on 19 July 1943, with night attacks as unexpected as they were unprepared for. There was damage, death and injury and more again during the following forty-eight hours. The raids came as such a surprise that many people didn't take cover and were hurt by friendly fire: shrapnel from the thunderstorm of artillery anti-aircraft shells. The Luftwaffe turned up again, like a bad nightmare, on 20 July and again at night on 26 July; like Dracula, they just didn't want to stay dead. As they dropped their bombs, the artillery barrage in the Grand Harbour opened up like a firework display and when that eased, only for moments, the sky reignited as the barrage was joined by the guns of the ships in the harbour. We were more like lions than mice now. A young artilleryman, Vincent Attard of Żabbar in the south-east of Malta, was the last person to be killed in an air raid. I remember that, for it was symbolic to us. It's strange, the memory. I also recall it being so hot that July and August, the heat more fierce than ever in high summer. With all the destruction, the ruins and rubble, the dust was always whirling up so you were uncomfortable, sweltering, filthy-skinned and fearful. And always thirsty. With friends, I risked sneaking through the rusty barbed wire on the beach to swim. Swimming and sunbathing with the war going on was quite something. There were always a group of us – earlier in the war, it would have been my friends Tessa and Bella and the boys we gathered around us. We'd have picnics. There were always pilots or submariners or sailors. They'd take their shirts off in the Malta sun and their white skins would redden in no time. Our shirts stayed on!

Most of them wanted to marry me. But I didn't want to get married. Not all of them were my boyfriends. Bella had stolen some of them. She was very pretty and I was so jealous of her that I scratched her face out of some of our snapshots! I never told her, or anybody else. I became clever at keeping secrets. When my children come across any of those photos now, angry biro marks defacing some poor creature, I do feel a bit guilty. And they are quite shocked!

With the Allies in charge of Sicily, the Fascist Grand Council had given a vote of no confidence in Benito Mussolini on 24 July 1943. He was removed from office by King Victor Emmanuel III, arrested and replaced by Marshal Pietro Badoglio as Italian head of state the next day.

Secret negotiations sprang up between ABC Cunningham's office and the commanders. Italy was, as far as Hitler was concerned, officially still at war, but Marshal Badoglio now regarded the cause as futile and wanted Italy out of the conflict. Badoglio and the Allies, aware that this had to be kept quiet for reasons of strategy and safety, began secret negotiations. After an intricate series of events, the armistice was announced on 8 September 1943, with the Allies holding Sicily. For me it had been like being in one of Eric Ambler's spy thrillers. The atmosphere was very much need-to-know until that formal radio broadcast.

I had a front-row seat for another epic moment in the history of what everyone now calls the fortress of the Middle Sea. About forty-eight hours after the surprise armistice was made public, the Italian fleet sailed into the Grand Harbour – watched over, I like to think, by Grand

Master Jean Parisot de la Valette and monitored by the defenders who had kept out Suleiman the Magnificent and all other would-be invaders. Sir Andrew Cunningham, our beloved ABC, had a touch of Lord Nelson in his character. That day, as Admiral of the Fleet, he sent a signal to the Secretary of the Admiralty reading: 'Be pleased to inform their Lordships that the Italian battle fleet now lies at anchor under the guns of the fortress of Malta.'

Those seventy-six Italian vessels anchored in Malta's harbours were under the command of Admiral Alberto Da Zara, a neat, manicured man and wearing a sparkling white uniform when I met him. He gave away his nationality by having a little jaunt to his naval cap. He landed at the Customs House Steps at Valletta and was met by an honour guard and ABC. The official meeting was to be held in the Lascaris War Rooms, the underground command centre comprising a network of mechanically ventilated tunnels, and communications and cypher rooms.

It was a matter of a few steps to the rooms designated for the signing of the formal documents of surrender of the Italian fleet, but Admiral Da Zara was taken on a short tour by ABC. He was determined the Italian admiral should see close-up the impact, the horror and destruction that the Axis bombardment had inflicted on Malta.

I know he felt that by doing so, Admiral Da Zara would consider he was doing the right thing. He was then escorted to our naval headquarters.

As though I was simply being asked to 'take a letter', I was called in to witness the formal signing of the 'surrender' documents. At the time, I recall there was much hustle and bustle and then the solemnity of the moment – and this remains an amazing event in my mind: Admiral Da Zara, handing over his ceremonial sword as part of the ceremony, is the clearest image I have. There were smiles and handshakes, but it was subdued. It was a pivotal moment in the war; as it took place, the true significance was most certainly beyond me. It is only now, as I am recalling so many of the events in my life for this book, that I have mentioned the episode to my sons for the first time. Of course, they are a bit shocked that such an historic occasion should never have come up before. When I talk about it now, everyone is amazed and I suppose I realise how important that moment really was. But when you're living the moment, there's no time to be thinking about it. And then something else happens. It's like the telephone always ringing when the kettle's boiling.

When you've been present at such events, it's difficult to regard them at the time as such important history. I was also there when the plans for the invasion of Sicily were discussed and other 'secret' events too. I never signed any papers; I was never sworn to secrecy. I was simply trusted.

Time seemed to speed up for me. For all of Malta. It had been us against them for so long, but now we felt part of a team and charging forward together. No longer alone. That evening, ABC Cunningham and Admiral Da Zara met at the Lascaris War Rooms, where they agreed to take most of the Italian warships to Alexandria, in Egypt, for safety. The armistice remained delicate, because the Allies very much wanted the Italians to be in the fight against Hitler – with us, rather than on the fence.

The Italians were compromised and had to surrender their shipping under the Allies' terms, which included British use of their ports and merchant shipping. All this was contained in the 'Long Document of Armistice Terms' and ABC was host when Marshal Badoglio and America's future president, General Eisenhower, signed the document, witnessed by General Alexander, 1st Earl Alexander of Tunis, on board, appropriately, the British battleship *Nelson*. What became the Badoglio Proclamation was signed in Grand Harbour at 12.45 p.m. on 29 September 1943, and officially took Italy out of the war. Now the navy could deploy in strength from the Mediterranean.

We were also getting stronger, healthier. Supplies were arriving and food was better and sometimes it even had some taste: there was more flour than dust in the bread! It didn't stop our concerns, of course, for after three years of the bombs and everything else they threw at us, we knew it was far from at an end. Many walls in Malta had crumbled (75 per cent of the houses in Valletta were damaged or destroyed) but I still felt squeezed by a suspenseful claustrophobia. There seemed no way of escape. And Malta was once again getting crowded with new arrivals of our young overseas defenders.

The war was close, but the imminent threat of invasion was over. People were able to safely move around more; there were church bells not sirens sounding in the air, and the sailors and airmen, American as well as British and Australian, instigated a nightlife in Valletta. Laughter replaced hysteria and the clubs and bars became popular and loud again.

It was a different atmosphere, but it still remained one of war. I couldn't relax. Much of that was to do with my family. My father had not been well – the shortages had played badly with his health. His face, the sallow skin, reflected inner problems that the doctors could do nothing for. The irony was that although we now had the food, my father couldn't eat much. His weakness didn't mellow him, but the fractious relationship we had did not ease my concern for him.

My mother nursed him and my brothers helped all they could, but he was fading before us. Yet I remained 'on curfew' and the excuse of 'duty calls' was of no interest to him. I was busy, for war dictates its own paperwork and usually in triplicate; there wasn't always carbon paper, so often documents had to be typed several times. There was no quick fix for mistakes, they had to be typed again. I learned that in all vital duties, the detail requires attention; everything must go in the diary. I also learned that there is always change.

ABC moved on to London to become First Sea Lord, replacing Sir Dudley Pound, who was dying. Sir John Cunningham, his good friend (and not related), was appointed Commander-in-Chief of the Mediterranean. We had a departure parade for ABC and he had tears in his eyes – understandable, for this man had held so much life and death in his hands.

When my father died in 1944 he was, in his way, another casualty of the war and I mourned him in that way. He died from emphysema, brought on by smoking; he was a habitual smoker, non-stop and, in time, it killed him. For me, my father seems such a distant figure, as he was emotionally while I was growing up. He was protective and caring but not in a 'loving' way.

I had made many friends in the naval offices and I was offered the opportunity to go and work in Sicily, using my language skills in dialogues between the British and local Italian officers. My friend Tessa had been given the chance but couldn't take it, so I grabbed it with both hands. Many of the pilots I knew in Valletta were back and forward to Sicily all the time and I knew many of the girls working there. My mother encouraged me to go, as it was a chance to escape from all that had happened. It was true, for I'd had enough of Malta. I wanted to get off the island. I'd seen enough bombs and bombing but I'd also been told so much about other places – London, the English countryside, the Scottish mountains, and New York – and places I'd only read or talked about.

My father's death gave me freedom, but I felt my mother should have that too. Frantic as these years had been, it had been a lonely life for her. I thought it would be good to give her some time with herself; she was a young woman and I knew she would meet someone else and marry again. I didn't want to be in the way.

It would be my first trip away from Malta, from home; my first journey abroad on my own. My mother put the fear of God in me: all Service people – Army, Navy, RAF, anyone in uniform – were up to no good, no good whatsoever. I suggested that I'd survived the Great Siege, so could take care of myself. My mother told me: 'That was a rehearsal.'

In the beginning, Diana with her brother Antoine.

Off-duty: Portrait when for a moment the bombing stopped in 1944.

The Navy Lark on Malta before the war in the Mediterranean.

The ace RAF pilots who kept flying and fighting and below...

The soldiers who held fast as Malta became the most bombed place on earth.

Diana with Tony Clarkson and, right and below, some of the servicemen she befriended as part of the war effort.

Spitfire pilot Sandy Powell.

A Lancaster bomber.

A page from Diana's wartime scrapbook including a news report of Arthur Donaldson's air attack survival and David Milford Haven.

King George V1 on his visit to Malta to present the island with the George Cross.

The bombed-out Opera House — Diana was nearby and blown off her feet by the blast from the aerial bomb.

Diana's photograph of the Queen and Prince Philip dancing at the 1967 Gala Ball at the Government Palace in Malta and below...

Wartime distraction, the opera: Tito Gobbi performing with Diana's sister-in-law Alice Falzom [Antoine's wife].

Diana and Ian Mackintosh dancing at the same event.

Diana with her brothers and mother.

In Love and War: Mrs and Mrs Ian Mackintosh
and below...

High jinks for ENSA and...

Chin-up — champagne for the
happy couple.

The Mackintosh clan in post-war Britain.

Donald Neville-Willing with Ian, Cameron and Robert Mackintosh.

Diana's 'boys', Cameron, Robert and Nicky.

Let's get this show on the road — the 'boys' put on a revue.

THE GREAT SIEGE – CHRONOLOGY

The last air raid on Malta occurred on 20 July 1943. It was the 3,340th alert since 11 June 1940:

1940
10 June: Italy declares war on the United Kingdom.
22 June: The first six Hurricane fighters arrive on Malta to join the three Gladiators in the Malta Fighter Flight.
November: The 10th Heavy Anti-Aircraft Regiment arrives on Malta.

1941
January: The 7th Anti-Aircraft Brigade is formed under the command of Brigadier N. V. Sadler.
11 January: HMS *Illustrious* (aircraft carrier) limps into Malta's Grand Harbour for urgent repairs.
16 January: A large German air raid by about seventy Ju 87 and Ju 88 aircraft attacks Grand Harbour, targeting HMS *Illustrious*.
17 January: Second large air raid on Grand Harbour.
19 January: Third large air raid on Grand Harbour. Only one minor hit on HMS *Illustrious*.
23 January: HMS *Illustrious* sails for Alexandria.
31 January: Brigadier Cecil John Woolley, MC assumes command of the 7th Anti-Aircraft Brigade.
February: A series of daylight and then night raids commences attacking Malta and the airfields at Luqa and Ħal Far in particular.
18 April: Anti-aircraft defences are reorganised with the formation of the 10th Anti-Aircraft Brigade (commander: Brigadier D. A. H. Hire), which takes command of all the heavy anti-aircraft regiments, leaving the 7th Anti-Aircraft Brigade (commander: Brigadier C. J. Woolley) in command of the light anti-aircraft and searchlight units.

June: German air forces in Sicily and Southern Italy are reduced by their redeployment in operations against the Soviet Union.

November: German air forces are again deployed to Sicily and Southern Italy. A new phase of air attacks against Malta begins.

1942

8–9 March: Malta endures over twenty-one hours of continuous air attacks.

April: German air attacks start targeting the anti-aircraft gun batteries. Casualties in the 7th and 10th Anti-Aircraft Brigades reach 149 killed and 290 wounded.

7 May: Lord Gort arrives on Malta to assume his appointment as Governor. He brings with him the George Cross on behalf of His Majesty the King to be presented to the people of Malta.

June: The level of air attacks decreases.

October: Another air offensive starts, focusing on the airfields and defences.

1943

January: Large-scale air attacks decrease significantly, but are replaced by periodic German fighter-bomber sweeps.

March–April: No air attacks reported.

July: Two air raids are mounted against Royal Navy shipping in the Grand Harbour. Allied forces invade Sicily.

August: There are no further air attacks on Malta, and the British forces on the island begin to be scaled down.

3 September: Allied forces invade Italy. The Italian government agrees to an armistice.

8 September: The Italian armistice is announced to the public.

7

PRIVATES ON PARADE

'Fasten your seat belts. It's going to be a bumpy night.'
BETTE DAVIS AS MARGO CHANNING,
ALL ABOUT EVE (1950)

I'm not going to tell you his full name, because I can't remember it. Tommy was an RAF pilot, a twenty-three-year-old and therefore 'veteran' of the Spitfire, and he thought rather a lot of me. He was a daredevil and one of a crowd of us who went on dates in Palermo. The Germans had taken over most of Italy and there were constant concerns over which Italians retained allegiance to the Fascists. There was much myth and gossip around in the months following the 'liberation' of Mussolini by one Hauptsturmführer Otto Skorzeny. He had led some eighty German paratroopers (Fallschirmjäger) on a potential suicide raid to free 'Il Duce'. Skorzeny was personally chosen by Hitler for the mission, so it was pretty much do or die for him. His own team of top commandos overwhelmed Mussolini's Carabinieri captors (about two hundred of them) without even a shot being fired. We read the story with a mixture of wonderment and fear. You can hear the myth beginning.

It stated that Skorzeny knocked out the radio operator and his equipment, then formally greeted Mussolini:

'Duce, the Führer has sent me to set you free.'

'I knew that my friend would not forsake me,' replied Il Duce.

The grand success of these exploits high in the Apennine Mountains (the rescue was all skis and gliders and intrigue – real James Bond stuff) gave Otto Skorzeny a bit of bogeyman status. The RAF pilots used to claim their whole aim in life was to protect us girls from a raid on Sicily, led by him and his SS troopers. Of course, anything was possible: Skorzeny had paraded Mussolini in Rome and Berlin, with the newsreel cameras capturing every moment. The arrival of the Hauptsturmführer

Otto was a fearful prospect. Tommy pledged to protect me from the German paratroopers who, if he was to be believed, would be swarming into our lives at any moment. Nevertheless, the doors on the apartment block where I was staying were locked by 9 p.m. Yes, there was a metal escape staircase, a spiral contraption at the back of the building, but after a nineteen-year-old RAF boy broke a leg on it, it was never used again.

Upon my arrival in Sicily, I was billeted with several other civilian and enlisted women, all of us working out of naval headquarters. Everyone was most respectful towards us, which seemed extremely kind and chivalrous – and strange: it was totally out of character for Sicilian men, and many of them worked and gathered around our building and in the local cafés.

Sicilian men are born with a Casanova code of conduct, so to be free of their constant seduction attempts was like going out in the rain without a coat: it wasn't normal for them to keep their hands to themselves. If anything, I felt more threatened by the lack of bottom pinching. Through curiosity, I found out we were under the protection of the Mafia – the area 'godfather' was collaborating with the Allies, and so we were a protected species. He'd been influenced by a Mr 'Lucky' Luciano. It was a strange time.

Italy had changed sides, but the sympathies of Italy and of the Italians were ambiguous at best. I spoke the language and often found myself translating for British officers. It was after a long day of this that I went for a drink with Tommy. He said I wasn't my usual cheerful self.

'I'm concerned about my mother, I haven't heard from her.'

'I'll take you to see her.'

'Don't be silly, there's no transport.'

'Come on, I'll fly you to see her.'

As I said, Tommy was keen on me. Foolishly, for it was an offer I should have refused, I agreed, and when my boss was on furlough, I found myself flying above the Mediterranean between Sicily and Malta. I couldn't see much as I was 'sitting' on the floor of the Spitfire cockpit, which is definitely a single seater, concertinaed like a collapsible toy. The heels of Tommy's flying boots were all that was in my eyeline.

It was all very stupid and it was only because I am so small that I was even able to get into the cockpit of the plane. And I was young and fit – flexible enough to twist and turn into the space that was there.

It is only a hop, skip and a jump across the water to Valletta, and my mother was thrilled to see me, even if I was a little crumpled – with a stiff neck and cramp in my left leg. We'd just had our tea when I got a call from Tommy:

'Diana, I'm afraid the weather's bad and it's rocky up there.'

'But I've got to get back.'

'There's very bad weather, rough conditions.'

I got concerned and made it clear: 'My boss will be back in the morning and I have to be back there tonight.'

'It's going to be bumpy, really bumpy.'

'Tommy, I really have to get back!'

So, that was that. The bonus for being squeezed in so tight in the Spitfire cockpit was that I couldn't be thrown around by the turbulence. There was no room in there to be bounced to. I felt the rock and roll, but I didn't have half an inch either side of me to be moved about in. But Tommy was indeed an 'ace' and we landed softly, like a bird.

There was much more turbulence on the ground in Sicily to be fearful of. Corruption was part of business. The Cosa Nostra, with Mr Luciano's instruction from America, 'advised' the Italian government and the Allied troops tried to keep order. And all the time there were whispers that Otto Skorzeny was loitering around the corner.

But it was Tommy who got me into a spot. I was with him in the control centre, bringing in the planes to land in Sicily. There was a Spitfire on the way and suddenly he shoved some papers in my hand and said: 'You land it.'

I protested, but as I was doing so, the Spitfire pilot was asking for instructions and Tommy argued back with a smirk on his face: 'Just read out what's on the paper.'

And I did. I talked the Spitfire down to a safe landing.

I was remonstrating with Tommy when the CO (Commanding Officer) appeared. He had heard me giving instruction and told me: 'Never do that again!'

I pointed at Tommy: 'He told me to do it.'

Later, I was in the officers' mess and I heard the CO say: 'That's what comes from fraternising with the Eyeties.' He thought I was Italian, because I spoke the language without any accent. I was furious with his attitude. I was very young, but I did have the rank of officer and some days later I received an invitation to go for drinks at another mess. The invite was signed from this CO. I thought: 'Oh Lord, I think I am going to be rude to him.' I went. Upon arrival he greeted me and I told him: 'Excuse me, but I'm going to demean myself and fraternise with the

British!' But I decided to leave with a final passing comment: 'What if I was an Italian? Why shouldn't I speak to Tommy?' I was as offhand as I could be with him – I didn't care. I was quite a strong-headed girl and he had really annoyed me.

But I had to be careful. On Malta you knew the bombs were on the way, but here in Sicily, everything was unknown. We were given an official guide to the unknown – or rather the soldiers were, but there were always copies in the offices. *The Soldier's Guide to Sicily* was edited in Britain and contained an introduction by General Eisenhower. It brought me no comfort with 'headlines' like these:

Morals are superficially very rigid, being based on the Catholic religion and Spanish etiquette of Bourbon times; they are, in fact, of a very low standard, particularly in the agricultural areas.

The Sicilian is still, however, well known for his extreme jealousy in so far as his womenfolk are concerned, and in a crisis still resorts to the dagger.

An American report maintains that 'gangsterism' in the USA had its origin in Sicilian immigration.

The native, living as he does in primitive conditions, has become immune from many diseases which British soldiers are likely to contract.

The insanitary condition of the island is one of its best defences against an invader, and casualties from disease could well be higher than those caused in the field.

Venereal disease thrives on the island.

Contact with the civilian population may bring other diseases such as those mentioned above.

I felt homesick. But instead of going home, I went to Naples and into show business. On the 'business', not the 'show' side; my piano and dancing days were over. I joined the Entertainments National Service Association (ENSA), which was established at the start of the war as an organisation to give concerts and shows for the troops. It was my baptism into a new culture, with names such as Mantovani and songs like 'We're Going to Hang Out the Washing on the Siegfried Line.'

I met a host of characters like the (later to be) distinguished actor Nigel Patrick, who was my first ENSA boss. I was his secretary and, in time, partly responsible for getting the performers for the shows. Even with bombs falling or tanks aiming big guns at one another, war or no war, the main concerns of the entertainer is billing, where they were going on, when they were going on, who would be on before them, and on after them. It was a quiz and a challenge.

It was also my introduction to the British class system: the troops wanted comedians with racy jokes, their routines decorated by showgirls; the officers (supposedly) wanted more high-end material. Mostly, the entertainment was provided by very brave people who, in peacetime, wouldn't reach the end of the pier. But in the horrors of wartime, it was a much-needed distraction at any level.

But there were also the great talents such as Gracie Fields and Joyce Grenfell – and 'new' entertainers such as Tommy Cooper, Tony Hancock, Eric Sykes, Spike Milligan and Peter Sellers – whose names meant nothing to me. It didn't matter in wartime what their names were, as long as they were willing to get on stage – the audiences loved them. They appreciated them. I enjoyed the work, for it involved me in organisation, making sure everything and everyone was in the right place at the right time. I think it set me up for the life ahead. I seem to have spent much of my life organising – boys, men, everything.

It was a necessity of wartime that you had to be prepared for any eventuality. Nigel Patrick could be a little snooty about the less talented members of ENSA, but he was also kind-hearted in wanting the entertainment to be just that: entertaining. He did have difficulty concealing his disdain for 'the amateur dramatic contingent'. There would be gripes that some war zone got a Gielgud or Laurence Olivier and Ralph Richardson (honorary army lieutenants in ENSA in 1945), while we were allocated half a dozen showgirls and a 'blue' comedian. To be entertained, or not to be, was never a question for me. I thought they were all rather wonderful to be somewhere they didn't need to be.

In Naples, most of us ENSA girls were living in a ramshackle, ancient building. It had been someone's castle once upon a time, and we were told it was haunted by a beautiful princess who had met an untimely and unpleasant end. I soon learned to understand the way of entertainers. Depending on who was telling the tale, this ghost carried her head under her left or right arm. Late in the evening, after drinks, she often carried a head under each arm. We were quite a happy bunch with or without the ghosts.

Nigel Patrick had a grand, patrician manner, but was an amiable character and as his secretary I worked closely with him. Putting on a show is never easy, but in wartime 'bombing' has an altogether different meaning. Our Naples posting covered quite a substantial area, and so there were also several divisions of soldiers and airmen around at the same time as the Fleet. We did all our own planning and the shows were created around who was available and could get to us. The Germans were keeping armies out of Italy, so it was just as tricky to smuggle in the song-and-dance men and women. We did have a warm camaraderie. Jayne, one of the ENSA girls, invited me on a blind date in 1944 – it went on for more than half a century. For me, it was just another evening out and, as always, I was happy to flirt, but not in the least interested in getting into anything serious. My family were back in Malta and my intention was for us all to survive until this horrible war was over. I didn't have room in my life for some great romance; eating out and dancing and flirting was fine, but nothing else.

I met Captain Ian Robert Mackintosh of the Fife and Forfar Yeomanry Regiment on that blind dinner party date and after two weeks he proposed to me.

Now, I'd been proposed to (and I'd accepted) many times before, but this time I was wrong-footed. It wasn't love at first sight, but when you know, you know. Fate! Chance! Kismet! Ah, it was a complication. Where's your brain when your emotions get carried away? And vice versa? It's like wrestling fog, a Maltese curse, and I may have said that many times. It didn't solve the situation. I knew nothing about Ian other than he was quite dashing and polite, fun and very kind and nice to me. He had a cheeky smile decorated with a neat moustache. Still, my mother's warning rang in my ears, and I turned him down – or rather, put him on hold. He was happy to talk about his family, their London home, his Scottish background. It was more difficult to discover the details of his war. When that subject came up, he'd start talking about music, about jazz and about his great hero, Louis Armstrong.

I did discover more because of his mania with jazz. He was the fifth of six children born to Aeneas and Minnie Mackintosh. He'd started playing the trumpet when he was sixteen years old and it was a natural thing for him; he wanted to play – and he could. His mother, Minnie, believed it was because when she was pregnant with Ian, she would sit and play the piano, play Scott Joplin, give her future son some ragtime. His precious Selmer trumpet was his talisman; it went everywhere with him. There are many stories from wartime friends of how it never left his side. So, of course, it was at Dunkirk with him when the great evacuation took place in June 1940. Ian was twenty-two, an ambulance driver with the Royal Army Medical Corps; he wasn't conscripted, he'd joined up. He'd wanted to do his bit, he said. When all went wrong and the craziness of Dunkirk was happening and the rescue was underway, Ian, along with another ambulance driver, was cut off from the beaches by German snipers. They had to leave their ambulance and make for the beach on foot. The bombs were dropping and the German gunners were rattling bullets about. Ian suddenly realised he'd left his trumpet back at a café where they'd stopped and hidden while a German patrol went by. He announced he was going back for it…

So, while all the Dunkirk evacuees were fleeing from the Nazi army, Ian was beetling back towards them and his beloved trumpet. Where angels fear to tread, Ian would go. He made it and returned to the beach just a little north of Dunkirk, where the little boats, this amazing rescue flotilla, were arriving. The bombs were dropping all the time but this tiny boat got him out to one of the big naval ships. There, he was lucky again. The sailors were herding the army boys into the holds 'for safety' but Ian thought he deserved a cigarette – he always thought he deserved a cigarette – and insisted on staying on the deck 'to have a fag'. Well, that particular fag break saved his life. A bomb went into the hold and did deadly damage. Ian was rescued from the icy water, his hand tightly gripping his precious trumpet. Henri Selmer, who made the damn things in Paris, would have been proud, having such a tenacious keeper of his instrument.

The bombing was hell, and I had some idea of it from what I'd been through in Malta; but I had no conception of such horror, where your fellow man is blown to bits beside you. Or instead of you. For Ian, for many of these men, it was so often brushed aside, their generation's way of coping with the terror of it all. The stiff upper lip manifests itself in many ways. But there are side effects.

His family home was 103, The Chine, Grange Park in north London; and the house, which I was told was a 'Just William' home, mirrored the address. Others might think it a little more grand. It was very large, quite dark and austere, but felt very homely with so many bustling family members in it. It had been around during the First World War and was still fitted with blackout blinds. The Sunday morning when the Second World War was declared, Ian's aunt Mary had raced around the house pulling down the blinds; she expected the bombs to start dropping immediately. He conjured up a comforting picture of the house, of this extended family calmly taking care of any unpleasantness that arrived. Ian continued to want to do his bit to take care of Hitler. After Dunkirk, he went to a training school in Scotland and received a commission in the Fife and Forfar Yeomanry and a trip to North Africa.

Which is why you will fully understand my distaste for Erwin Rommel, who tried to annihilate my future husband. The full story of Ian's North Africa campaign is unlikely to be fully recorded: so many of those who witnessed it died in battle, while others put it from their minds. I know men were barbecued to death trapped in tanks, and that was only one of the atrocities of those bitter battles in the desert. There were stories of Ian's bravery – but never from Ian – and how he'd saved a life or a situation. There are many other stories – some told by Ian – of trumpet playing and the 'musical evenings' trying to escape the warfare for a little time.

Every engagement in that conflict was vital and, in time, proved decisive for the outcome of the war. But Ian retained his own priorities, and the first of them was Louis Armstrong – he was the boss. He was somehow always able to tune into Forces radio and was listening to Louis Armstrong and His Hot Five playing 'West End Blues' when he was alerted to take his tank into action at El Alamein. He let 'West End Blues' finish before ordering the advance: Hitler, Montgomery, it didn't matter who, everyone had to give way to Louis, pronounced, correctly I'm told by Ian, as 'Lewis' – like the island in the Outer Hebrides. Their tanks won the day. But Rommel – well, one of his men – got Ian anyway. He was sent on a dispatch mission, rushing orders to another tank commander, and was roaring about and, I expect, enjoying himself on a motorcycle whizzing through the desert, when a mortar shell hit his bike and spun him into the air. He never knew a thing. He was blown up and lay there to die. The Germans left him for dead, but a group of Bedouins found him alive and took him into Cairo. He woke up in an army hospital with severe injuries to the head.

He also, astonishingly, found his trumpet by his bedside. One of his Arab rescuers had brought it for him. He didn't care about his missing watch, cigarette lighter and other trinkets, which found their way into some passer-by's pockets. Ian was told to sit back and rest. He did that and, after a few weeks, entertained the other invalids by playing the trumpet. A little later, he received something he did like to talk about – a royal command. King Farouk, who was a couple of years younger than Ian, was a jazz fanatic and, hearing about this trumpet-playing invalid, summoned

Ian to play for him. He loved that: an audience and a Royal Command Performance. The King was schooled in England, at the Royal Military Academy in Woolwich, and as a City of London School graduate. Ian liked that too. They could talk jazz and public-school life, a winning combination. But Ian wasn't winning the health battle. The mortar had shaken him about and although he recovered, the army believed his injuries were such that they should invalid him out.

Ian was appalled at the thought. He wanted to stay, so he joined ENSA, Central Mediterranean Force, where he could do his bit for the war. And play his trumpet. Music, ENSA and a soupçon of serendipity brought us together. We became a couple. Now all that was in my ears was Ian's trumpet playing (and his marriage proposals). I didn't listen to any of it very carefully.

The most important ENSA duty was to boost morale and get servicemen involved with the shows; staging talent contests provided a quick way of doing both. Ian, because of his personality, musical ability and openness to any excuse for a jazz session, was recognised as a talent; he was also very considered and so regarded as a fair man. ENSA (known as Every Night Something Awful) was a test even for him. Still, he saw the best in everyone. Unless they didn't love and believe in Louis Armstrong – which narrowed the constituency, but only a little. His belief was that if he played Louis enough and at full volume, you'd convert.

Ian could discuss anything, but whatever the subject, it was always jazz that had the last word. His nickname, 'Spike', followed from his admiration of the popular black bands of his time, led by the likes of Duke Ellington, Count Basie, Fletcher Henderson, Chick Webb and Don Redman. I know all this because he told me many times. But the nickname 'Spike' was an acknowledged theft, a direct steal from Spike Hughes and His Negro Orchestra. Hughes went off from Britain to New York – a great adventure in 1933, when Ian was a teenager – and Ian adopted the name as a tribute. He thought there was no greater loyalty than following the music. In Naples, another Spike wasn't half so encouraging, though...

A new addition to the world of entertainment in Naples, the 56 Area Welfare Services' Dance Band Competition at the Bellini Theatre was heralded as something special. It was special. And noisy. It was also lively, with eight bands in competition on Sunday, 3 June 1945. The master of ceremonies was Captain Philip Ridgeway, the son of Philip Ridgeway, who was a British radio star with *The Ridgeway Parade*. Lieutenant Eddie

Carroll (pre-war he was the BBC dance band leader) and Ian were the judges. Someone has to win. Which means someone has to lose.

Gunner and future 'Goon' Spike Milligan was a band member. He was a man who spoke his mind. Of one ENSA performer who was a singer at the Windmill Theatre in London, he offered: 'That was like being a blood donor at a mortuary.' So after he got the thumbs-down from Ian and his fellow judges, he held a grudge. For a long time. In fact, he detailed it in the fifth volume of his war biography, *Where Have All the Bullets Gone?*, in 1985:

> The compère for the contest is Captain Philip Ridgeway, the announcer. He is as informed on dance bands as Mrs Thatcher is on Groin Clenching in the Outer Hebrides. Other judges are Lt Eddie Carrol [*sic*], famed composer of 'Harlem' and Lieutenant 'Spike' Mackintosh, famous for not writing 'Harlem'.
>
> Can you believe it – we didn't win! WE DIDN'T WIN!!! I wasn't even mentioned!! Why were the 56 Area Welfare Service persecuting me like this? At the contest I heard shouts of 'Give him the Prize'. No one listened, even though I shouted it very loud. Never mind, there would be other wars… !

An example of one of those quiet wars for Ian: if we were in an area under threat of being invaded and taken over by the Germans, he'd 'enlist' Jewish musicians to the ENSA entertainment troops and smuggle them to safety. He just did it and never talked about it. Many of these people were desperately afraid for their lives and Ian, as usual, tiptoed around bureaucracy and helped. It took guile and a brass neck.

We did fight noisier wars but, happily, they were short-lived domestic ones; for the moment, my family were very much at war. My brother Victor had distinguished himself as an artillery officer defending Malta. He was promoted and sent off to England on a British Army officers' training course and his ship stopped in Naples. We all met to tell our separate stories. Victor brought news of my mother and the rest of the family. Despite the world events, with the constant bombing stopped it seemed peaceful in Malta. The surrounding seas still held danger, though.

Ian and Victor enjoyed each other's company; they got on well. Ian invited Victor to go to 103, The Chine, Grange Park in London, and visit his family. It was a clever trick to get to me through our families. I was still avoiding Ian's marriage proposals. He made one every day, sometimes half a dozen. We were together every day in Naples, but the work was constant and some weeks went by before Victor returned to Malta. As Captain Victor Tonna, a weapons expert, he was going to be based with Ordnance Care at Donnington in Berkshire. He told my mother how kind and warm Ian's family were. And they had given Ian a five-star rating. My family thought this was wonderful and I thought: 'Well, they would, wouldn't they?'

Anyway, I knew that if there were any skeletons lurking around, they wouldn't be attached to Ian. But I suspected Major Donald Neville-Willing, who was an ENSA producer, wanted there to be. He adored Ian. The Major was an extraordinary character whom we all called 'Neville Ever Willing'. He was a very 'gay' gentleman, in both senses of the word! He was one of the ENSA officers recruited from the entertainment world and I thought he was wonderful. I met so many people through him – such as John Le Mesurier, who I'm sure got much of his *Dad's Army* performances from his ENSA days.

Someone said, correctly – my son Cameron, I think – that Neville-Willing was as camp, or more so, as the outrageous character Denis Quilley played in *Privates on Parade*. Neville-Willing could have walked into any production of that Peter Nichols play and not been out of place. He was one of so many everlasting wartime friends we met through ENSA. The situation was so uncertain that we all hung on to our friends. I always thought that if someone was out of sight I might never see them again.

I was promoted or demoted, I was never sure which, to being Ian's secretary. Nigel Patrick had gone off to Cairo. We, in turn, were moved on to Florence, a place where it is difficult to turn down marriage proposals. Still, there was a bump in the road. We were driving to Florence, Ian with the wheel in one hand and a cigarette in the other, talking and talking, and then there was a skid and the car crashed. We agreed that the answer to this difficulty was lunch, which calmed us down. The car was bashed in but, like us, not knocked out of action so, as always, we kept on going.

Florence was a delight, with the privilege of remarkable accommodation. We were both billeted at the Excelsior Hotel, which was the ENSA HQ in Florence. It was a spectacular spot next to the Arno river, overlooking the Piazza Ognissanti and a few minutes' walk from the Ponte Vecchio bridge. Even with such a romantic setting, in those days, marriage never came into my mind. I didn't want to get married. And I never lacked for attention, there were so many people always around.

When Ian first met me he told me: 'If I know you for another week, I'm going to ask you to marry me.' And he did. Again and again. It went on for week after week after week until he just wore me down. Nigel Patrick had got in on that act, telling people that Ian was going to marry me. He put a sign on his desk and eventually, I ran out of 'NO!'s. I got engaged. I'd been engaged before, as I liked having lots of boyfriends, though I didn't really want to get married, but when you're young and you fall in love, that's it.

Ian and I had our moments, of course, but he was lovely. And, in turn, everyone loved him. Why should I be different? I accepted Ian's proposal of marriage on the rooftop terrace of the Excelsior Hotel. I wanted my mother to be at my wedding, all my family, everyone I'd ever met to be at my wedding, as Ian did his, but travel was impossible for our families. It was the start of 1946, the war had only been over for a matter of months and the situation remained chaotic and dangerous.

Still, we wanted to marry, for who knew what would happen next in the world? We'd survived our share of battle – we decided to begin our matrimonial one. I was very happy and very sad. A wedding is such an important moment in your life; you feel those closest to you should be there. We longed for that, but we also felt a need to be married: so much was unknown, especially the issue of when all the bother would be over. It wasn't long since bombs dropping on both of us had been part of daily life. We had to take our chance when we had it, snatch it from the mess that was none of our making.

We married without our families, but a Prince gave me away.

My friend Marisa, who worked in the ENSA offices with me, was the daughter of an Italian aristocrat, Count Pasetti-Huntington. She knew Prince Giorgio Rospigliosi (he was a real prince) and his wife. The Prince agreed to act as 'father of the bride'. Marisa sat opposite me at work – we were good friends – and she said the one question she wanted the answer to was why the Prince was always in the bathroom. When I got the chance at his villa, I looked. He had dozens of bottles there, full of gin. Well, a lot of empty bottles too. He used to come out of the bathroom sloshed. But he wasn't a drunken prince – simply sloshed, and charming with it; he wobbled, but his manners never did.

Count Pasetti-Huntington had a superb home, the fourteenth-century Villa Mercedes in Bellosguardo, outside Florence, with its own chapel. Ian and I were married there. He was in his uniform with the Eighth Army badge and looked very smart. It wasn't so easy for me.

I had a grey suit and the Countess Pasetti-Huntington lent me a very nice blue hat that I wore with a veil – something borrowed. And she gave me some orchids. It was impossible to buy anything decent and I bartered by cigarette ration, of more value than cash, for a deep-blue silk blouse. Tobacco was like currency and, thanks to people craving it, I was presentable.

It was sad and happy, but moving; and Ian added levity. For all his time in Italy, he had none of the language. If he felt he wasn't being understood, he spoke more loudly and in his very mannered way. As for his language skills? 'Si' and 'No' was his vocabulary. He couldn't understand a word of the service, which was conducted by a very nice priest, the Rev. Father Cechiezzi, who was puzzled by Mackintosh colloquialisms, such as 'How are you, old cock?'

It began at 11 a.m. on Sunday, 27 January 1946 in the chapel and it was quite an elaborate service. Ian kept asking where we were in the ceremony and I repeated: 'For better, for worse…'

'Where are we at, Diana?'

'For better, for worse…'

'Are we married yet?'

'For better, for worse…'

To this day, I remain sad that none of my family was there, but they couldn't get out of Malta. And we couldn't get to them. Ian was still in the army and stayed on in Florence. I reluctantly went ahead of him, went alone to my new home in England where, with some remarkable gusto, my sons – and Louis Armstrong – were to join the family. I continue to puzzle over who made the most noise.

ACT TWO: JAZZ TIME

'Louis Armstrong was the third person in our marriage.'
DIANA MACKINTOSH, 2017

8

THE MUSIC MAN

Richard Bellamy (David Langton): 'What on earth is that noise?'
Hazel Forrest (Meg Wynn Owen): 'It's a gramophone,
I think, Mr Bellamy. Coming from upstairs.'
Richard Bellamy: 'Must be my son. He's keen on the latest
ragtime music, this dreadful syncopated jazz. Like everything
else from America, it's too fast, too noisy.'
UPSTAIRS, DOWNSTAIRS, LONDON WEEKEND TELEVISION (1973)

To begin my new life, I had to first find Glasgow. Or rather, the battered and bruised troopship that took me and many other officers' wives from Italy to the west of Scotland had to navigate the waves and the new rules and order of life on the world's oceans. Travel anywhere remained something to be nervous about in the early days of 1946. People were frantic, bereaved, wounded and all, in one way or another, suffering. Shipping had to avoid areas that might have been mined and I spent much of the journey looking into the sky, watching for bombers. There were bunks and sleeping areas, but there wasn't much sleeping. The seas were rough that February, with heavy swells adding a see-saw effect to the ship's movement. I had carefully folded as much as I could into one of my father's old suitcases, but there hadn't been that much to bring. The war had left most of us with not much more than a change of clothes. I was glad of my ENSA-inherited overcoat when the ship reached the Scottish coast and I saw land.

The landscape looked bleak, a place enveloped in greyness, but, you know, I didn't care. I felt a resounding freedom. Freezing cold, but free. As such, there was nothing to complain about, but I was sure I'd be able to find something to get started with. It was an overhang from the war, a time when you learned to grumble automatically on good days and with despair on bad days. I was on automatic.

I arrived in Glasgow on 14 February, St Valentine's Day, 1946. After being bounced about in heavy seas, I was glad to reach Glasgow Central Station finally and board the steam train to London. After the dust of Italy and Malta, I was covered in whirls of soot, but I was too exhausted to be concerned. The other passengers were wrapped up and their clothes were better than I expected. I anticipated instant evidence of austerity. Most carried their own food and flasks of tea, as I did. The tea warmed me up, but fatigue overwhelmed me. I felt I was carrying the train as it whooshed and whistled its way south. I was that terrible thing, too tired to sleep. Or too awake. How did I look? How much of a mess was I? I felt like a zombie, so I must look like one too. It worried me more and more as we got closer to London and my first meeting with my in-laws.

'They'll all love you,' Ian had said as I walked up the gangplank to the troopship. But he wasn't here to do the introducing. I didn't get off that train looking like Celia Johnson – goodness knows what my brother-in-law Bill, who came to pick me up at Euston Station, thought of the new bride. He was gentle and straightforward and I found myself and my suitcase in his car and on our way to 'home' in what seemed like one grand sweeping motion. There was plenty to talk about – how was Ian? How was the trip? – but all the time I thought the big question was what were they going to do with me, this stranger who had arrived in their lives? I wasn't a housewife. I couldn't even boil an egg. I'd been to boarding school. Toast was a mystery dish.

My mother never let me in the kitchen – too many cooks – and my inclination was never, never to argue with her, or anybody, about that. As Bill's car turned off into the driveway, I tried to conceal my fearful eyes and smiled.

All my Daphne du Maurier chills vanished when I arrived. This wasn't Manderley. It was like walking into an enchanted forest, all wonder and delight. When I saw my troop of in-laws for the first time they were all lined up outside 103, The Chine to meet me, like *Upstairs, Downstairs*. There were brothers and sisters and uncles and aunts and I was quite in awe. No one rushed forward to greet meet me; it was altogether orderly and all the more caring for that. They were all smiling. They queued up to shake hands. But, oh, it was cold and damp and chilly and not at all like the climate I was used to. The welcome warmed me up like a cashmere blanket, though. They were all kind, the sort of people who made their own fun, took their own enjoyment out of life, entertained themselves with their own singing and music-making. I was soon put at ease. Ian's father had died from cancer when Ian was eleven years old, so he'd spent his teenaged years in a female-dominated household. Which worked in his favour, for the stories I heard said he'd got away with just about anything he wanted. They were certainly tolerant of him. They still were. Ian's mother had given us her bedroom and we had the run of the house, which had plenty of rooms and a big garden and was a bit like the people in it: honestly welcoming.

It was a middle-class after-the-war home; clean, but you could see where the brittle linoleum had been polished up. Everyone was making do. When I arrived in London, the main complaint was the lack of food. Queues for rations, from biscuits to bacon, were constant and there were cutbacks on poultry and eggs, something aggravated by the government's decision to stop importing dried eggs; this was unwelcome déjà vu. Yet there never seemed to be an obvious lack of food at The Chine. There were always people being fed – family, strangers, and all sitting down for lunch and dinner. It didn't seem to matter how much or what food was on offer, everyone tucked in and talked and chattered.

To live on a small island and then arrive in England and live with a large family was a huge leap for me; it was very strange, but I got into it quite quickly. Nobody fussed, which was perfect for me. We were certainly all in it together at the beginning of this family life. It was a communal set-up with my in-laws and very loving and very Scottish. They all had stories to tell about Ian. His youngest sister, Sheila, was the first. She told me how she and Ian, on an ENSA trip home, had walked up The Mall and gone to the gates of Buckingham Palace to watch Winston Churchill and the Royal Family on the balcony waving to the crowds celebrating VE Day on 8 May 1945. On the way – and this was typical – he took her to a theatre where the Crazy Gang (Bud Flanagan, Chesney Allen, Jimmy Nervo, Teddy Knox, Charlie Naughton, Jimmy Gold and 'Monsewer' Eddie Gray) were playing. Ian loved them, almost as much as their other great fan and clearly a man of taste, King George VI – who'd awarded Malta the George Cross. Sheila and Ian went behind the scenes, where the Crazy Gang were sitting chain-smoking Senior Service cigarettes – Ian was stuck with Woodbines and envious – and drinking whisky in between going on and off stage. Ian had one or two drinks with them. He had a penchant for crazy gangs. There was a conga line dancing along Piccadilly and Ian, who was in uniform, wanted to join in. And he did. Ian always wanted to join in – that was the wonder of him, he was always an enthusiast. He ran his life in excess. I think the family thought I might slow him down a bit.

But I didn't have hydraulic brakes!

For me, it was a time of constant discoveries, for I was living in a wonderland with many encounters larger than my life had been. Life was changing for everyone during our first year of married life in north London, though.

There was a man on the radio called Wilfred Pickles, who got laughter for the way he spoke to someone called Mabel. I tried not to listen. Most of BBC radio sounded like ENSA shows and that's probably because that's where the talent came from. Instead, we had our own Mackintosh Follies. The household provided its own entertainment. Ian's mother sang beautifully, as did his sister Jean, and Auntie Mary played the piano and everyone played games in the garden. I was even allowed to experiment in the kitchen, that's how brave the family were. It was a honeymoon in how carefree our life was. The only anxiety I had was for my mother, but we wrote all the time. She had met a nice man – I knew she would with me out of the way – and it wasn't too long before they were planning to marry. Ian's brother Bill ran the family timber business and Ian reluctantly joined up for that. After the war ended, Ian had pondered going to America to become a professional musician, following his much-admired Spike Hughes. Now he had commitments and marriage, and the business run by his brother, all of which persuaded him to stay in England. The timber industry was flourishing – Europe was rebuilding, and the firm was doing very well. Ian adapted easily to the business, but not the office environment: for him 9 and 5 were more the Devil's numbers than 666. He could do his job with ease, but Ian burned the candle at both ends, working all day and playing jazz many evenings and into the night. He did seem indestructible, for he never tired; his energy was everything.

He was so happy when I became pregnant, instantly making plans for schools and job prospects for his first child, and all before that child had appeared. There was a new maternity hospital near Enfield, Middlesex, which the gynaecologist looking after me was about to open, and Cameron was born there on 17 October 1946. Indeed, he 'christened' the establishment – the Windmill Nursing Home – being the first child to be born there. He got even more attention at The Chine, with a household of 'mothers'. Cameron was thoroughly spoiled by his grandmother Minnie and Aunt Kate, his grandfather's sister, and Ian's two sisters, Jean and Sheila. He was my son, but they certainly loved sharing him. When I was pregnant I was asked whether, if it was a boy, he could be called Cameron in memory of his first cousin. When I heard the story I was happy and honoured to oblige. The other Cameron Mackintosh was an RAF squadron leader, who had volunteered to carry out one more operation in 1944 and was shot down over a village in Belgium. This Cameron Mackintosh was on a pathfinder mission to Germany that was aborted. The Lancaster was damaged, crippled by flak, and most of the crew baled out. This Cameron Mackintosh stayed with the plane, which was crash-diving directly towards the village where scores of people lived. Miraculously, he managed to pull the aircraft out of the dive and steered it away from the village, saving many lives and houses. He had no thought – and no hope – for himself and died in a fiery crash about a mile from the nearest house. Many years later, the village erected a monument to his memory and they asked Ian to unveil it.

The present, it seemed, never, ever completely eradicated the past. Ian and I were bonded by it. Ian marched not so much to a different drummer as a different band. Sometimes to a different orchestra. He was (I grew to appreciate) a brilliant jazz musician and he played in the style of his idol, Louis Armstrong. Louis Armstrong was the third person in our marriage. I had to compete with that man all my married life. I had to hear his music all night long; nothing – well, almost nothing – would induce Ian to turn the volume down. He never left the house without an armful of 78rpm jazz records, usually Louis, Ellington, Basie. It made for tension and, because of our different personalities, we would get ourselves going. It did get heated, but never for too long.

In 1948, Ian went to the Nice Jazz Festival and it proved a momentous occasion for him: he met Louis Armstrong and, just as importantly, his lifelong friend and musical compatriot Wally Fawkes. They hit it off and played and recorded jazz for many years. It was at the Nice festival that Louis heard the French song 'C'est si bon', which was played there in public for the first time. He arranged to buy the English rights to the song and his recording became incredibly popular. 'C'est si bon' was something of a theme song for Ian and Wally, a musical mascot. Ian was bonded to his music as well as his family. He'd say: 'I'm just going out for a drink and to blow the trumpet.' Everyone in the jazz world knew him and he played with the best – his idol Louis, and other British greats like Chris Barber, George Melly, Humphrey Lyttelton, Mick Mulligan, Ian Christie and, of course, Wally Fawkes, who was also the cartoonist

'Trog' for the *Daily Mail*. Ian had the best of times playing with Wally Fawkes and the Troglodytes, before Wally announced the break-up of the band with: 'I believe in quitting at the bottom.' They were an amusing bunch of men – a sort of music version of 'The Goons'; intriguing and rebellious, although I didn't like their lifestyle because of the way it entrapped Ian. But Ian, their 'Spike', thrived on the lifestyle – *duck to water* is definitely the wrong analogy – and, astonishingly, he coped. Even on three hours' sleep a night, when the phone rang in the early morning concerning his timber importing business, he could quote timber prices and do deals and be entirely civilised without even flinching. Before actually picking up the phone, he would have rummaged for a cigarette, lighting it as he verbally came to attention. He snapped into it without any complaint or apparent bother. He operated as though he'd had eight hours of undisturbed and blissful rest. I always had to admire his stamina, infuriating as it could be and usually was. Ian was like so many people after the war: he was 'fitting in' to post-war conditions about which he and so many others had built up apprehension. Lots of his friends seemed to feel that peace had broken out, rather than war ending.

Daily life was a new battle complicated by new tensions and rules, but it was the strict licensing laws forcing pubs to close at 3 p.m. that got the most complaints. Ian, however haphazard he was in so much of our affairs, could sort some things out. When we moved from The Chine to establish our own home, we went to the village of Cuffley in south-east Hertfordshire, between Cheshunt and Potters Bar. The headquarters of the timber business were there. Our first home in Cuffley was Brow Cottage on Plough Hill – and a hundred yards from the Plough which, of course, was a pub that he could easily and quickly walk to.

In Britain in the late 1940s and early 1950s, there was much hardship, and ration cards restricted what people could buy; yet there was room for jazz clubs and what Ian and his friends called fun; there was room for fun even if things were shaky. Being 'suburban' appeared to be a great sin, but here we were outside London being just that. Ian and the jazzmen seemed emancipated, however, and wanted to get on with playing their music. Possibly, they thought all the generals and politicians had not made much of a fist of their world and they were going to spread some good times; certainly, their attitude was low key – it was mellow. Given what most of them had endured, there were few who could offer them novelty. We'd all seen or experienced far too much at that point. Although I wasn't that friendly towards the jazz fraternity for tempting

Ian away, I understood that, even without them, he'd have gone to the clubs and played on his own. It was a passion that required attention. Still, the places they played, the buildings, the pubs, seemed to leer at you. The trumpet and the whisky and the jazz were, as Wally Fawkes said, part of the contract.

With Ian, it was an acceptable fallibility, his living and thinking differently, for he was so loving and warm that people responded in kind. His life was a kindness. But not always to me. Sometimes he would disappear for a couple of nights playing at jazz clubs with his friends; no money exchanged hands, and if it did he used to give it to the professionals, who he said needed it more than he did. He never seemed to have tuppence to rub together and when he did he'd give it to somebody else.

I never knew how he kept going with so little sleep. It didn't bother him at all. Some nights I'd wake up early to look out of the window to see if there was any sign of him. Once I couldn't believe what I saw. We had a very long drive to the house and just as you got near the front door overlooking the garden there was a drop of about ten feet. The car was balancing like a variety act on the edge; a couple of inches more and it would have toppled and overturned. There was no wall there to stop the car, not even a little brick barrier. It was a clear run into oblivion. There was no 'there' there.

His excuse was 'the brakes don't work,' but the smell of whisky suggested otherwise. Ian was what wasn't working. It was quite normal for him to lose his house keys and attempt to use a ladder to get in through the bedroom window: one night I was woken up by the noise and, thinking it was a burglar, I nearly pushed him and the ladder off the windowsill. It surely would have killed him.

On many occasions, he would forget where he had put his car and report it stolen; the police would search for it everywhere. In the end, he would be too ashamed to admit that he'd mislaid his car, as it were, at the end of a very blurry night out. After a couple of days there would be a knock on the door, with a policeman saying they'd found the car in London, but it wasn't on the street he'd said it was. It was just as well he didn't find the car, as the fact that he'd been drinking wouldn't have stopped him driving for sure.

There were no seat belts back then, and although there were drink-drive laws, they weren't stringently enforced. The police could be lenient if treated in the right way. And Ian was certainly good at that. Ian once got a car almost halfway up a lamp post, claiming he 'thought it was just a very steep hill'! He was generous with his hospitality, even in the middle of the night. The household would be asleep and I'd hear banging and crashing and know Ian was home from playing at Ronnie Scott's or another jazz club somewhere. Not infrequently, Ronnie Scott used to ring up and ask me to collect Ian. I'd tell him in quite clear terms: 'You entertained him – you bring him home.'

Often, Ian arrived with the band and out would come the brown liquid hospitality and the Louis Armstrong records. They'd go on at full blast. I'd shout down the stairs and tell Ian to be quieter. He would turn it down for a time and then up the sound would go again on a favourite record or track – or just because it should. I would get so mad and I recall sometimes marching downstairs and dismantling the whole damn noise-making apparatus.

That was our married life and it was never dull. We had our rows, but these sort of dramas were over as quickly as they started. A Mediterranean thing, I guess. We both had a great energy and that, I'm sure, provoked the drama, the energy coming from both sides.

My ongoing concern was the worry about money to pay the bills, pay the school fees; that nagged at me. I was horrified if they were left unpaid. Eventually, I had to take over the financial affairs of our lives, as it was not Ian's forte. I had been brought up to always be prompt in taking care of such things and I was embarrassed when I saw final demands in brown envelopes, often stuffed into Ian's jackets or dressing gown. I got so wound up at one point that, in a moment of sheer frustration, I did consider leaving him, but nothing ever came of it – probably because, essentially, I knew that we belonged together no matter how complex life was.

All that seemed inconsequential, for we had been through so much in the past with and for each other. We had forged this common destiny. And, of course, we had the boys. Cameron was growing and Robert was also born at the Windmill Nursing Home, three-and-a-half years after him. Somehow, Ian managed to keep everything ticking over financially, no doubt partly due to his undeniable personality, and we moved to a bigger house in Cuffley, not far from Ian's brother Bill's house. We moved there after Nicky was born, nearly five years later. I was not really equipped to run a house with a very large garden and three children, but I had to cope. The boys loved the house and when they were home from school, they spent most of their time running around the garden.

Cameron was quite a handful. He and Robert shared a bedroom. They were close, but not always totally loving, and enjoyed providing me with scary moments.

I can see Cameron running after Robert in the garden with a pair of scissors. He was intent on giving Robert 'a trim'. Thank God their father was quicker than Cameron and a nasty haircut was prevented. Cameron certainly wanted to be Vidal Sassoon. He was quite a naughty boy. I used to dread leaving him with his brothers, but on shopping days I had to. I'd have a local babysitter there to keep an eye on them, but the boys were sometimes too quick. On one occasion, I came back from shopping and I was driving slowly down the drive, when I was greeted by a heartwarming sight: baby Nicky was in his pram, while Robert was sitting on a stool next to him and Cameron appeared to be overseeing them. When I got closer I realised what he was up to. He had a large pair of scissors in his hand and he had cut Robert's hair in large chunks and left him bald in the front, his eyebrows hardly left on, and no doubt eight-month-old Nicky was next for the 'barber's chair'. I was livid and shouted at him, especially as Robert was having his portrait painted by an artist friend of mine and – well, that wouldn't work now. Cameron never liked to be punished, so the next thing I knew he'd packed a few things in a satchel, put it on his shoulder and announced he was leaving. He went to the end of the drive, waited fifteen minutes and then thought better of it. After another argument, he lay 'dead' on the floor in the hallway to gain attention. We all just walked around him for the next half-hour until he got bored. I don't know where he gets it from!

They all followed Ian to public school (private in financial terms). In no circumstances would Ian have it any other way. He was a Conservative and conservative; he liked things as he knew them, but others were free to do as they pleased. He just believed that that was the best for his children. And when he was not borne away into his heady world of jazz music, Ian took the family timber business seriously enough. At 9 a.m. he was in the office, which was in the timber yard in Cuffley, a couple of hundred yards from the Cuffley Hotel. However, that acted as a second office, but with a limitless supply of drinks to conduct 'business' with like-minded customers. And in business, he was just as affable. I can see why he was so liked by everyone, as he never had a complaining attitude; he would always work something out in the event of a problem – even if it meant a loss! Ian was so happy-go-lucky. He would say 'jolly good chap' about everyone. I was a touch more cynical. Ian thought everyone was a good man until it turned out they were a rotter and then he'd go completely against them. Anyone Ian initially met was seen by him as 'top drawer', so he would hire them to do all the jobs. And after much complaint from me that we needed more room in our house, now with three children, he agreed to add on a garden-room extension. It was to be his greatest coup. He announced: 'I did a great deal.' When it was finished and the builders – after being paid – had vanished, literally, I pointed out that all the windows had been fitted the wrong way round. Not that they just opened the wrong way. The sills were inside the house. Typical of Ian. With a degree of embarrassment, the 'jolly good chap' was now a 'rotter'. But Ian went through life thinking everyone was basically good. It got him into terrible trouble. Apart from the drinking, a social habit that he felt was perfectly normal and should be encouraged, he was a very fine man – kind and generous; and he became even more generous in drink.

He'd give his last penny to help a stranger; he also had a strong code of right and wrong, but always gave a person the benefit of the doubt. When he received the occasional windfall from his business, he would then tell you that 'so-and-so' just bumped into him in the pub with a desperate story of a life-or-death need for some cash, which would be returned by the end of the week. We are still waiting. I was furious when he acted like that, because I had to keep the family going on often inconsistent funds. And the newspapers kept telling us we were in 'the golden age'. I did feel more secure with Winston Churchill as prime minister in 1951. But Churchill wasn't up for the school fees.

We had a fairly tumultuous time as a family, but driving us all was the challenge of sticking together and for so much of the time enjoying life. I know that has always given me the spring in my step to go on, the zest for life; Ian wanted everything for the boys and they adored him.

He had enjoyed his own school days and was determined that they should too. He wanted them to be privately schooled, yet finding the fees was always a problem. When Cameron went to board at Prior Park College in Bath, Ian was asked: 'Now, Mr Mackintosh, how would you like to pay the fees?'

Ian looked politely at the man and, smiling, answered: 'In arrears.'

9

THE QUEEN AND I

'It was all very merry and agreeable, but there is always, for
me, a tiny pall of "best behaviour" overlaying the proceedings.
I am not complaining about this, I think it is right and proper,
but I am constantly aware of it. It isn't that I have a basic urge
to tell a rude joke and say "f★★k" every five minutes, but I'm
conscious of a faint resentment that I couldn't if I wanted to.'
NOËL COWARD (ON LUNCHING WITH
QUEEN ELIZABETH II), 1969

I won't say it's like yesterday, but there's so much still the same about Malta, the geography of the place, the people, the smells and the atmosphere and attitude, that wandering or driving around can't help but bring the memories flooding back. I never dwell on the past, but I've not forgotten it either. The Queen revisited Malta in November 2015, and while others saw the image of her as she is today, my mind froze the evening news for a moment. I saw instead a photograph I took of the Queen and Prince Philip dancing at the Governor's Palace in Valletta. I danced there that evening too.

The Queen and Prince Philip have always been charming but easy-going with me on those occasions when I have been fortunate enough to meet them through my life.

Oh, I would never break protocol or say the wrong thing and be familiar with them, but our conversations are never strained. I believe that is partly because of our shared love and memories of Malta where the royal couple had what I think were the most relaxed moments of their married lives. And later, when I found myself in their company, the topic about having children of similar ages became a natural part of her familiar conversation, by someone who has an extraordinary gift of memory, as though it was weeks rather than years from the last meeting.

I had 'escaped' from Malta by 1949 when Prince Philip was made First Lieutenant and second-in-command of the destroyer HMS *Chequers*. As such, the future Queen was able to live – well, as much as officialdom allowed – as a navy wife. They were a young couple in the sunshine. Philip had his navy duties and his Princess had few cares – and her independence from duty.

Prince Philip's first cousin, David, Marquess of Milford Haven, had roller-skated with me when he was based in Valletta with the British Mediterranean Fleet before the siege of Malta proper began in 1940. He was going out with my friend Tessa DeDomenico and he organised us in groups, in teams to compete in roller-skating races. No one paid much attention to who was who. It was simply fun. On Malta, with its easy-going atmosphere, other family members were just as casual as Milford Haven. There were also days with the horses and polo matches. Malta was so British, with the contradiction of the devotion to ceremony and the rebellion against too much authority. The naval dances and official balls were grand affairs but more pomp and pageantry were involved after Princess Elizabeth became the Queen. Then it became 'the full ceremonial'. But those very early days were relaxed and what the Queen is known to have called 'the happiest days of my life'.

Of course, she was the focus of so much interest on the island. Everyone wanted to know what she was up to, where she was going, what she was wearing – and all those miles away in England I wanted to know too. Luckily, I got letters most days. I missed my mother and my family and friends and they were all very good at keeping me up-to-date with the royal news. There was plenty of gossip about who had seen Princess Elizabeth and who had not. Also, all the details about how they were living. My friends at the Malta *Times* sent me clippings, so I was well informed.

My Maltese correspondents said the young Princess was enjoying a genuinely worry-free time. She had left England six days after Prince Charles's first birthday, in time to join Philip for their second wedding anniversary. They had been told that 'conditions in Malta' were not suitable for the infant Prince Charles. I never fully understood what that meant at the time, but I was told in the letters I received that the idea was to help the royal couple have freedom to 'bond'. They certainly had a lot of freedom on Malta and for a time enjoyed some anonymity. Margaret Rhodes, the Queen's cousin and bridesmaid, friend from childhood and everlasting confidant, explained in an interview before she died, aged ninety-one, in November 2016: 'I think her happiest time was when she was a sailor's wife in Malta. It was as nearly an ordinary a life as she got. She socialised with other officers' wives, went to the hair salon, chatted over tea, carried and spent her own cash.'

My friends wrote and said that shopkeepers noticed how she was nervously slow when paying in the pounds, shillings and pence of the day. She was handling cash for the first time in her life. That little thing made everyone like her even more. She wanted to be normal. She wanted to join in with daily life. She really loved Malta because she was able to wander through the town and do some shopping, and whenever the Fleet came in, rush over, as we all did, to the Barrakka (the public gardens on the seafront) to see it. A far cry from the protocols of life back in England. The Hotel Phoenicia, which opened in 1947, was a favourite of the Queen, and she and Philip were like so many of the other young couples dancing the evening away. They did, however, have a different lifestyle than most.

Through Lord 'Dickie' Mountbatten, they had as their home the Villa Guardamangia, on the outskirts of Valletta, and lived there for long periods between 1949 and 1951; Malta, I say proudly, is the only foreign country in which the Queen has ever lived. Tragically, the Villa Guardamangia is no longer the grand structure it was. Time has caught up with it, a reminder to us all, and it's a shame such an architectural heritage is in disrepair. When the Queen and Prince Philip saw it in November 2015, she told the officials showing her around: 'It looks rather sad now.' I was glad she was reminded of the glory days of the Villa Guardamangia when Malta's president Marie-Louise Colciro Preca presented her with Edwin Galea's watercolour of the villa in its prime. 'Oh look,' said the Queen. 'Guardamangia, that's very nice to have.'

When I met President Marie-Louise Coleiro Preca in June 2016, she recounted to me how really pleased she was, about how much the Queen had enjoyed the visit and her present. She does like remembrances of good times. I know that personally. When the Queen visited Malta in 1967 as part of a Commonwealth tour (she remained head of state of Malta until 1974), I was asked by our ENSA friend Philip Ridgeway to work with him in making a documentary film about her visit, as I 'had all the right connections'. There was no pay except for travel costs and I could see my family. I was the location 'scout', whatever that is.

So, off Ian and I went. I was able to get the film crew into locations where the Queen would be present and my biggest help was my 'uncle'

Hannibal Scicluna, who was very influential and much involved in the arrangements. He couldn't help enough and through him and other contacts I was able to help Philip Ridgeway get proper access to events. When it came to the gala ball at the Governor's Palace, 'Uncle' Hannibal said: 'Come along, dance and enjoy yourself.'

One minute I was helping the cameramen set up in my work clothes, and the next, all dressed up, Ian and I danced at the ball alongside the Queen and dozens and dozens of other glamorous couples. That evening I was able to get a photograph of the Queen and Prince Philip on the dance floor and very much the centre of attention. It is a wonderful picture. The Queen is wearing a sparkling suite of jewellery – Queen Alexandra's Kokoshnik Tiara, antique Girandole earrings, the Coronation necklace and Queen Victoria's bracelet. But it was the happiness, that special glow, which captured the most attention. It was a wonderful evening and I held on to that photograph of her and Prince Philip until an opportunity arose, some thirty years later, to give it to her at a Royal Gala event, produced by my son Cameron, at which I was also present – and sitting next to her!

I believe they were both truly surprised and delighted at the photographic reminder of such happy times.

When the Queen visited Malta again in 2015, the news channel found and screened film footage of the 1967 Gala Ball at the Government palace and there I was dancing next to the Queen. My son Robert got several calls saying: 'Your mother's on the six o'clock news – dancing with Ian.' I didn't even realise the camera was rolling!

Someone suggested on television that the 2015 visit might be the Queen's last trip to Malta, but I'm not too sure. Lord Mountbatten's daughter and the Queen's friend, Lady Pamela Hicks, spoke to the newspapers during that trip and told them: 'The Queen loves any moment she can spend in Malta because she led such a free, independent life there, without a care in the world.'

The Queen also made lifelong friends and connections on Malta. Mabel Strickland and *The Times of Malta* were superb supporters. One of Mabel's proudest and longest traditions was sending a basket of Maltese oranges, mandarins and avocados to the Queen each Christmas at Sandringham. I saw one of the thank-you letters made available by Mabel's family, one sent in 1979, which Mabel received from the Queen. It was personal, heartfelt: 'Dear Mabel, thank you very much indeed for a lovely Maltese Christmas present of oranges and mandarins – in spite of the weather and the small crop available. Your gift is always much appreciated by my greedy family, but Philip and I always think back on those happy days when he was serving in Malta and I was able to travel about all over the island and see what was going on in every area while we lived there. Life changes so much these days and who knows what 1979 may bring to us all, however, we have our memories. Elizabeth R.'

Mabel Strickland used to terrify me more than the Nazis, but time emphasises what a genuine and good person she was. When my son Cameron saw a photograph of Mabel, he thought it was the actor Alastair Sim playing the headmistress character in drag, from the *St Trinian's* films. He's right, there is a strong resemblance. Ian would have none of it. To him, Mabel was a 'fine, handsome woman'. Give or take the moustache. Ian was incorrigible, but there was no malice about him – he had a Pollyanna attitude that all would be well, things would work out, and it was best not to worry. Of course, I worried all the time. Happily, Ian's family were able to help out when reality knocked Pollyanna off his feet.

If there wasn't the money for the school fees, even in arrears, his sisters, who were pretty successful, would help. They really were a proper clan in that sense. His older sister, Auntie Mary was later a director of the Hong Kong Shanghai Bank before it became HSBC. Their father, Aeneas, was determined that all the girls got a proper job and introduced them to his London banking contacts, a business world in which women were accepted to some degree.

Mary blossomed, particularly in the area of tax as it affected banking. So much so that with her London bank's relationship with Hong Kong (British at that time), she was sent over to help set up and oversee the Hong Kong Shanghai Bank's new tax structure. She was very high-up there. She lived in Hong Kong for many years. His sister Catherine (Aunt Kitty) got first-class honours at her university and later became a company director at a time when women rarely became directors. Kitty was a super mathematician and was working as a maths teacher when she was seconded to work for the UK government. It was all very hush-hush at the time, but she was most involved with Operation Pluto (Pipe-Lines Under The Ocean) during the war.

Through that, she worked with the major oil companies, the army and specialist engineers to create oil pipelines underneath the English Channel to help the Allied invasion of Normandy, Operation Overlord, in June 1944. It was typically British and inventive – the engineers adapted submarine telephone cables. Don't ask me how it worked. Kitty did explain once, but all I knew was that it saved lives and fuel by taking out the reliance on oil tankers, which were slow-moving targets for enemy submarines. Kitty was awarded an MBE for her contribution and my son Robert now keeps it brightly polished. Just after Kitty died, he had found the medal sitting out of view in an old filing cabinet. She was never one to make a fuss about things like that. Kitty had a brilliant mind, becoming very important in the male-dominated world of the oil business. This brought her into contact with two men in particular, who owned both the Manchester Oil Refinery and the Peruvian-initiated Lobitos Oil company: Norrie Fuller and Stuart Jarvie. Her skill at negotiating international oil licences granted by the UK government did not go unnoticed and this led to her being invited to join their board of directors, based in the very fashionable Jermyn Street, just behind Fortnum & Mason, Piccadilly. Their offices were above Quaglino's restaurant, where we were often taken for glamorous lunches. In time, she would receive another invitation from Stuart – this time for marriage. They were both intellectually suited; he had film-star looks and was from a very aristocratic family. They lived a pretty high life in a beautiful country house where we and the children spent many enjoyable times. Their housekeeper and cook was a wonderful German lady called Emma. With her thick accent, and being by no means a small woman, she was a real *Sound of Music* caricature. When we stayed with them for weekends, she loved to make huge meals and large cakes for the children to build them up! 'Mrs Mackintosh – zzay need feeding!'

Fairly early in their careers – the two of them were only in their fifties – the companies were bought out by Shell Oil and Stuart accepted the golden handshake. But Shell wanted Kitty to remain, such was her talent, which she did – for a while. However, leaving Stuart at home, just pottering around on his own in their huge garden and grounds soon caused him to be restless, as he was so used to the high-pressure world of the oil business. It was not conducive to a happy life for them both, so she gave them notice a year later to enjoy early, but extremely comfortable retirement at fifty-five.

With no children themselves, Kitty and Stuart loved to support our family and Ian, as much as possible. Their lifestyle was always quite extravagant, eating at the best restaurants around the world and likewise, staying at the best hotels. With Cameron and Robert instinctively following their creative paths, our youngest, Nicky, was developing a 'lucrative' interest in the culinary arts at school. He had always loved watching me in the kitchen, where I became much more at home after nearly a year of cooking duties at The Chine with Ian's family, and now he apparently saw the opportunity to supplement the lacklustre school menus with some tasty treats, for which he duly charged his fellow pupils. He even managed to get teachers as customers! Hearing of Nicky's exploits and interest in cooking, Stuart made some phone calls and introduced him to a few prominent people in that world. So, after Nicky left school, he was invited to join the staff at a well-known London hotel – and found himself moving from one five-star establishment to another in order to learn the catering and cooking business from the ground up. He hated many of his early duties, which mainly consisted of picking and cooking boxes of fresh spinach, but dues have to be paid. With a few early wobbles, he persisted, training at the very famous École Hôtelière de Lausanne and the Cordon Bleu School in Paris to become a very fine chef, owning restaurants in New York and London. Kitty and Stuart, of course, were delighted that they were able to help set him on his journey and watch him use his skills and determination to carve out his own career path.

We spent a lot of time with them in the early 1960s, often enjoying weekends in their beautiful house in Westerham, Kent. They had a friendly neighbour – Winston Churchill. He admired the fabulous gardens they created, which were now their passion, often leaning over his fence, when he was painting outside. It gave Stuart and Kitty great pleasure to have our children running around their rather grand and sprawling house.

It was there that I met Sarah Churchill. We hit it off. Sarah asked me to translate some documents from French and because of that, we got to know each other quite well. I tried to help her with spoken and written French and she worked hard with it, but she had distractions. I'd see her in Westerham, but later, when we moved to St John's Wood in London, she'd come to my house for lessons. When she was writing her autobiography, *Keep on Dancing*, I did the copy typing for her – I could, and can, type quite quickly. That was the first thing I learned and I've never forgotten. I used to bash out Sarah's words. She was fragile. I liked her and I have a book of her poems that she signed for me, a rather lovely memento. She got on well with Kitty and Stuart; they were carefree people and Sarah needed a lot of caring.

All four Mackintosh sisters were very gifted, very bright and all naturally mathematical. Ian's youngest sister, Sheila, is as smart as they come and made a wonderful teacher; she was a head teacher for many years until she retired. Ian enjoyed learning, but was not scholastic. He was not the type of father to sit on the boys' beds telling them stories, but he would go out with them and have fun. He was very happy to sit with Robert, who had a natural interest in the piano, and encourage him. He made much of us all being together, of playing the patriarch as well as the trumpet. Sunday was the day for family gatherings and lunch was always a big event. We trooped off to church for a mid-morning service – without Ian, who would start to make the lunch. After church, we drove to one of the local pubs – usually the Coach and Horses in Newgate Street. On these Sundays, Ian was usually on good form and never strayed. I think it was his own form of 'church' ritual, which he didn't care to miss. Upon our return home for lunch, the boys usually had a radio show on that kept us all in good spirits, whether it was *Round the Horne*, *The Goon Show* or *The Billy Cotton Band Show*. But often we would go over to visit Ian's family in Enfield, where food was always in abundance right the way through to a big tea in the garden. They were wonderful, golden family days.

He was very proud of the children and they all had elaborate educations in many ways. We were lucky with our sons, for they were happy boys. All three of them went to St Dominic's Priory Roman Catholic School, in Ponsbourne Park, near Cuffley. That was the one condition I gave to Ian upon agreeing to marry him. Whilst I accepted his non-religious views and lifestyle, the children had to be brought up as Catholics, as I had been. He accepted, unconditionally. But whilst Cameron went to a boarding prep school, Robert and Nicky went to a day school. The boys will tell stories that I dumped them at St Dominic's and left them for weeks at a time, as I chased around Europe, but that was never the case. They all exaggerate and try to malign me! Although, yes, the nuns spoiled the boys and the boys loved them in return, so it was helpful for them to stay there, occasionally, when any of them had catching illnesses and could be isolated in the dormitories. And there were times when I needed a rest too!

In the middle of Cuffley was the Cuffley Hotel, which was a typical country hotel of the time, and Ian's timber yard business was across the road. Jack Cohen used to drive around there, having bought a piece of land from Ian and Bill's timber yard to build his first new-style warehouse for his company Tesco.

Robert, who was mad about cars from a very early age, used to secretly back Ian's car out of the garage, when we were indoors and out of sight. I think he was nine. So on Saturday mornings, when he went with his father to play at the timber yard, he was fascinated by Cohen's electric-blue 'Chinese-Eye' Rolls-Royce, which glided by Ian's office to the Tesco headquarters opposite. Robert was always spotting the car. Ian's business hours were from 9 a.m. until 6.30 p.m., excluding the opening hours of the Cuffley Hotel lounge bar. The St Dominic's nuns became part of Ian's circle of friends. They had a little minibus and would call Ian's office to ask where they should drop the children off after school. Ian would tell them: 'I'll be at the Cuffley Hotel.'

Sometimes they'd bring Ian home too – in good Christian spirit – realising his spirit was mainly from a bottle on that occasion. Technically, the boys weren't allowed in the hotel bar and they'd be jumping up and down at the bar window, wanting to get going. Ian would bribe them with packets of crisps – they'd turn up at home with all these used blue wrappers of salt in their pockets. The nuns weren't troubled. They recognised the kindness of the situation and of the person central to it. If the nuns wanted to go up to London, they would come to the pub and ask Ian for a lift and he'd put his drink down straight away, and they'd be off. He would not concern himself with set appointments. He believed in doing what he thought was right at the time – any time. If St Dominic's wanted him, he was there.

There was a wonderful humanity about Ian. He'd ask the nuns to have a drink. He knew they wouldn't touch alcohol, but it would be: 'Come and have what you're allowed to.'

For an atheist, Ian was in many ways more Christian than anyone I knew. I had to balance our lives out so that the boys had a fairly comfortable and positive upbringing, even if it was fairly knife-edge at times. They were never much trouble at school and the family house in Cuffley had a welcoming garden for them. They always wanted to be outside. They'd play cricket and games, and being boys, they got a little rowdy. But one looked after the other: Cameron watched out for Robert and Robert was protective of Nicky; musketeers, all for one and one for all. Ian was determined about their education, the importance for their future of going to good schools. I had been sent to boarding school and I wasn't impressed. When, in turn, each of them went off to boarding school, I used to sit and cry for a time. When Cameron became a boarder at prep school, he was only eleven years old; he didn't like it at all. He missed home and tried to run away a couple of times. The grand gesture, I am sure. He told me later he adored the melodrama and the tears. But at the time, for me, it hurt. For all of them, the nuns, like any collection of people, could be 'goodies' or 'baddies'. But all the boys were resilient. Still, it was a concern.

I had four boys to worry about, when I included Ian. I was also fearful about money, yet the boys themselves were not a daily strain on the purse strings. I was careful and they didn't ask for much in the way of toys or 'things'. The family entertained themselves. Cameron had experienced that way of life at The Chine with his grandmother and aunts, whom he adored. Cameron and Robert sang for their supper, as it were, while Nicky, in time, learned to make a proper gourmet job of it. Still, they were on rations for quite a time. Ian was lucky to have a job in the family timber business. He would never have made any money as a musician – he'd have just given it all away.

The boys were themselves lucky to have such generous aunts. It was Aunt Jean who got Cameron into the world of theatre. But he was the one who made the most of it. And, I suppose, that's all my fault. I was the one who agreed to take him to see Julian Slade's *Salad Days* for the second time.

Magic piano, indeed!

Aunt Jean had taken Cameron, who was reluctant to go, from school to see *Salad Days* at the Theatre Royal, Bristol, in June 1954. It's a lovely musical featuring Minnie the Magic Piano, which gives anyone who hears it playing the urge to sing and dance. There's nothing challenging about *Salad Days* other than to join in the escapist fun, for it's a work of great love and enjoyment, full of silliness and flying saucers. It was a great gift and Cameron was truly enchanted by it. When his eighth birthday came around and Ian and I asked him what he wanted, he was quick: 'I want to see *Salad Days* again.' I wasn't that keen. He'd already seen it. And it certainly didn't sound like my cup of tea. No one, not even me, nags like an eight-year-old. But Bristol? It was another trip we didn't need during half-term. Ah, said the smarty pants, the show had transferred to the Vaudeville Theatre in The Strand, London. Ian gave in. I resisted. Cameron repeated the story of the magic piano. He was curious. He wanted to know how it worked, what went on behind the magic. Who, I suppose, was pulling the strings.

At that moment, it wasn't me. I agreed to take him again, if he looked smart. He dressed up in his kilt (Mackintosh tartan) and jacket and we went off to a matinee performance as a birthday group. One of his aunts pointed out that the composer, Julian Slade, was playing the piano in the orchestra pit. After the show's hero and heroine, Timothy and Jane Dawes, take off to live happily ever after and the curtain drops, Cameron took off too. Before I could stop him he was at the orchestra pit.

I chased after him, but by then he was introducing himself to Julian Slade: 'I'm Cameron, please may I see the magic piano?'

He all but demanded, in that desperate-to-know little boy way, how the piano worked. Instead of just patting his head and signing an autograph, Julian – he was twenty-four years old at the time – showed Cameron how they mimed the magic piano on the stage and how he played it in the pit. Then he showed him how the flying saucer was actually attached to wires and where all the scenery went. As we walked back into the theatre, Cameron told me: 'This is what I'll do when I grow up.'

Now, I believe it would have happened whatever, but this gave him an incredibly early interest in the theatre. Julian, who died in 2006, was a constant supporter. Ever since that birthday on 17 October 1954, Cameron has always known that someone has to make magic happen.

But what really set off the whole thing were the Pelham puppets, which Cameron and Robert adored. Their aunts took them to a show and these puppets were so lifelike that Robert and Cameron were hooked on them. Robert had been to see *Salad Days* and loved it, but it was not the landmark experience it had been for Cameron. Robert adored the puppets, though – and he could work them, all the strings and movements. Cameron was not mechanical, but he knew what he wanted to happen. Both of the boys nagged us to buy them puppets and their aunts were so pleased with the theatrical side of it that they kept up a constant puppet supply.

Cameron and Robert created puppet shows; they had a script and Robert, who was only about eight years old, could follow and play the music perfectly on the piano. Robert could hear it and then play; he was a natural – he got that from Ian. He'd be moving from the piano to the puppets and back again. The Pelham puppets were their real introduction to practical performance. It was great fun watching them making so much out of it and now, looking back, there was Cameron clearly becoming a producer in front of our eyes, knowing what would make a show work, seeing the big picture.

Cameron was also lucky in that his grandmother, great-aunt, and especially his Aunt Jean and Aunt Kitty all loved the theatre. His aunts both worked in the city, and they took Cameron to shows in Palmers Green, or to the West End, where he saw Frankie Howerd in *Charley's*

Aunt; Howerd played Lord Fancourt Babberley and that 1956 revival was a huge success. The seed planted with *Salad Days* was growing. Cameron was smitten by it all and, well, he and we never got over it; a total conversion. He was evangelical; he created little theatres everywhere we went. Making seats and setting stages. He began presenting his own shows when he was eleven years old. He was, as he is now, absolutely insistent about details. Everything had to be perfect – as he saw it.

We all had to be in our seats on time; we had to have our tickets – the stubs, not the full tickets, which had to be ceremoniously 'checked' by Robert – and to applaud at the appropriate time, along with Nicky, which was most of the time, as he was a toddler and thought the puppets were his little friends! And there had to be a packed house.

Instinctively, Cameron knew that it did not matter how wonderful your show was if no one was there to see it. We had to round up the relatives and 'pack' the audience, with aunts and uncles and next-door neighbours, who were persuaded into coming. I asked him: 'What if they don't turn up?' That didn't bother him: 'I will keep the doors open until they do. And I won't let them out until the show has finished.' Possibly, my stubborn streak was passed on.

Later, when the organisation became more sophisticated, they started a puppet theatre in the garden shed, with the timbered walls covered with theatre show leaflets he collected from friends and relatives. And every Sunday there would be a performance with about ten tickets for his friends. Cameron would write the script, Aunt Jean would type them, Robert would pull the strings and again Nicky would be seated in the back row to encourage the applause. Everything was done very professionally.

Robert Mackintosh: Cameron already had a sense of the impresario, which included 'billing'. Apart from 'Presented by…', it was also 'Stage management by…', 'Costumes by…', 'Lighting by…', 'Scenery by…' and 'Direction by… Cameron Mackintosh'! That left 'Puppetry by Cameron (just about) and Robert' and 'Piano by Robert'. That was one credit I got on my own – hands down, so to speak! Cameron issued tickets, printed on a John Bull children's lettering set, which had to be paid for to gain entry. And most importantly, the 'audience' had to be on time. Punctuality was essential to Cameron. He was really obsessed about it and got quite cross with anyone who was late. He would tell them that unless they were seated on time they would not be allowed in to see the show. Cameron took that notion to his production of *Cats*. Anyone late for the curtain up had to watch the show from a TV in the foyer, until a suitable moment in the show.

And he still believes in escape, in escapism, in that world of theatre where a piano can make people sing and dance, wonderful whimsical fantasy. By now, he wasn't just enjoying school but organising the theatrical endeavours of Prior Park College. There, he was nicknamed Darryl F. Mackintosh after the colourful Hollywood producer Darryl F. Zanuck. He loved it. Other boys might have wanted to be farmers or scientists or spacemen, but Cameron wanted to put on a show – at the end of every term.

The school didn't have a huge theatrical budget, but Cameron talked them into doing 'small' productions. And instead of giving tickets to the captive parents, he'd sell them. Tickets were one shilling in advance, two shillings on the door.

I credit all my telephone box 'Push Button B' training for that. This 'box office' cash helped pay for lighting and props. The key to his early contentment is that at the age of eight he knew he wanted to be a producer and by the age of fourteen he was one. The cover of a 1963 theatre programme from his school reads:

Darryl F. Mackintosh
Presents
The Annual
Prior Park College
REVUE
Christmas, 1963.

What indeed had I produced? But he has always taken 'making people happy' very seriously. When Robert and Nicky were on their half-term, Cameron, who was just turning twenty, was opening a show called *Bell, Book and Candle* at the lovely old Kenton Theatre in Henley, and we were all invited to go and see it. As we were leaving and going down the stairs to get to the car, the phone rang. It was Cameron: 'If you're still there you'll be late and you won't be allowed in.'

Well, nothing his father could say to assure him we would be there before the curtain went up would do. He was adamant. And we were late. So we took Robert and Nicky to the pictures instead and they enjoyed it.

They were growing up too. While Cameron favoured musicals like Charles Cochran's production of *Bless the Bride*, Robert was more into pop music, and Nicky preferred racing around the garden. It was the beginning of the Beatles and Rolling Stones era. Music was definitely in the air and in our house.

Life was changing in so many ways. We had a wide circle of friends, many from the ENSA days and so not so rock 'n' roll. Robert's godparents were Nigel Patrick and Gracie Fields's personal assistant, Mary Davey; she had met her husband, Leon, whom we all called 'Ding', during an ENSA tour. Of course, Ian's jazzmen were making a name for themselves appearing on television and Wally Fawkes and George Melly's comic strip *Flook* running in the *Daily Mail* had a great following. Humphrey Lyttelton and Chris Barber were household names – especially in ours.

We'd be out with Nigel Patrick and people would stare at him. He was very well known from television by then, one of Britain's top ten stars. He'd been the lead in the 1960s drama series *Zero One*, in which he played an airline detective. It was in black and white, much as I saw all of Britain at the time – all black and white, everyone striving to bring some colour, some joy, into their lives.

Zero One was very popular for three years. Nigel was also in films with Jack Hawkins and Richard Attenborough. *The League of Gentlemen* (1960), about disgruntled former army officers robbing a bank, was a family favourite – and the boys still enjoy it. As they did the visits, every Christmas, of Major Donald Neville-Willing. Christmas, we all agreed, would not be complete without Ever Willing. He never changed, and because he was so much a part of our extended ENSA 'family' Ian and I were always going to parties with him. It was always quite a crowd and I'd find myself dancing with people I'd seen at the cinema or on television, which was quite exciting. Jack Hawkins – easily one of the world's top cinema stars of the time – was always a fun dance partner and cheerful, although even in the late 1950s he was having treatment for throat cancer. We just didn't call it that then. I sometimes found him hard to understand after his throat operation, but he always charmingly persevered without embarrassment. He was the ultimate English gentleman. He was extraordinary. He carried on working – and chain-smoking, even though he lost his voice box – with his voice having to be dubbed. Jack, John Le Mesurier, Nigel Patrick, it was a very British crowd. Like Ian, they all had quite a stiff upper lip, contained. But with Donald Neville-Willing around, they all shared that ENSA camaraderie. And through him, Ian and I found ourselves at the most stylish and glamorous parties.

Major Donald Neville-Willing was responsible for bringing the nightclub Café de Paris, on Coventry Street, Piccadilly, back to life after the war. Famously, when it originally opened in 1924, Louise Brooks – who performed there – made a little dance history by introducing the Charleston to London. Many there danced with the man who danced with the girl who danced with the Prince of Wales before he abdicated to become the Duke of Windsor. The heir to the throne was a regular, as were the Aga Khan, Marlene Dietrich and Cole Porter.

But later, on 8 March 1941, two Blitz bombs fell into the basement ballroom of the Café de Paris. They dropped down a ventilation shaft and exploded in front of the stage, killing over thirty people and severely injuring eighty others. Following this carnage, Donald made it his mission to resurrect the club, which he did in 1948 as one of the great theatre spots in London. Dietrich and Noël Coward returned and showcased their cabaret acts and Donald lured new names such as Frank Sinatra, Grace Kelly and Tony Hancock.

'Ever Willing' knew everybody and because of that, Ian and I met them too, as frequent guests of Donald. People like the portrait painter Raymond L. Skipp, a sort of bohemian bachelor who became part of our jolly crowd along with Bea Henderson, who was a fashion model, a beautiful girl who was often in *Harper's* magazine. Raymond painted all sorts of people, from Grace Kelly, when she was a Hollywood star, but yet to become a princess (he said she had a perfectly symmetrical face), to jockey Lester Piggott and… me! My portrait has pride of place in my sitting room and it's only when I see the date, 1953, that I remember those times and the painter are now long gone. But, naturally, I haven't changed that much! Ray and Bea were very close friends. One day they told Ian and me about a beautiful property, the Tower House, in Regent's Park. It was owned by an artist friend of theirs, Annigoni – famous then for painting the Queen – and it was up for sale. At the time, it was priced at around £2,000. Actually, not too much for what it was. But, being a Crown Estate property, there was a very onerous repairing clause as part of the lease, which would have been crippling. But the real reason we gave at the time for turning it down was the fact that one of the bedrooms, which would have been the children's, was at the top of a very steep and winding staircase. A more acceptable excuse for saying no than a repairing lease! But that wasn't the end of the Tower House story.

And anyway, living in the Hertfordshire countryside was a good enough reason to make lots of social trips to London to see our friends. A much more fun place then, I think, than it is now, being so overcrowded. We went to the Stork Club and other nightclubs in the West End, when they were fashionable nightspots, not the rather sleepy establishments they later became. It didn't cost much to go out for an evening to meet up with and be a part of our show business ENSA gang.

I used to raise an eyebrow a little at Donald, as he was so over-the-top camp, but Ian and the boys loved it when he visited. He was fun. In those post-war years, most of life was unframed. But I wanted to be busy too. The boys were growing up, and Ian was involved with the timber business or playing his trumpet. I was stuck in the middle of them. I wanted to do something for myself, and make some money for us all. From a small windfall left me on my side of the family, I did make an investment in a new whitewashed property we called Villa Mercedes (named after the villa where we had got married in Florence) in Menorca. I thought it would be good for a rainy day. We ended up having many enjoyable family holidays there, and it was also used by the boys after they left the nest and didn't want their parents cramping their style!

I began to get restless when Ian was out during the day – and at night when the music called – and at the point when Nicky was also at school. I tried many distractions, including local lampshade-making classes, dressmaking and a host of suburban pastimes that various friends invited me to. Robert recently reminded me of another event:

> I dropped by my mother's house for a cup of tea a while back and she brought out the biscuits. They were in the usual container, which for some reason caught my attention that day. It started by me noticing how old it was and I remarked that it had become quite tired-looking – a sort of greying rubbery plastic. Then I looked at the lid and saw it had the Tupperware logo on top, with the date 1954. I couldn't believe it. Over sixty years old. And then it dawned on me. Of course, the Tupperware party. Suddenly, a vision of fifteen to twenty ladies drinking tea in our garden room in Cuffley, being talked through a pyramid of various different-sized and coloured containers, by a smartly dressed Avon-style saleswoman, demonstrating the perfect seal made by pressing the centre point of the lid, to extract the air from inside; thus creating a totally air-free environment. It was all the rage in the fifties and sixties and as the host, Diana was given a free set of her choice. And now, the seal still works! However, the biscuits need to be eaten pretty swiftly, or they do taste a bit plasticy. Those were the days.

But with the three boys now at boarding school, what I really wanted to do was get a job. I joined the holiday travel company Wings as a tour guide. I also did some work for British Airways Tours and an American company, Olson. My qualifications were my languages; my geography was, to be kind to myself, rather limited. But I've always been a bit of a conjuror, which has been just as well, especially as I was now to be Mrs Mackintosh, escort to the VIPs!

My first experience was a six-week stint in Portugal, although I knew not one word of Portuguese, which was not the best start to my new career as a travel guide and ambassador for the good times ahead. Still, I found I could learn on my feet and I was able to communicate effectively when it came to currency exchange and any hotel bookings – which often went wrong. There was also the advantage that people kept giving me money – cash. I didn't understand it at first, when restaurants and shops kept giving me envelopes with cash. Then, silly me, I twigged that it was my commission – or possibly a simple 'incentive' to take my groups of tourists to certain venues. I would return home with my handbag stuffed with different currencies. I saved it up as a nest egg. In time, I made various trips to Italy, France, Spain, Germany, Romania and Madeira.

Madeira! That was the beginning of the end. I will never forget the place, not for its beauty but the hell I went through from day one. It was my first visit, but my Spanish was good, so I anticipated no problems. The plane left late, so we missed our connection between Lisbon and Madeira and the hotel was overbooked when we arrived late in the evening. Only after a huge fuss – I said all thirty of us would sleep in their lobby until they found us rooms – were we accommodated. Bright and breezy the next day, I discovered that all domestic flights were cancelled because of a strike and the rest of the tour was not happening. My enthusiasm for seeing the world this way was quickly diminishing and soon ended when one of my customers died. It wasn't so much his death, but his wife's reaction.

People believe that the Mediterranean Sea is always nice and warm; it's not, as my holidaymaker with a weak heart soon discovered. He plunged into the Mediterranean and his heart literally almost stopped on the spot. He stayed under until we got him pulled out of the water. He was alive, but terribly distressed and he died shortly afterwards in hospital. With some trepidation, I asked his wife if she would like me to organise an extended stay at the hotel, as we had to continue, but she was unperturbed by the events: 'I've paid for the holiday so I shall carry on. My husband? Oh, I'm sure the authorities here will deal with the funeral. Probably cheaper than taking him back home.' She was off touring while her husband was being buried in Italy. I was shocked. And it gave me my own subliminal alert. I thought I should be back home looking after the boys, including Ian.

It was just as well. In my absence, Robert encountered the sharp end of his father when he was at The Oratory School in Woodcote, Berkshire, and a simple trip by Ian and his music friends to perform at his school was about to make school history.

It was a very traditional old school way out in the countryside, about twenty minutes' drive from Reading, but a fair journey from Cuffley, Hertfordshire in 1964, without the crow-flying aid of motorways. A beautiful building founded by Cardinal Newman in 1859 and run by the Benedictine monks. Quite the 'Tom Brown's School Days' school with ancient halls of learning and lush lawns and parks. It also boasted a new auditorium, which had been added to the original building. Dad was playing quite a bit at this time with various regulars on the jazz scene. Even though the music on the 'pop' scene was Beatlemania, a concert opportunity arose at the school for which I proposed my father, as being able to bring his All Star band to perform for the entire school. It created quite a stir and even propelled me to a level of popularity that was no bad thing at a boarding school, where life can have a snakes-and-ladders mentality. This was definitely worth a brownie point or two. So it was all set and posters were printed for 'Spike Mackintosh and His All Stars'.

Prior to the date in question, arrangements were discussed – times, meeting places for the band – about eight of them; of course, in those days all directions were via this or that pub, three doors down from the Drum and Monkey or the George and the Dragon. It was that type of route which no doubt Dad delivered to his fellow band members, to ensure a seamless gathering of the troops for the journey to The Oratory music event. The plan was they would first have lunch at the school and perform for the pupils and their parents – an audience of around 350 – in the afternoon.

Now Dad loved real cars and he'd recently bought an Armstrong Siddeley, which had three gears and an engine so powerful that he could take off in third gear. It had those doors which opened in the middle – pillar-less. It was to be the band's 'tourbus', as it were. A smaller car trailed behind with the instruments and drums and two of the band. No doubt with extra liquid supplies for the boys too! Arrangements had been made to pick up Wally Fawkes and Mick Mulligan and Ian Christie and other 'All Stars' at various places en route down the A4 to The Oratory School.

From the explanation I managed to extract from Ian upon his return the next day, typically they got the wrong pubs to meet in (there were no mobile phones), and after a circuit around the pubs and drinks in all of them, with Ian driving, the band miraculously somehow found each other and headed to Robert's school in a hazy convoy. But, of course, everything (in their saturated minds) was thought to be going 'splendidly'.

Robert had telephoned me to ask when Ian had left. He was anxiously waiting outside the school, now way past the expected time for their pre-lunch arrival, really quite worried and nervous, for quite a fanfare had been made and it was all-important to him. And it was his father who was coming to play!

Embarrassment was now gnawing away at him:

By about three-thirty, peering across the school driveway, I heard a distant growling of a car. It was impossible to miss; a bit like a Sherman tank. And sure enough, the two-tone green Armstrong Siddeley made a slow, stately climb up the long drive. By this time, there was quite a gathering of teachers and pupils. There was a chrome-top arrangement on the bonnet of the car glistening in the sunshine, which nudged up to the brow of the hill. The car pulled up in the middle of the driveway, just in front of the main entrance and the central doors opened in a single flourish. They all spilled out, along with half a dozen empty half bottles of whisky – the liquid of infallibility.

There was a fermented shine in the air around the car from the alcohol, like the high octane haze of a plane on the tarmac. Dad announced: 'Hello, old cock, we're here!'

I was horrified 'Oh God. They're all sloshed.'

At that moment it was the worst day of my life. I was the organiser. It was all down to me. It would be my fault – my disgrace. The school had set out a lunch, a proper lunch – lamb chops with all the trimmings – for the band! And the new school hall was prepared for them; it was a really big event. And here they were appearing one after the other from Dad's car with their choreography seriously askew. One of the teachers, a really nice chap, obviously understood the predicament and took charge. He arranged for them to go off and have their 'late' lunch – with plenty of coffee. He told the audience that there had been a delay – a technical hitch! But the show would go on – at 6 p.m. It would be an evening concert. He wanted to be on the safe side of sobriety. They did sober up quite well, but when they went on, they were still in a very jolly mood, almost giggling like schoolboys themselves; which is exactly what they were really. But, oh yes, they could play. That was never a problem. It was foot-stomping stuff.

When you get a great jazz band going full tilt, there is nothing like it and they were on top form that night. When I was SURE it was going well, I dared to look around and gently nod to my school friends – 'Yes, that's my dad up there' – he was not going to let me down. It was so good, everything was forgotten or, at least, forgiven and they received plenty of hoots and hollas at the final bow and farewell. I was quite the hero of the day – and night!

I gather the show didn't finish until 10 p.m. and Ian and the rest of the band stayed the night at the school, which saved me from having them all at our house. That's one of the things I had to put up with in our marriage. There would be people I knew sleeping on the couch and sleeping on the floor and also people I didn't know sleeping and snoring too. Ian would go off with the band playing somewhere and we were the first stop on the way back to London. He and Wally Fawkes and others would be brought in and Ian would put on his Louis Armstrong records. Full blast. He couldn't hear for toffee, thanks to the war effort. But even without any particular love for jazz, I knew Louis was his hero. Of course, I knew full well that he played with Louis Armstrong and, at one impromptu gig, Louis borrowed his treasured Selmer trumpet so he could join in. The Selmer became almost a religious icon after that.

In the liner notes for the CD *Flook Digs Jazz*, Ralph M. Laing noted: 'Half a dozen of Britain's finest trumpet players, including Spike [Ian] congregated to greet Louis on the Heathrow tarmac when he briefly flew into London in December 1956 to play for the Hungarian Relief Fund at the Royal Festival Hall. The player who caught Louis' ear was Spike.'

When they were in their prime and performing at concerts in London, Ian would take us to see so many of the legendary jazz performers. After the concerts he'd introduce us backstage: Duke Ellington, Earl Hines, Count Basie, Louis Armstrong and others; quite an extraordinary line-up. We once went to Ronnie Scott's to see an intimate performance by Ella Fitzgerald. There were other performances and funny (to them) stories – featuring Ian, told to me time and time again by many of his musician friends. They mean it fondly, but they're not the ones who had

Diana with neat little boys, Cameron and Robert.

Kitty Mackintosh and Stuart Jarvie's wedding.

Diana and Ian hosting a garden party.

London life: Ian and Diana with painter
Raymond Skipp and partner Bea Henderson.

Sir Cameron Mackintosh presents *Les Misérables* — and his mother.

Diana tells Princess Anne the latest gossip as son Robert listens in at Abbey Road Studios for a Save the Children event.

On the town — never a dull moment.

The Queen and I, a reception with Prince Philip making the jokes...

With Cameron at Buckingham Palace in 1996 for his investiture.

It runs in the family, Prince Charles always makes me smile.

With the wonderfully talented
Bernadette Peters and my childhood
friend, Pat Naggiar.

With Cameron, Michael and my
longtime friend Gillian Lynne.

Having a carry on with the great star
Jim Dale.

With the delightful and wonderful
Stephen Sondheim at Cameron's
apartment in New York.

On the set of the film of *Les Misérables* with Cameron and one of its great stars, Russell Crowe.

With Plácido Domingo and...

My on-and-Hoff toy boy David Hasselhoff.

Lord Andrew Lloyd-Webber.

A night out with Cameron and Michael and friends including Michael Ball, Elaine Page and Nickolas Grace.

With my son Nicky and daughter in law Cindy, and 'Fab Five'
members Andy and Steven, having fun at sea and...

Reliving my past.

Into the sunset after a day at sea.

With the boys, left to right: Robert, Cameron
and Nicky at my 99th birthday party...

Which led on to fun and games with Christopher Biggins and the
conga crowd.

Happy Family, left to right: Nicky, Jayne, Robert, Morgan, Lauren,
Cindy, Cameron; front row: Michael, Angel, Diana, Max.

King George III from *Hamilton* presented my 100th birthday wishes at my glorious party at Claridge's.

Too many zeroes — officially.

Another century begins — I'm off on the road again. My love to everyone.

to track down the cars left somewhere in London or who woke up to a stranger – or strangers – sleeping on the silk sofa with cigarettes burning holes in my carpet. I always liked to keep the family home looking smart, with occasional antique pieces of furniture that I could find, from saving money whenever I could. I didn't do this in order for vagrant musicians to pass out on them for the night!

ACT THREE: SHOW TIME

'My salad days,
When I was green in judgment:
cold in blood,
To say as I said then!'
WILLIAM SHAKESPEARE,
ANTONY AND CLEOPATRA,
ACT I, SCENE V
(FIRST PUBLISHED 1623)

10

RELATIVE VALUES

'Advice to aspiring young producers: never put a show on for audiences; always put it on for yourself, and do it as best you can. Only then, maybe, will an audience come to see it.'
IMPRESARIO SIR CHARLES BLAKE 'C. B.' COCHRAN, 1935

While Ian was getting on with all that jazz, I had the children to entertain. And vice versa.

For Cameron's seventeenth birthday we all went to see the West End production of *My Fair Lady* with the original cast of Rex Harrison, Julie Andrews, Robert Coote and Stanley Holloway. All eyes were out like bottle tops. It was the most amazing show and, proving everybody else thought that too, the production ran at the Theatre Royal, Drury Lane for around six years. I think it's still Cameron's favourite show. The Theatre Royal is most certainly my favourite theatre and you'll know why very quickly.

Ian and I both wanted our children to get solid educations, maybe even to go to university, which the antics of Mr Hitler and his friends had made quite difficult for us, under the circumstances. But at Prior Park, the Catholic school where we sent Cameron, he had been more interested in escaping to the theatre in Bath or the Bristol Old Vic. We often got enthusiastic letters enclosing 'reviews' of Van Johnson in *The Music Man*, Chita Rivera in *West Side Story* or Harry H. Corbett playing Macbeth, rather than an update on his class studies.

Cameron was just wanting to talk about play this, theatre that, music, scripts and an endless quest to do something about it. He wanted the theatre, to be in it and part of it; but his mentor, Julian Slade, whom I suspect he thought would think differently to us, convinced him that university was the path to success. It had worked for him. But only Bristol and Manchester ran proper theatre departments, though.

There was just one major snag. Cameron had spent so much time going to the theatre, he didn't have the 'A'- or 'B'-level grades to get in. He knew Ian and I were anxious that he went to university, a known and solid route to making a career and a living. Well, I was very anxious. But he tried really hard and finally got a grant and entry to the Central School of Speech and Drama in Swiss Cottage, London. A sort of university for theatre. It would be the best of both worlds – ours and his. At first, he was full of praise, excited about the facilities they had and obviously saw it as the pathway to his dream But as soon as he got the measure of the place, it was chalk and cheese. He was impatient to get on. He probably learned very quickly about how it all worked and wasn't interested in doing the exams. Cameron just wanted to 'put on a show'. Nothing new for him! The tutors, of course, wanted to explain the foundations of theatre, from the Greek playwrights to the street entertainers of medieval times. But our boys are not ones to sit around, and Cameron was true to his promise and did try, and try. He lasted a year, left (his version of his exit was, I think, a little questionable) and had to find himself a job. Ian was very relaxed about it, as usual, but I was desperate. I told him: 'You'll never make any money out of the theatre business, you'll need to get a proper job.'

Cameron knew what he wanted to do. He knocked on all the stage doors of London's theatreland, but there was nothing doing. Then, by chance, after being told there was no job available, he was offered work out of the blue: two weeks as a stagehand. It didn't sound so much, but it was for the show *Camelot* and the venue was the Theatre Royal, Drury Lane. Maybe my father's snobbery had rubbed off a little – the Theatre Royal! Well, that was it; abracadabra, pure magic. For me, it was not about being in the theatre, which I know he wanted so badly, but the fact that he was in employment. He got £7 a week, but managed to earn more, by cleaning carpets and polishing the brass rails around the dress circle. The sheer joy of keeping him in the world of theatre completely outweighed any thought of it being work, which might be considered unusual, after six years of private education. I was quite proud of him for that.

Once he fully left home, we knew he would simply immerse himself in this passion he had for theatre. Nothing was going to stop him. He worked for touring companies and had a little role in *Oliver!* during a British tour in 1965–66. It was his one and only time on stage. He was a very well-fed waif. His proper job was assistant stage manager. He was living in a flat in London then, cooking for himself (I had always encouraged him and his brothers to experiment in the kitchen) and soaking up everything so that he could create his own *Salad Days*. For the time being, though, he was to remain an orphan in the cast of *Oliver!*

That experience proved to me that you should always follow your ambition – chase happiness, even if you don't find the pot of gold straight away; keep the rainbow in your sights – he made lots of friends and contacts with people who could help him on his journey, he would enthusiastically tell us over the few phone calls we got. He became very friendly with a boy during the *Oliver!* tour – and in due course I found out that it was more than just a friendship. I was upset. Remember, it was a very long time ago, the early 1960s, and after my strict Catholic upbringing and living in Britain through the 1950s, it was difficult for that news to be anything but a shock. There were many tantrums and much hand-wringing and all of that, but it was a reaction to the shock. Yet, what at first had seemed out of place, at least in the world Ian and I had come from, became a normal part of all our lives very quickly. Ian had tried to warn Cameron of the perils he might face in the theatre, although I know now that he didn't handle that too well. But we both took it on board as part of our lives and, importantly, we saw it was what made Cameron happy. He immersed himself in the world of theatre. The contacts he made on tour and at Drury Lane, where he later worked on *Hello, Dolly!*, stood him in good stead. That camaraderie eventually paid off and he was given the use of an office at a talent agency. But with no money, expected to live and eat very frugally, he suggested that I should help him in the office, on a low salary – zero! So I worked with him there. I used to cook exotic lunches in the office on a makeshift electric oven. It was a very different life for me, this London West End of the Swinging Sixties. Cameron quite liked the Beatles, but he didn't want to be one of the Moptops. The musical *Hair*, on the other hand, seemed to be more his cup of tea – the cast all take their clothes off under a hairnet canopy and sing to the sun. This was more than enough for a Maltese Catholic.

Cameron never wanted to be famous for anything but putting on a show. The true definition of an 'impresario' – a name he loved to introduce himself by, when asked his profession. He was clearly addicted to pulling the strings (he had had a little practice at that with his brother Robert at quite an early age) and the detail, how it all worked and then making it work. So he set himself up as a producer in the West End of London, putting on all sorts of shows, scraping whatever money he needed from friends and family in the early days. Many of them lost every penny. He'd get knocked back time and time again, but his confidence never suffered. He was irrepressible. He was a master of the soft sell; everyone seemed to believe in him, in his enthusiasm and grasp of the theatre. But what worked for him most of all was that if he said he'd make something happen, it did. Whatever he built might crash down around him, but he delivered what he said he would. I like to think that's part of what I taught him: if you say you are going to do something, do it. Now!

Robert and Nicky were given the same advice and it has worked for them too. They got on with creating the lives they wanted.

To be a producer, Cameron had to have a show – and a cast. There was an aspiring talent company run by a man called Barry Burnett and Cameron telephoned him, saying he was producing a musical based on Oscar Wilde's *The Picture of Dorian Gray*. The response from this Mr Burnett was a snooty 'Send me a script.'

Well, Cameron was his own shoestring and an hour later he delivered the script to Barry Burnett, who obviously saw a very young man and told him: 'Please tell Mr Mackintosh, I'll be in touch when I've read it.'

'I am Mr Mackintosh.'

They spent the rest of the day becoming friends and talking about musicals, which they continued to do over the next fifty years. Barry Burnett, as Cameron discovered, was the son of Al Burnett who owned and ran the well-known Stork Club (which Ian and our friends often frequented), and he offered Cameron a desk in his office, which was two rooms in the heart of Piccadilly, across the road from Fortnum & Mason, where his Aunt Kitty had often taken him as a child. It would be £9 a week. This was a big breakthrough for him – and me, for as his 'secretary', we'd been like nomads camping around in various offices for a few weeks here and there. I think people were fascinated by him, his authoritative innocence, and so we got away with more than we should.

I don't think Cameron ever actually paid the rent on the office, so it was no great surprise that he couldn't afford a secretary – me, the unpaid secretarial status symbol. I, of course, had more in my purse than Cameron.

I could never be 'my mother'. I had to act as a detached and quite imperious secretary, the gatekeeper to the great producer. I had to be more dragon lady than mother, fielding difficult phone calls and placing hopeful ones. But it was fun, this scraping about to create a professional front and helping Cameron. And all these men chatting to me. I don't think I encouraged them. I fielded them off, although there was one famous nuisance whose name I won't remember.

This producer asked me out for a drink and I was mortified because I knew I was going to meet him at a first-night show. And I did – much to his embarrassment, as he was escorting his rather famous wife. I had other 'friendly' producers quizzing me about how Cameron could afford a secretary (presumably because we owed them money) and if I tried to explain who I was, Cameron would scream: 'Don't tell them you're my mother!' It was a little like *Dad's Army* and 'Don't tell him, Pike!' It was a world of cheques chasing one another and, fingers crossed, one managed to catch up with the other before it was cashed. Not so easy nowadays with instant Internet banking. I was not unaccustomed to dealing with such matters with Ian, who was never too worried whether cheques bumped into each other. I hated it though. I believed you should only buy what you can pay for. The nostalgia effect makes it hard for me to recall having doubts, but I suppose I must have had concerns, the protective instincts. It's just that I buried them deep, for all the boys went off and did their own things. None of them took conventional routes and that is, I think, from the encouragement and love they had growing up. And, of course, the odd ten shillings I was able to give them. Robert was off being a musician: he was a talented pianist and songwriter, now a theatrical producer and artist manager, but in the early years he was quite the family rock star. I worked for him too after Cameron. At least with Robert I was on the payroll. But before Robert got into the theatre business, when Nicky was still at boarding school, I had free time to help Cameron at the office. Often he'd ask me: 'I've got an important meeting, have you cash for the taxi?'

'Take the bus.'

'I must arrive in a taxi, put on a show.'

Reluctantly, ghost mother handed over the cash. I gave him money for his taxi fare, because I did understand the importance of wanting to arrive looking the part of the successful producer. Or I'd pay and send flowers or champagne to some financial backer or star. It provoked a tizzy now and again, especially when some of Cameron's rather more lusty contacts attempted to inveigle me out on a date. That was not the role I was there to play. And I was led to believe the theatre was full of gay men. Where were they when I needed them?

If he didn't want to use an actor or actress, I was the one who had to tell them they 'weren't quite right'. There were some talented people, but not every talent suits every job. I did the dirty work at the sharp end.

I don't, and didn't, have much influence with Cameron, but I did, and do, tell him what I think. If I'd seen someone in a play or on television who wasn't much good, I'd tell him. Still do.

The boys have their father's charm, and Cameron could keep ideas and plans afloat; everyone was always willing to give him that extra chance for, instinctively maybe, or by some supernatural osmosis, they knew he would come good. That's a conundrum that I can't solve. We had some bumps and I'd lose heart, but then we'd be up and at it again with something new or a twist to the project in hand. I found myself deeply into this theatrical world. Well, I had had a taste of it with Nigel Patrick at ENSA. During the day, I'd be mixing with very successful film and television people. We were, financially, the poor relations. But it seemed Cameron was an intriguing and passionate newcomer on the theatre scene. It was difficult not to take him seriously and he soon walked and talked amongst the 'establishment', even if he was penniless. Still, Cameron found money to buy Barry Burnett the occasional lunch over the road at the downstairs bar of Fortnum & Mason – and we held our breaths and held on to the office desk and space.

It wasn't forever, but it was long enough for Cameron to work on a revival of Cole Porter's *Anything Goes* with the jazz singer Marian Montgomery and James Kenney. That was my baptism of fire. And Cameron's too. Polishing the brass handrails at the Theatre Royal was now behind him. West End, here I come.

One of Ian's friends knew an investor with a huge flat in Knightsbridge. Cameron had a financial supporter, a backer who pledged 80 per cent of the money needed to put on this show in the West End. All appeared well, but the man was a fantasist and the money from this elaborate prankster never appeared. Cameron was racing around trying to get funds. The first leading lady left; the musical director followed her.

I put in some money; it all looked very promising, the real thing. I thought it would be nice to get a cheque, even a small one, from its success and so did others, including one of Cameron's friends – a West Indian greengrocer who, curiously, designed and made jumpsuits as well. The greengrocer's deal was that he'd invest quite a huge sum of money if one of his jumpsuits was worn during a scene. So, it was on with the show, sixteen Cole Porter songs, a story I can't recall and a fluorescent jumpsuit – which, like the quiche at the opening-night party, looked better than it was. It was our debut West End production and I helped arrange the first-night party on 18 November 1969, at the Unicorn pub near the Saville

Theatre. Cameron had put on two plays in 1967, *Little Women* at the Jeannetta Cochrane Theatre in London and *The Reluctant Debutante* in Henley. This was the big time and I was an investor – money I'd put away for that 'rainy day'. Well, it rained on this parade. Firstly, almost everyone at the Unicorn party got food poisoning, which was a haunting omen, and the show closed after two weeks. *Anything Goes* lost £45,000 in unsecured loans – the bank and other people's money – a huge amount of cash in 1969; that might have made Cameron pause in his tracks, but it never stopped him. One of his theatrical partners, Richard Mills, who worked with the theatre owner and producer Bernard Delfont, told him: 'I know you are heartbroken, but if you can survive this, you'll survive in the theatre business.'

We were back at our desks very quickly. Cameron's backers still believed in his ambition. One supporter in particular, the late George Borwick, then heir to the Borwick Baking Powder empire, was a Cameron enthusiast. He helped him get the rights to a play based on the successful BBC radio soap opera *Mrs Dale's Diary* and written by Charles Simon, who'd played Dr Dale forever. It was a great idea. One of the most popular radio series at the time.

The problem was that radio listeners had their own images of Mrs Dale and her friends and family and had little interest in leaving their own homes to go to the theatre to see *At Home with the Dales*. On the first night of the long tour, at the Winter Gardens in Blackpool, the takings were ten shillings – not 50p, but ten shillings, old money. The first week we took £220, the second £225.

It was with some exasperation that Cameron told me about the theatre's house manager who, on seeing him looking glum, told him: 'Cheer up, Mr Mackintosh, at least it's building.'

Cheer up, indeed. And he soon had cause to. The show was a financial mess, a disaster The National Westminster Bank, who had believed in him, could either give him more money – unsecured money – to pay the cast and the theatricals involved or Cameron would have to declare bankruptcy. His father and I didn't have the money to help. Going bust would have meant the end, as he would have been blacklisted by Equity, the actors' union, and lost his chance of being a producer for the foreseeable future.

The bank clearly believed he would make good and backed him – again. But he had to take stock, and not add to that overdraft – I was getting rather heated at this time. He took a job in Scotland as a publicist for a touring company's production of *Hair*, to keep afloat. But his heart was always being dragged back to what he really wanted to do. He enlisted his brother Robert to play in the pit for a touring revival of Julian Slade's musical *Salad Days* (no puppets!) in 1971 – and they all did well. Julian had written the score for another show and that became *Trelawny*, which Cameron produced with Gerald and Veronica Flint-Shipman. I went to a charity evening at the Sadler's Wells Theatre and, true to the Victorian theme of the show (based on Arthur Wing Pinero's 1898 play *Trelawny of the 'Wells'*), we were dressed in the costumes of that period for the opening night, all very grand!

And it was well received. There was hope at last!

Cameron, I was so happy to see, was gently moving upward. Robert was forging a career in the music industry (when not down the pits in Cameron's shows), Nicky was training to be a chef, and Ian was blowing his trumpet (and blowing hot and cold over the timber business). I was juggling the family and family finances, yet I felt we all had a grip on our lives.

Cameron returned to the West End in 1973 with his first original musical, *The Card*, with music by Tony Hatch and Jackie Trent and the book by *Billy Liar* team of Keith Waterhouse and Willis Hall. *The Card* launched Jim Dale as a theatrical superstar and the cast included Millicent Martin and my favourite Miss Marple, Joan Hickson; that made critical waves, if not great profits. Yet, they did well enough. Cameron was then enthusiastic about a female version of *Beyond the Fringe*, but it was never a threat to the beloved original featuring Alan Bennett, Dudley Moore, Jonathan Miller and Peter Cook. It was a musical revue, now renamed *After Shave*, and it did well at the Haymarket Theatre in Leicester. Whatever it had, though, didn't travel. It was an all-woman, leather-clad cast involved in a lot of feminist sketches. That all died rather quickly, after two weeks at the Apollo Theatre in London.

Even Cameron didn't want to go to the first night. But I always believed he had a special insight, love, even gift for the theatre and I tried to show it by backing, as a modest 'angel', all of his shows. Veronica Flint-Shipman, who also believed in him, became a good friend and in 1974 she and Cameron produced a *Winnie the Pooh* musical adapted by Julian Slade, which Veronica directed and choreographed. The jolly Christopher Biggins was the title star and captivated the audience. It was Cameron's persuasion that captured the investment of the other producers, Bristol Rovers Football Club Ltd, to help oil the financial wheels. It was a vagabond life, but a busy one. Like everything that had happened with my life it was one ruled by chance, by happenstance, fate, kismet, karma, luck – call it what you will – but there's an element of the unknown in all we endeavour. I suppose life's the same – capricious.

Cameron Mackintosh: As soon as I left the school in Bath, I got an interview at the Central School for Speech and Drama, which was to be my university in theatre, as my mentor Julian Slade had suggested. When I was accepted, I then couldn't wait to leave home. I couldn't wait. I was counting the days down until I was at the drama school. After the initial excitement, I should have realised, in the title alone, that a lot of what I was being taught was a waste of time. I wasn't going to be an actor, I wasn't going to direct. I just wanted to produce and that's all I had ever wanted to do. So after several vocal encounters about my plight and numerous suggestions as to how certain things could be done better, I was asked to leave after one year. Well, I knew then that I had to be where the action was – in the heart of theatreland: London. Goodbye Cuffley.

The first job I got was to be a stagehand at Drury Lane, because I wanted to start in the theatre. I was paid £7 as a stagehand, which was the standard rate for doing seven or eight shows a week. I got it as a holiday job, and of course I knew I couldn't live on £7. They said I could get another £7 if I was the cleaner in the front of house, and so I used to clean at Drury Lane. So, I had £14 a week. In those days you could get fairly decent accommodation for about £3 a week – not in the centre of London. You could get a two-bedroomed flat or something like that. I didn't fancy going to Muswell Hill, so I sort of told myself: 'My job is in the West End and I have to be in the West End in the morning to clean,' I was supposed to be there at 7 a.m. or 7.30 a.m. Never got there before 8 a.m. or 8.30 a.m. 'I've got to be at the theatre in the evening.' My rationale said to me: 'I'll get an apartment in the West End.' I managed to find the choice of – in a lovely old house in Half Moon Street, Mayfair – a bedsitter plus bathroom, or a bedroom plus sitting room and you shared facilities. I, of course, went for the bedsitter and the bathroom with my little Belling. In Shepherd Market, which the house backed onto, there was a greengrocer and a fishmonger's. I could go and get everything I needed. There was the most wonderful atmosphere. I had sort of learned to cook, because my mother used to let the three of us experiment with the leftovers. Not with anything else. If we burned it, we didn't eat. That was it. We got used to creating anything out of scraps that were left. For me, a little Belling with a tiny oven was quite enough. That's where I learned to cook with woks. I paid £7 a week for the bedsitter, which was half my salary. It was interesting in those days, because I could cook, I could feed myself for £1.50, maybe £2, and by the time I had bought little bits of clothing, I was able to save £1 a week. Something I wasn't able to do again for twenty years until *Cats*. That would still give me £2 or £3 to go out for a drink with friends. I didn't need a taxi. I occasionally took a bus, but from Green Park to Covent Garden, which was my world, was not a long walk.

When I got the job on *Oliver!* and was going on tour, I met my father after one of his luncheons at one of his restaurants in Romilly Street, Soho. He was plucking up courage to tell me to be careful of theatrical types and the dangers to my innocence, but he was so worse for wear that he fell off the stool, and I went: 'Oh don't be silly, Dad. Of course I know what's going on!' My father hated talking about anything to do with sex or sexual orientation or anything of that sort, as that generation were very Victorian. He dealt with it completely normally because he did have some camp friends. Donald Neville-Willing would come to us every Christmas. He was adorable. Christmas would not be the same without having Donald spend it with us. He adored both my parents, but he in particularly adored my father and very likely fancied him as well! This my father took completely in his stride. My mother was slightly worried, but Dad didn't care about things like that as long as one was a good person, honourable and not a rotter. That's what mattered. But he was so funny that day, embarrassed to come forward and talk about it. Those were the days.

I remember, I must have been twenty years old, and my mother found a letter from a boy I had met on tour with *Oliver!* There were a lot of tears. Of course, very typical of my mother: 'What are my friends going to say?' That's where she went straight to. The shame of what she was going to say to her friends. I told her it was no problem. I told her if she wasn't prepared to meet my friend, then I simply wouldn't come home to visit. It was fine with me. After the initial shock, she calmed down and took it in her stride – as she always does with everything in her life.

Knowing exactly what I wanted to do with my life, I couldn't wait to be on my own two feet. My brothers were the same. But to buy, you couldn't get a mortgage unless you put 25 per cent of the capital down. People forget now. You had to have that lump of cash before you could buy. You had to either earn it, or have it from the family. I had my independence from my parents, but I would still see them a lot. The marvellous thing was, between my granny and my aunts and my parents in Cuffley, they were all less than an hour away, I had this wonderful safety net. Not that I needed it. But having it there was just that, a safety net. We were a very close family and we remained a very close family, even though my life was now immersed in the world of theatre and the often late social nightlife that went along with it. That has been the bedrock for us all. Don't forget, as I started very early, my mother didn't know the depths of the odd flop that happened.

In 1969 I was bringing *Anything Goes* into the West End, which was a flop. After that, I was touring all sorts of shows. By the time I was twenty-five, from my parents' perspective, it appeared that I was a seasoned producer. Everything I had set out to be. Except for making any money. They weren't aware of how big the debts were at the bank from the occasional failure. I had shows going on and therefore it was a profession and they knew I was not making money on some, but there was always something going on. I had a bank, the Leicester Square branch of the National Westminster Bank, which was the famous impresario Harold Fielding's bank. Harold Fielding was always moving money around. In those days, the relationship with your local bank was absolutely crucial. They were high standing and you had a very personal relationship. If they liked you, they could be very flexible, unlike the computerised system today, where either you have the money in your account or you don't, and it's available to see on the press of an iPhone button. Therefore, if they had faith in a customer, which they did with me, they were supportive – as they were with one of my very early disasters, *At Home with the Dales*.

It was a stage version of *Mrs Dale's Diary*, and well done, but no one would go and see it. They wanted to listen to it for thirty years, but they didn't want to go and see it on the stage, and at that point the bank manager said: 'Look. Can you pay the actors?'

I went, 'No. I haven't got nearly enough.'

They gave me – just on my signature – £500, which was a great deal of money in 1969. It was also a tremendous amount of faith. They gave me the £500 so that I could pay the actors, because the bank manager at the branch in Leicester Square – home of show business – knew the ropes and told me, 'If you don't pay the actors, you will be drummed out of this business.' I'd been sensible enough to move my bank from Piccadilly to this bank. So, I was saved from that particular disaster.

I remember earlier, my bank in Piccadilly, which was also the National Westminster, bounced a cheque for £5 and I said that this was ridiculous. Therefore, I looked for a bank that had theatre savvy, that understood the yo-yo nature of the business. I said any bank that could deal with Harold Fielding would understand what I was going through. They did. That was one of the reasons why I have partly stayed with the National Westminster for many decades. In those days, it took two to three weeks for cheques to catch up with your bank account. If you had two or three bank accounts, by the time you had cleared all of them you might have actually got some money in your account. There was a chance that something would bridge the gap. It's so different now. The bank, even though I had losses, didn't really catch up to it until years later.

At the very beginning of the shows, *Little Women* and tours of Agatha Christie plays with *Poirot* and *Captain Hastings* would cost me £250, because you only had short rehearsals, so it was £20 from my mother, £25 from my aunt, five quid from him or her and goodwill from many. That is where I got some of the funding from. And a couple of friends. My mother's investment was always linked with the question: 'How much will I make?'

Invariably, if the show succeeded she used to blame me for not letting her put more in, and, on the few occasions it failed, she blamed me for not telling her it would fail.

I was with a partner called Patrick Desmond, a wonderful character. He was an actor, manager, a writer. Wonderful man. He taught me everything I ever knew – and lots of things I shouldn't – about the theatre. He was brilliant. In those days, you didn't have to rehearse a show for long, only a week. I remember I would be rehearsing actors and going to Lisson Grove, where you got your dole. I forced myself out of bed and would go there at 8 a.m. before the actors got there. The actors wouldn't like to see their producer on the dole as well. Not the greatest confidence booster. I had to, though, to make ends meet. There was one actor whom I quite liked and wanted to employ, but I couldn't, because he lived opposite in the mansion block near the dole queue and I didn't want him to see me going in there collecting my unemployment benefit. I wasn't on the breadline, but neither did I have the 'golden spoon'.

I have never been backward in coming forward with my thoughts, and as a producer I don't think I was ever humble. I think I was more of a bumptious little squirt. I'm a terrible interferer. There isn't an element of the show, from the design of the poster all the way through to the curtain call, that I don't have a go at, at some point.

Even as a stage manager, I made a nuisance of myself and insisted on having my name on the playbill, which I did at the Kenton Theatre in Henley in 1967 where they were doing *Jane Eyre*, with a sheet of red shiny paper and a hairdryer to stage the fire scene. Name in lights. Think big!

It was about this time that my mother was working for me. I was in *Oliver!*, where I met Larry Oaks who was the associate director, a brilliant guy. He and this other friend, Geoffrey Ferris, became some of my longest friends, but sadly Geoff died a few years ago. He had also been in the original production of *Oliver!*

Geoff and I became very good friends. He had an agent friend called Phil Payne whom he introduced me to. She represented him and lots of young actors. She liked me and she said I could work out of her office for a bit. My mother came to help.

She used to 'make lunch'. She would take the electric heater, put it down, put a pan of water on it and boil eggs She did bits and pieces for me on and off for two or three years and came with me when it got a little busier and I went to Barry Burnett, who kindly gave me a free office.

We shared an office for several years, one in Piccadilly off the Arcade, and then in Maddox Street off Bond Street. We shared for many, many years. He never charged me rent or anything. Neither of them did. They liked me and I got my foot in the door.

So, for some of those years Diana worked for me and when Robert went into the business, then she started to work with him – paid, as she never lets me forget! It was wonderfully helpful to have her, in her mad way. There was no bowing or scraping to anyone. Whoever wanted our attention, however important, they had to prove they were to be listened to. She had her opinion.

I remember when my brother Robert was an agent and a call would come to discuss representation and Diana would take the phone and say: 'Robert. So-and-so is on the phone.'

'Don't see them.'

'I saw them on the television.'

'They were terrible.'

11

SALAD DAYS

'Bit by bit, putting it together...
Piece by piece, only way to make a work of art.
Every moment makes a contribution,
Every little detail plays a part.
Having just the vision's no solution,
Everything depends on execution.
Putting it together, that's what counts.'
STEPHEN SONDHEIM, 'PUTTING IT TOGETHER',
FROM *SUNDAY IN THE PARK WITH GEORGE* (1984)

I know many people regard the theatrical composer Stephen Sondheim with awe and all but worship at his feet, and I admit I am very fond of him and, of course, all his wonderful shows from *West Side Story* to *Gypsy*. Yet, what I will always adore most about him is his ditching a dinner appointment in New York with Angela Lansbury and meeting me for drinks instead. That I call a compliment. I was only in New York for a little time and when Cameron mentioned that I was coming over, Stephen changed his arrangements to see me.

My son Cameron thought that if anyone ever wanted to make a film of my life, Angela would be perfect.

'Too old,' I told him.

Sorry, Angela!

Stephen comes across as quite a shy man – considering how most of his shows portray so brilliantly the personal relationships between men and women – in words and music. Yes, I am very fond of him and really enjoy chatting about anything in life. I do smile to myself, in the knowledge that Cameron and Stephen's friendship so obviously came about through their mutual passion and love for musical theatre, and through that I got the chance to meet him too. And, of course, recall how the germ of that relationship started by a quirk of circumstances, back in 1976, which brought Cameron together with a show called *Side by Side by Sondheim*, celebrating the songs from all his shows. It was put together and performed by David Kernan, Millicent Martin and Julia McKenzie, with Ned Sherrin as the narrator, for a one-off concert in Wavendon, Buckinghamshire.

Cameron was invited to this special performance, but sadly (as he would later recount when quizzed), his sense of direction was a bit like his driving – erratic. He had set off towards the M1, but after an hour and a half down the M4, realised he was going in the wrong direction. He made it for the interval. But having to fly to New York the next day, he thought he should get a few of his trusted friends to see the whole show when it was performed in London a few days later, just to be sure. It got the thumbs up and so encouraged Cameron to get the British rights. Of course, it became one of Cameron's first real successes. Stephen Sondheim came to London and worked with the cast, where I first met him, I suppose. It ran at the Mermaid Theatre from May 1976 for eight weeks and actually made him some money at last, then moved to Wyndham's Theatre, where it ran for a further two years. This particular association with probably Theatre's most revered contemporary composer was undoubtedly a landmark step in Cameron's career, of which others would take closer notice. And I liked him too.

And now, as musical theatre interest has deepened into great friendship, Stephen sometimes comes with us on holiday. He likes hiking and although he's getting on (he turned ninety in 2020, so with him I have made a one-off exception), he can still keep up with me! In the first days of my friendship with him, the theatre people were trying to keep up with Cameron. And I was trying to keep up with all the boys.

Cameron was enjoying the glory of *Side by Side*, with his name up in lights in the West End. From his success with Stephen's songs and music, Cameron got the job of producing the 1978 Society of West End Theatre Awards (SWET – now with the grander title of the Laurence Olivier Awards), which led to what became a well-documented bitter feud with Andrew Lloyd Webber. Blow by blow, we were to hear Cameron's side of the story.

Evita had won the award for Best Musical that year and Cameron naturally thought the main attraction should be Elaine Paige performing 'Don't Cry for Me Argentina', which reached the top ten of the pop charts. Andrew, whom he had never met, apparently wanted a string of songs from *Evita* to show off his score. He got his way, but the sound system broke down and the *Evita* hits did not sound the way their composer had intended. He was furious and aimed the blame at the producer – Cameron. Andrew had never heard of Cameron Mackintosh and probably imagined him as some ageing, Scottish producer, who had little understanding of the finer points of sophisticated musical theatre. As he accepted the award, he felt it necessary to add: 'It's a shame that a real producer like Hal Prince isn't around to run this show.'

Well, Cameron was around. And it appears that he had enjoyed a glass or two of wine and found an empty bottle which he was going to use as his formal response to that barbed remark. Calmer heads prevented any confrontation that night, but the feud began and circulated the theatre world of the West End. It was silly and they both knew it. But I understand Andrew was the first with the olive branch (Cameron is very stubborn) and a letter of apology. I think they sensibly both agreed to forget the whole thing. We've always been a cat family (even Ian's family crest is a cat showing its claws, with the motto 'Touch Not A Cat Bot A Glove'), and I have always found amusement in Abraham Lincoln's words 'No matter how much cats fight, there always seem to be plenty of kittens.' The cats had made contact.

And, then, when Ian and I were wondering about the future – and I was having my own kittens – the musical that had started it all for Cameron, *Oliver!*, proved how serious our son's success was becoming. He loved that show – touring with it in the late1960s – and became very fond of its creator, Lionel Bart. But he also talked about and marvelled at the stage set, which had been designed by Sean Kenny. Cameron wanted it and managed to get that set and everything else kept in storage – even his own London orphan's jacket, which still had his name stencilled inside it from his days as assistant stage manager on the show. He was always a very determined boy. Bart's production had been so popular, and had such a long run in London, that the theatres weren't that keen to see it back in the West End so soon. Nevertheless, Cameron created a wonderful new production, as if it were a new show opening in London or New York. But then he wouldn't do it any other way. It opened at the Haymarket Theatre, Leicester in 1977, with the very popular Roy Hudd as Fagin. We all trooped up there and enjoyed the first-night festivities. It got such a good reaction out of town that the production was invited into the West End – again. He's like Oliver, Cameron. He's always asking for more. Or, rather, not for more but to do more. He would be devastated if he let an idea for a show, for anything, escape. Cameron was, of course, living away from home through all of this, but with his continual excitement about everything, he would always be on the phone updating us, or when he managed to come home for a family Sunday lunch, which he still continued to do.

I didn't work to give the boys confidence by telling them: 'You are going to be great and wonderful men when you grow up.' I didn't tell them to work hard and do their best. I tried to do it by example, to make them feel as valued as they were. I didn't tell them – I tried to show them.

I believe if you treat your family, or indeed anybody, as if they truly matter and what they do or achieve is important and valued, only the best can result. We didn't go in for sermonising, certainly Ian never did, but for creating the emotional tools to be happy and to succeed. Atmosphere rather than hard-and-fast rules can be effective, for all children want their freedom, want to earn their spurs, show what they can do.

So, when Cameron was doing just that, the 'establishment', unexpectedly started to take notice. In a good way. There was much financial front required in putting on shows, although Cameron was still living frugally in a little flat on Wardour Street, London – a better address than ours for his impresario lifestyle!

But there was money around. The British Arts Council offered funding for him to produce a show to tour the theatres which had been refurbished with local council cash. It certainly helped take the pressure off us! They had bright new venues, but no shows. It was a delicate balance on the see-saw between 'art' and 'entertainment' – they believed Cameron had an eye for the commercial, but classy show. I think that has always been his trademark. Finally, *My Fair Lady* was deemed suitable. Cameron had mentioned *Pygmalion* and George Bernard Shaw to a few of his financial 'angels', convincing them (and me too) to loosen their purse strings for what he would sell as a fresh production with integrity (his), which he was determined to apply. He wanted a 'new' adaptation and with the help of Alan Jay Lerner (who, with Frederick Loewe, had created *My Fair Lady* in 1956) he got everyone to agree. Alan Jay Lerner wrote great musicals and liked to get married all the time. He married Liz Robertson, whom Cameron cast as Covent Garden's most celebrated flower seller, Eliza Doolittle, and whom Lerner clearly approved of: he made her his eighth wife. He must have been trying to outdo Henry VIII!

I was especially fond of Peter Bayliss, who played Eliza Doolittle's father. He was a real scene-stealer, a true character of the theatre, and always fun to see. Peter was a familiar face from films like *Darling* and *From Russia with Love* and did a lot of television work – 'Pays the bills, darling' – in series like *Lovejoy* and *Coronation Street*. His telephone answering machine had him mimicking a parrot: 'Peter Bayliss is not available. He's gone out to get my bird seed.' When I worked for Robert in his management agency, we represented him for a while. It was always interesting to receive a phone call following any interview he attended, as to what had actually taken place. I would get a call from Peter to meet him in town, when I was living in St John's Wood. He was such a lovable character with a funny and wry sense of humour, both on and off stage. We often met at Fortnum's, his favourite tea place, but this time he said meet me at his flat. I knew I was quite safe! And when I went into his 'room', there were hundreds of pictures and cuttings of me in one area – yes, like a shrine. I think I even saw a candle! There was a brief mixture of being flattered and shocked. But I always knew he liked me and was quite eccentric in a lovable way, so I was not too concerned. But I suggested we make our way to Fortnum's before there were no tables!

He was an eccentric, a dedicated and totally English one. For some time, he went everywhere with an invisible dog. He could throw his voice slightly and his barking was uncannily accurate. One famous story is when he took the dog with him to Fortnum & Mason's tea room, where he was meeting Cameron to sort out his contract for *My Fair Lady*. He asked the waitress for a saucer of water for his dog, and included the invisible animal in negotiations. Every time Cameron suggested a weekly amount, the dog would bark. Peter would tell Cameron: 'My dog doesn't think that's enough.' For his sheer inventiveness, I think he did get a better deal than he could have hoped for. He was worth every penny – on and off the stage.

Cameron Mackintosh: My mother flirted with all the leading men. Peter Bayliss, the actor I had in *My Fair Lady*, was completely devoted to Diana. His top-floor flat, his whole apartment, in Jermyn Street, was completely enshrined to Diana. She adored him. He died, aged eighty, in 2002. His last words were 'My space suit has developed a fault.'

There was joy around. For me, having taken Cameron to see the original *My Fair Lady*, it all seemed as if it should be. Life might actually be imitating art and vice versa. Real success breeds itself and the Arts Council were delighted, so Cameron followed on with another big revival production of *Oklahoma!* Ian's and my diaries were beginning to fill with first-night invitations and soon our friends were seeing his name being mentioned on posters. We were very proud parents.

But then the two creative talents of my son and Andrew Lloyd Webber were to collide and make some very special magic, with a little help from one of the greatest American poets – T. S. Eliot.

Ian always argued that what happened next was all down to the wisdom of having a long lunch and adequate refreshment. Which is what Cameron apparently had with Andrew Lloyd Webber at the Savile Club in Mayfair. They tottered out into Brook Street some time after 6 p.m., as Cameron vaguely recalled to me. They had agreed to pursue a 'daft idea' about a musical, inspired by a book of poems involving cats. Now that idea would need nine lives.

Not a great reader of poems, I had to look up *Old Possum's Book of Practical Cats* by T. S. Eliot and, I suppose like many other people, I did wonder at first, what on earth would be appealing about a musical about cats. Weren't dogs a man's best friend? Anyway, I did find the poems amusing and full of character. And I assumed they had some brilliant theatrical idea of how to pull it off. It was intriguing, so different from anything else ever attempted on the stage. Of course, between Cameron and Andrew (with so many hits before him), they managed to attract some of the best for their creative team. The designer, John Napier, brought a gasp to the first audience, who saw the larger-than-life rubbish bins and old cars everywhere on stage, and Gillian Lynne's choreography, with all the cats and the flashing effect of the cats' eyes looking out from every corner of the theatre, was sheer magic – for young and old. Whilst the cat stories were a delight, it was the look, the feel, the atmosphere, the sets scaled three times bigger than normal to 'shrink' the cats. And Andrew's music charged it with musical electricity. That was a wonderful exhilarating experience. It changed musical theatre – for everyone, probably forever. And Cameron was the producer. I was a little bit in shock. It seemed now to happen so suddenly. Only yesterday we were sharing an office with Barry Burnett, with me paying for his taxi. Was this a crossroads for Cameron – for all of us?

At that point in time, Ian's brother wanted to retire from the timber business and move to Scotland and in truth that meant that Ian would be retiring too. So, our lives were changing; time was moving on.

But before the horses (or cats) were out of the gate, and in the face of a lot of professional pondering as to its likely success, I did have faith, to a degree. A musical about cats? Hmm. It was all very well to have belief, and I put my modest money in, but even with Andrew's success in *Evita* and *Jesus Christ Superstar*, and Cameron's recent good luck with *Side by Side*, they did have quite a job raising the capital for *Cats*. Many had the same thought. Cats singing and dancing? Would this be feline panto? Which now, with the show having been such an extraordinary success around the world, seems strange. It wasn't at the time, it was terrifying. Cameron was trying to get people to invest up to the last moment.

Robert recalls a particular, if not peculiar incident, when there was just that last-minute call to 'angels' arms:

I had also invested my little bit into the show, but knowing there was more needed, I went to a few of my music friends, one of whom was the youngish right-hand man of the owner of a very big music publishing company. He told his boss about the show and a few days later I got a call to say that he had agreed to invest £50,000. A very large amount at that time, probably the equivalent of half a million in today's show investment money. Anyway, I told Cameron, who was delighted. As the show got closer to opening, there was a lot more interest, also with Elaine Paige (fresh from *Evita*) joining the cast. I thought no more about my friend's investment, except that just after the show had become such a hit, I happened to bump into him walking along Oxford Street. With a smile on my face, I said his boss must be overwhelmed at what was like winning the theatre lottery. In hindsight, a £50k investment would be worth a return in millions now, being around 6% of the profits. Somewhat sheepishly, he replied that his boss had mentioned the intended investment to his wife, who reminded him that she hated cats. A bad omen, which convinced him not to invest. Presumably she ended up in the doghouse – on a very short leash.

They ended up with over two hundred small investors like me, to get to the half-million or so pounds they needed. Homes and reputations were mortgaged. Not one person, I am certain, actually believed this would be the genesis of a show that would go around the world in ten translations and then go around again and again – and, in the twenty-first century, be in the history books of theatre. Of course, the clever thing is that *Cats* had no boundaries, no borders, to music and dance. It would play as well in Tokyo as London. Finally, I thought, Cameron had opened a new door and in the words of Cole Porter, 'Anything Goes'. And it did.

As Cameron would tell me, this was going to be the beginning of the modern musical that could be copied in any language and in any city around the world. And that's exactly what happened – often with Ian and me in tow. It was so wonderful for us then, and still looking back now, that he wanted us to join in his experience and enjoy the incredible ride with him. This was the birth of the big-budget tours. He had that sort of Barnum and Bailey excitement about him. I'd like to say I knew all this then but, as I said, I doubt anyone could have. Ian and I could now see Cameron moving in grander circles. I didn't expect to be invited along for so much of the extraordinary journey ahead. And this was just the beginning.

Cameron Mackintosh: I don't do shows because I think they will be a success. I do them because I think they've got something original there. My own tastes happened to be in tune with what the public wanted. I think that's the reason my batting average is so high, not because I've discovered some brilliant formula. I love musical theatre, it is the art for me. I suppose it has to be the very heightened theatrical experience it provides. The musical is the one area of the theatre that can give you the biggest buzz of all. I'm still as mad about it as I was when I started, indeed when I was a schoolboy seeing magic pianos and dreaming about doing it.

Which is why my parents were so important, because of being such brilliant fun. For joining in.

(On *Cats*): I was still living in a £5-a-week rented flat in 1980 when I met Andrew Lloyd Webber for lunch to discuss a musical based on some T. S. Eliot poems. We were nearly the same age and we had an absolutely pissy lunch at the Savile Club. We were tossed out at about five or six o'clock in the evening. We went back to his flat and he played me some of his settings of *Old Possum's Book of Practical Cats* and I went: 'Oh, there's something there.' The idea of the British doing any musical was fairly risible, but doing a dance musical was considered total lunacy. Only Americans did that.

Cats got the box-office cream in the West End and on Broadway and the 240 investors in the original London production received £26.8 million over its two-decade run – a sixtyfold return. The investors were people who'd been told: 'You mustn't put money into show business – it's dangerous.' Yet they were taking out Post Office savings. I would say, 'You can't,' and they replied, 'We believe.'

Of course, *Cats* changed my life and lifestyle forever, as it did a few others involved in the show. And whilst it gave me the freedom financially to test my creative instincts, without the same pressure of requiring investment, I was also able to spread the comfort factor elsewhere. At this time, around 1980, my father was sort of asked to retire when he was fifty-five, which was pretty young; he was at a loose end apart from jazz, and it was a very tricky time, and luckily that coincided within a few years of the launch of *Cats*, when I could pay off my debts and, obviously, I could make it more comfortable for them. I'd always had an overdraft, I was never out of debt, and my career had been going on for ages. I was not an overnight success. But at that point, I was able to start sending them on trips and, actually, they were able to have the life that they didn't have before. In the few years before, they had been leading slightly parallel lives, my father being away a lot on his jazz expeditions, which sometimes lasted a few days. But usually back for Sunday lunch as though nothing had happened! Diana would religiously take us boys to church (leaving early before the 'offertory', when the plate for money was passed round), and dad would be at the pub. We all made our way back home for Sunday lunch. Then everyone fell asleep later in the day. A typical cycle of our family life. Now, they were able to go on trips and do things that were fun for both of them and enjoy life in a way that had brought them together in the first place.

12

SIX BELLS STAMPEDE

'Love is the sweetest thing.'
RAY NOBLE (1932). SONG
POPULARISED BY AL BOWLLY

I always tell the boys that if their father and I had not gone to the grand expense of having them privately educated, he and I would have lived in some splendour in Regent's Park from the early 1950s. The Tower House in Regent's Park was on a Crown lease for £2,500, but we gave up the chance of that and stayed in Cuffley. What could have been our home was a beautiful stuccoed villa, built in 1824 by John Nash, and we were told about it by one of Ian's arty friends. You could see Beau Brummell or someone like that walking out of the front door. It was splendid and I thought of it often as we struggled with education, education, education. But we knew it would have to remain a pipe dream and we found a more modest Victorian house in Swiss Cottage (but backing on to a railway line!), which made it a lot easier to accept our growing London invitations.

But following the success of *Cats*, Cameron helped us move into a much quieter street in St John's Wood proper – a lovely town house on a tree-lined street, near Abbey Road and the Beatles' zebra crossing. I could drive to Bond Street and all the shops in a moment and Ian could walk to the Drum and Monkey pub, which was in a tight, small street near Ryder's Terrace where Roger Moore drove around filming as The Saint in the 1960s. Ian raised eyebrows too.

Ian, as you now know, if you paid attention at the Intermission, was no saint, but our life together became more entwined. With Cameron's shows opening all over the world, Ian used to say he was a major export factor in Britain's balance of trade; we found ourselves going off with friends for opening nights or events in Venice and Vienna and everywhere

171

else, for the shows had opened up the world of musical theatre. Like the days of my schoolgirl opera outings in Valletta, the story and the music and the magic were way beyond this language or that.

My friend Stella Richards often went with us. We'd make up a little first-night party of people; she said it was like 'school outings'. We were like a little gang going off to enjoy ourselves and possibly learn something. Stella's right, there was something of the playground about it. She had always said that I should run a school for suitcase packing, but I'm tiny, so my clothes don't take up much space. It was an adventure. Such a relief for Ian and I to go away as a couple, and simply be comfortable and carefree. On those trips, we had our friends with us and you could always be busy doing something. I hate sitting still. Ian was as curious as I and we'd wander around places including some in Italy which we remembered well from the war; he said that, somehow, towns on the Continent had not changed as much as those in the south of England. He thought the north of England and Scotland had held on to past traditions with much more of a grip. After the somewhat claustrophobic feeling of growing up on Malta during the war, for me, this was like taking a deep breath of cool, fresh mountain air and seeing over the horizon. It was a heady feeling. It's not the having money, but the not having money worries which changes everything. Cameron's success was the family's success.

Oh, it didn't stop Ian going off to his jazz. He saw it as a duty to attend the Edinburgh Festival every year. There were still the Soho forays, four stops on the Tube, and regular meetings of the group known as The Codgers, that he helped found and who still meet each year, twenty-four years after his death. I may have referred to them in different terms from time to time, after they had led Ian a little too far astray. They would play all the same stuff and the records – Louis Armstrong, of course – and talk about jazz, a love of which, along with a drink or six, they all shared. They met in various pubs and the other drinkers seemed to welcome their musical celebrations. The other popular venue for Ian to play his trumpet was the Six Bells at 195 King's Road, Chelsea. He had an affection for that place and Robert would join his father there and play the piano. Wally Fawkes liked a particular room in the Six Bells and their friend Jim Godbolt had opened it as a jazz club in the 1950s.

For Ian, it would always be a special landmark pub, because of Spike Hughes, the jazz hero he'd named himself after, who spent many hours there. Of course, much of this passed me by because, to be honest, I saw it as the place where Ian could be completely carried off into a world where his family responsibilities became neglected. But what I later learned is that Hughes led a band called The Decadents (they recorded for Decca and possibly their lifestyle had something to do with the name) and after their recording sessions, they would quench their thirst at the Six Bells, recommended as a haunt for musicians. Many other musicians followed suit, a routine immortalised in Spike Hughes's recording 'Six Bells Stampede'. The Americans Jimmy Dorsey, Duke Ellington and his band, and the trumpeter Muggsy Spanier all recorded at the same studios and drank at the Six Bells. Ian and Wally Fawkes, Sandy Brown, Al Fairweather and Humphrey Lyttelton were all regulars or semi-regulars (as most of them were on my settee at 3 a.m.!).

The locals in the Drum and Monkey in St John's Wood were definite regulars. Familiarity of venue seems to be an important factor for social drinkers. As Ian could walk there, the Codgers would meet at the Drum and Monkey and indulge their passions. I'm indebted to one local anonymous chap, who knew the premises better than I and offered his personal assessment:

Pubs sometimes stand out because they're incongruous. This was certainly the case with the Drum and Monkey in St John's Wood. This is one of those upmarket areas that at one point had an unusual number of pubs, no doubt left over from the days when St John's was a wood and the travellers needed plenty of drinking houses to quench their thirsts. St John's Wood is an area imbued with what one writer described as plutocratic gloom. It has that sort of muffled quality you often find in very affluent parts of London, as if the air has been soundproofed. The Drum and Monkey was neither muffled nor plutocratic … The D & M had obviously once been a house, and having a drink there was a bit like sitting in someone's front room. It was a typical old-fashioned pub, dark, flock wallpaper – really, to call this place unpretentious doesn't begin to describe it. The locals were friendly, older people, including one chap whose party piece was sticking cigarette papers all over his face at the evening's end. It was a nice place to go. Since Ian's death, the Drum and Monkey is no longer. It has been turned back to being a family house. Indeed, a Codgers' dream location. Especially as the locals didn't object to Louis at full volume. Interestingly, the memory of those days now lives in those who were its frequent visitors and recall the little band of music heroes. Today, with the building turned back into a private house, I wonder if anyone is woken in the night by sounds of Satchmo and distant voices discussing which recording it was? They did and still do stick together, the Codgers.

When Jack Hutton, who was the editor of *Melody Maker* and co-founder of the Codgers retired in 1987, they all celebrated with a party at Ronnie Scott's and Ian played trumpet on stage in a jam session with Ian Christie (clarinet), Peter York (bass) and Hutton himself also on the trumpet. The Codgers also liked Covent Garden venues and bars, for jazz people attract jazz people, as theatre people attract theatre people. Of course, I do look back on those days with a little more humour now, but at the time, the mention of 'just going to...' a jazz club, a pub or the Six Bells filled me with my own alarm bells – and an almost uncontrollable urge to dial 999!

The boys' great-uncle Bill, who was a marvellous cartoonist and artist and ran his own gallery in Chicago, brought over lots of American records on his trips to Britain. Cameron loved one by Tom Lehrer and was captivated by its humour and wit. That led to them working together in 1980 on a revue of his songs, *Tomfoolery*, during the period he was working with Andrew on *Cats*. Tom Lehrer's work was a passion for Cameron and he turned it into a little gem of a show. It was a revue, not dissimilar to *Side by Side*, and he staged it stylishly. It was an omen.

Even as the doting parent, I was astonished at the immediate success of *Cats*, which made us investors quite hopeful. It began breaking all sorts of records in the early years including audiences, numbers of theatres, countries, continents – but still none of us could know what an incredible journey was actually taking place. Cameron excitedly talked about its future of international productions that could never have been imagined. Following *Cats* came *Song and Dance* (another of Andrew's and lyricist Don Black), *Little Shop of Horrors*, *Blondel* and *Abbacadabra* (to re-emerge in a different format as *Mamma Mia!*) and then the wonderful production in 1985 of *Les Misérables*. At this point, Ian and I needed a holiday, as a rest from all the trips to first nights around the world that we were invited to.

As *Cats* had proved such a huge international hit, you would think that, like winning the Lottery and so being financially set up for life, you should be bulletproof from future risks. *Les Misérables*, was, of course, Cameron's invention. The recipe of Victor Hugo, the RSC (and Trevor Nunn again) and a truly wonderful cast should have been a slam dunk (as they now say!). I invested – again. But of course, not everyone thought it was wonderful when it opened at the Royal Shakespeare Company's Barbican Theatre, London. The critics were very snobby about it, and with a do-or-die decision to transfer the production, in order to turn it into a commercial show, he came face to face with probably his biggest personal creative gamble. If it was wrong, it could cost him much of what he was currently making from *Cats* (still a kitten at this point). It was only with the drive and faith of the inner circle of the creative team – and huge personal investment from Cameron – that *Les Misérables* got to the West End and then the world. At that moment, he would have personally lost a huge sum of money if he'd given up on the show. We were all very aware of his situation, and naturally concerned, but I knew he had the inner strength and pure determination to do what he wanted, and I never saw any great signs of pressure on Cameron that he couldn't deal with. He had great instinct.

You also have to have a good story. Victor Hugo provided that. It was Cameron's job to provide the vehicle. I believe it took around seventy backers to put up the £600,000 for the original production of *Les Misérables* in 1985, and some thirty years later it had paid them over £50 million in profits. Unimaginable at the time. I was pleased to be a small part of that investment and get my little share! The success was reflected in Cameron's lifestyle. He was never brash, but he now had the funds to buy a little hideaway – a farmhouse in Provence. He felt, quite rightly, that he really did need somewhere to relax with his friends and to work with writers away from the pressure of a production office. But it also became a wonderful place which all the family could enjoy. Robert and his wife Jayne got married there in fairytale style. A lovely old local French church and ancient pony and trap to ride through the village definitely beat Caxton Hall and a Daimler limo! Lots of special memories from that time. Now, Cameron could think about moving to a bigger home in the country, as well as being able to keep the family close together, particularly at holiday times. He seemed to have the same outlook on life as Ian's sister Kitty, who enjoyed using her own success to make the lives of family and close friends as comfortable as possible. It has always been a big part of the same pleasure Cameron gets from his success, too. He loved to work with writers and others away from an office environment, so into his view came Stavordale Priory, an eleventh-century monastery in Somerset. He has been with his partner Michael Le Poer Trench for a long, long time and it was Michael who discovered the priory. He is a wonderful photographer and naturally something so historical and beautiful like the priory enchanted him and Cameron. It's quite ancient and they made it their mission to enhance it and preserve it – as they do me! Stavordale Priory came with lots of land, but Cameron managed to add to it over the years, with farmland that is stocked with well-nourished dairy cows. When Michael spent less time on photography, his interest was drawn to the beautiful gardens, which needed some attention. After a great deal of love and work, the gardens at Stavordale are some of the most beautiful in the country. It has caused so much interest that they now have visitors on quite a regular basis, with tea provided in the beautiful garden setting. All income goes to their pet charities, which is lovely. What has been a delight for me is that after Ian passed away, Cameron built me a lovely cottage on the estate, where I can spend weekends around the family, but independent of everyone! That is still very important to me, even at my young age! I never like to be a nuisance, although they think they need to keep an eye on me. However, I do think the cows have better mattresses than me!

The boys' connections to Scotland actually go way back through generations. Their great-grandfather was from Raasay, an island between Skye and the Scottish mainland, separated from Skye by the Sound of Raasay, and their great-grandmother from Skye. In 1980, following the death of his aunt Anthea, Cameron became the trustee of a property, Torran Albannach (Gaelic for 'little piece of Scotland'), near Mallaig. In her late teens, Anthea had been a celebrated concert pianist, who lived in a beautiful artist-galleried house in Chelsea, where she would invite Sir Malcolm Sargent and his concert orchestra to rehearse her solo performances for forthcoming concerts. She came from a pretty wealthy family and led quite an exotic life, although she was more at home in the local bar in Mallaig with her husband, Jim (whose brother Stuart Jarvie later married our Aunt Kitty), en route to their Loch Nevis retreat. Her mode of transport was a 1930s open sports tourer Bentley, and her imminent arrival in Mallaig was always known well in advance by the roar of its unsilenced exhaust system, delivering three and a half litres of unbridled power.

The log-cabin-style house was built at the foot of the steep hills of Tarbet Bay as it meets Loch Nevis. Bought in 1959 by Anthea and Jim Jarvie, its five hundred acres (at ten shillings an acre) have a spectacular view across Loch Nevis to the Isle of Skye. Cameron thinks it was meant to be and success enabled him to buy the 'twelve penny lands of Morar' for the estate. That included the view, a vast expanse in the West

Highlands, nearly fourteen thousand acres. Cameron is no newcomer: he first went there when he was about fourteen years old, joined later by his brother Robert and then Nicky, as they grew up; all of them have the fondest memories of their visits and have spent their Scottish New Years there continuously for over fifty years. But for all of our family, it was a wonderful place to spend time together. Even for Ian, whilst whisky (his favourite tipple) was almost on tap, away from London and his drinking buddies, he was as good as gold and it was a great way to recharge the family batteries. Cameron wants to protect every inch of it. It seems as though it was destiny that he would be able to continue taking care of this extraordinary place, and through his own success in life, be able to add to it for future family generations.

That said, any happiness was wiped off our faces at the millennium when Torran Albannach was burned out. It was such a shock. Since Cameron took the estate over, he has done so much for the area and here was this despicable case of arson and the devastation of the property. He had become responsible for nearly fourteen thousand acres by then, and was quite paternal about that place; it was part of his and our family history. And when the croft on the shore of Loch Nevis was completely gutted by fire, I wasn't sure he'd want to go back again. I know that when he first went up there with Robert, they arrived on the beach of Loch Nevis, where the croft had been, to see the charred and crumbled remains filling three blue skips sitting side by side. There was obviously a moment of anger and the thought of just walking away; but there was too much of a pull from the Highlands for him to run out with his kilt between his legs. So once the air cleared, Cameron knew he had to replace it – but this time he would make it bigger and better, following what I've learned to call my mantra: 'Get up, get going and pull yourself together.' What hurt Cameron most was that the police said there had been a hate campaign against him, no doubt brought on by local grievances, probably because he had become the laird and had spent a great deal of resources getting the surrounding land back in order, including new fences and generally upgrading buildings that were in poor repair. More than 1,200 yards of fencing that was put up to protect a tree-planting scheme was cut and a rowan tree on a small islet in Loch Nevis, opposite the cottage, was hacked down. Thinking that was rather strange, I was told that it was a clue that the vandals were outsiders, for in the Highlands the harming or felling of a rowan tree brings bad luck to those who do it. The police said at the time of the fire that they believed it was deliberate and had been caused by someone turning on the gas, setting some kind of long fuse device and making a quick night-time getaway; but nobody was arrested.

The repairing of the fencing which highlighted boundaries, for years overrun and now reinstated, caused some ruffled feathers. No doubt, heated discussions in the local pubs brought about a mindless determination to do something about the 'intruder' – although our family has been there as long as most of them. But it hurt Cameron more than he ever let on. I was very upset for him, knowing that he had supported a centre for elderly care, where he was due to cut the ribbon at the opening ceremony of The Mackintosh Centre in Mallaig. Previously, he made sizeable donations to the people of Mallaig for a health centre as well as a swimming pool, so the young people had their own recreation centre in the town; he did the same for the lifeboat facility, which can only exist on local funding. Cameron loved to do this, not just because he could, but because he felt it was the least he could do to give something back to a community and area that provided him and all our family and friends with such joy.

Torran Albannach on Loch Nevis is not an indulgence, but a demanding project to preserve and enhance. It's like a second family home too, where we celebrate every New Year. The journey up there is an event. Planes, trains, coaches and boats – quite hard work just getting there, but heartwarming (providing you have coat, scarf, hat and walking boots – and a wee dram!). When you arrive, the atmosphere in the fishing town of Mallaig is exhilarating and the final boat trip up Loch Nevis brings you into a world that hasn't changed for hundreds of years – a little older than me – but is gloriously tranquil. Not to say that we don't bring it back to life, when about a dozen of us move in and we invite the locals and anyone around, walkers, travellers to join in on any of the New Year festivities. I love it. It keeps me young, active and alive!

It's a little different from what greeted Cameron and all the boys more than fifty years ago, when he first stayed at his uncle and aunt's house in Tarbet, which was then a simple and charming hand-built log cabin. The facilities were pretty basic – calor gas and wood, and a lot of damp around the place. More like camping. The new building, which is made of the local stone and granite, is more like a mini castle. It feels very strong and certainly keeps us all a lot more comfortable – and warm! The locals are all friendly people and they always wave and say hello whenever we turn up. These were the regular Highlanders who had always welcomed us, and their support meant so much to the family, particularly after the incident. Many of them regard Cameron as 'a local' and that's a serious compliment in the neighbourhood. He calls it 'The Great Escape' (a favourite family film) and it is for us all.

And Cameron's success has taken me much farther than the Scottish Highlands. I must have been around the world a few times just with *Les Misérables*. And with *The Phantom of the Opera*, which brought Cameron and Andrew Lloyd Webber so successfully back together again, Ian and I became mascots – good luck charms, maybe.

It was life-changing for Ian and me, when it all took off for Cameron. He indulged us in everything. We were drawn into the glamorous lifestyle of theatre openings all over the world – Australia, Japan, Germany, wherever there were theatres there were Cameron's shows. And we weren't nervous about how they would be received: they were all hits before the curtains opened, so there was a sort of relaxed excitement about it all. It was first-class travel and hotels and a few days of jolly fun. We were part of a huge entourage at these things and I could see the pleasure it gave Cameron to make us part of it. We were a VIP couple for him. There was so much talent and enthusiasm around them. After all the financial gambling over taking *Les Misérables* into the West End, it was at a celebratory party that the French writers, Alain Boublil and Claude-Michel Schönberg, hinted at their next project, which would turn out to be *Miss Saigon*. It opened at the Theatre Royal, Drury Lane, in September 1989.

It seems such a long time ago now when we dressed up for the opening night of *Miss Saigon*, for so much has happened and all in a great whoosh. I find it easier to keep track of time and dates through Cameron's show openings or Robert's; or when Nicky opened a new restaurant and gave it the family name – 'Mackintosh's' in fashionable Chiswick – but he's more into family business now rather than the daunting hours demanded by cooking and running his restaurants. Being around your family is too important to miss. But I've always let them do what they wanted to do in life; as their mother, I would get worried in the past that they were not preparing for the future, but that's happily all wrapped up now, with a ribbon or two. That's a great pleasure to know. Yet even in the early 1990s, I would worry. Cameron had all the big hits, but even he could not predict public taste or whether one show would work as well as another. And I was well aware that however successful you were, a flop show could land you in huge debt. But for Cameron, it wasn't so much that he was lucky, he simply didn't take anything for granted. He has always talked about each new show or new production as though it was his first. Even after so many hits. He remembers when he had to borrow money from me, when he had to line up to get a ticket for two shillings and sixpence – I think that's about fifteen pence – to be in the gods at *Oliver!*

He's created everlasting productions, that's in his blood. It also makes you interested in what makes other people tick, what they like, what they want. As such, you enjoy all the pieces of the puzzle; Cameron revels in the computerised mechanisms that make a chandelier swing into place at the touch of a button, or a set of stairs materialise just as an actor puts his foot on the first tread; those are his magic moments. And it all probably started when he first saw the Magic Piano in Julian Slade's *Salad Days* all those years ago. Ian and I were there at all the opening nights and looked on as amazed as anyone else.

'THE ROYAL CIRCLE'

Many of his opening nights drew a royal attendance or two. One such couple were the Countess of Wessex and Prince Edward, whom Cameron knew well from the early days when the Prince worked with Andrew Lloyd Webber's Really Useful Group. They were his guests at an after-show dinner. Cameron quickly sorted out cars and a special restaurant for us to go to: 'Eddie, Eddie, this way,' he shouted to the Prince and we were off. When I arrived, Prince Edward and his party were all seated and I was opposite him. 'You got here first,' I said and he bowed his head with a smile. When his food arrived before mine, I laughed: 'And your meal first too.' He grinned at me, and circled one finger around his head, like a halo, or a crown!

I was thinking of Ian and Malta, where my heart has spent much of its time, when Cameron was asked by the Queen to put on a concert for the Combined Theatrical Charities and the Royal National Institute of Blind People (RNIB), of which she is patron. The event was to honour Cameron and feature performances from his shows.

It was called 'Hey, Mr Producer', originally thought up by his brother Robert, as a compilation audio recording of Cameron's shows, and what an event it was. It was staged at the Lyceum Theatre in London on 7 and 8 June 1998, and the second performance was the Royal Charity Gala in the presence of the Queen and Prince Philip. I was to be in the Royal Box with the royal couple and was guided towards my seat.

As I walked into the box, into the theatre proper, I could see all these faces at the end of a row of craning necks, looking at me. When I moved to my seat they all stood up. I didn't know where to look, it was most embarrassing: I was mortified. For all my bravado, I am really quite shy in those situations. I couldn't wait to sit down and be out of the way, but I had to wait for the royal party before I could do that. The Queen and Prince Philip glided in.

My face was red but, soon, everyone else was as flushed with excitement. The cast list would fill a shelf of show business encyclopaedias, from Julie Andrews to Andrew Lloyd Webber, Michael Ball to Elaine Paige, John Barrowman to Julia McKenzie, Judi Dench to Bernadette Peters, and all the alphabet between and beyond.

There was a segment devoted to my lovely Stephen Sondheim, and he and Andrew Lloyd Webber spoofed their own work. It was quite an evening, *Oliver!* and *Miss Saigon* and *Phantom* and *Oklahoma!* and *Cats* and *Les Misérables*. What a night!

And so special for me.

At Cameron's suggestion, I had framed that marvellous photograph of the Queen dancing with Prince Philip in Malta in 1967. During the evening I took the opportunity to present it to her and she called Philip over to study it. She told me, with a very honest smile: 'I shall treasure it even more as it has come from you.'

These are indeed very special memories to treasure and make you – me – realise how fortunate my life has been in so many ways.

Whenever I have found myself in the company of a member of the Royal Family, I have never had anything but a good time. Having met the Queen a few times in my life, she, in particular, is always kind and interested to ask me about ordinary things. I am sure it is the Malta background. At one dinner at Windsor Castle, which I attended with Cameron, Prince Philip asked who I was sitting next to. 'You,' I replied.

He smiled: 'Oh, goody goody.'

I never intrude with them and over the years that has made for a fond relationship. I wouldn't say anything out of turn or be over-familiar. Follow the rules and the warmth will follow, if it is meant to. When Cameron was knighted in 1996 and I went to Buckingham Palace, it was a sad time and the Royal Family were kind. Ian had died a few months before and we were all grieving.

Ian went off, as with all things in his life, stylishly. And without a fuss. He never liked a fuss. He wouldn't make one and you couldn't make one around him. He knew, and laughed that Cameron had 'become respectable', when his knighthood for services to the British theatre was announced in the 1996 New Year's Honours List. It was so sad that he wasn't at Buckingham Palace to see our eldest son being knighted two weeks before our fiftieth wedding anniversary. Typical Ian.

It was days before my birthday, on 18 January 1996, when he died. He'd had a jolly lunch with Robert that Thursday, some good wine and music talk, and then they went to Burlington Arcade to buy me a birthday present, which I have treasured ever since. After Robert dropped Ian back home, he went off for a haircut round the corner. When he got back, Ian went upstairs to do some leg exercises, because he was having treatment on his knee, which was giving him trouble, making walking difficult. When I went upstairs to tell him dinner was ready, I found him lying on the floor in the dressing room, semi-conscious.

I called the ambulance, but four hours later he was dead. He had suffered a terrible stroke. It was good that all of us, all the boys and me, were with him when he died. Cameron had been on a train to Reading, and so we made an urgent call to the station to try to reach him. They found him inside the train at the next stop and sent him straight back to Paddington; and he got to the hospital in time for us all to be together. So whilst Dad had spent a lot of his life escaping from us to follow his love of playing jazz, in the final moment he managed to bring us all together to say goodbye.

By chance, friends were on their way to London from Malta and America when Ian died. Cameron was opening a show in Stuttgart and had chartered a plane to take me and a few friends to Germany to celebrate my birthday. He had planned a lot of surprises on the flight, entertainment and special meals. Instead, I was kept busy while the boys planned Ian's funeral.

I felt angry when he died because his friends contributed to his decline by encouraging him to drink. That said, and I know it is awful to say, Ian wouldn't have wanted to be a sick person – he was always so hopelessly full of life. I think in his heart he felt that, if he was going to die, he wanted it to be the way it was, after a good lunch with his family around him, a glass or two of good wine and without any pain.

On my birthday, and what would have been our fiftieth wedding anniversary, less than two weeks later, there was a lunch in Deauville in France all planned as a surprise. I hadn't a clue where I was going until I turned up at Bristol Airport. At first, I thought we were going to Scotland but, no: it was a birthday lunch in France with my friends. It was nice, but it was sad. Still, my friends were there to talk about Ian and our adventure.

Robert Mackintosh: Looking back, the events surrounding Dad's sudden death are not always easy to recall in any order. They were lots of different mini events. Apart from our own personal feelings, our mother needed support from her sons. We were all there, every day at her house – their house. Leaving her to have a couple of hours on her own, one lunchtime on about the second day after his death, we decided to go round the corner to one of his local haunts – a wine bar, which we had heard he frequented but none of us had been to. We found it and trooped in. From the man behind the bar we each ordered a whisky, which seemed appropriate. The cheery bartender stood near us and we offered the fact that our Dad – Ian, 'Spike'? – came in here occasionally. He replied, 'Oh yes, Spike. You're his sons? We were so shocked. He was such a lovely man.' He pointed to a half-filled wine bottle on the wall: 'This is his.' Sudden thoughts went through all our minds that maybe there was an outstanding account to pay. 'Oh, do we owe anything?' 'Oh no, everything is paid up. He bought the bottle and just prefers to have whatever number of glasses he feels like, before he goes off to Hampstead.' Quizzically we asked 'To where?' 'To the pub up in Hampstead, where he meets Stan Greg and Ian Christie at one o'clock. He has a very particular routine, you know – gets here at 11.30 and always seems in good humour. I think he ends up in Kilburn at 3 o'clock at some other watering-hole. Every day. He gets a bus to each pub. Quite a character, though.' Well, this was all news to us. It seems Dad had a life and routine that was totally unknown to any of us. Later, we would find that his social calendar was a lot busier than we could ever have imagined.

Ian's funeral took place at Cameron's beautiful house in Somerset. We all took things to bury with him: his medals, his school tie, a bottle of single malt Scotch – though he would have drunk anything! It was a wonderful tribal thing. The funeral service was held in the thirteenth-century chapel attached to the house.

Ian was buried in the grounds of Stavordale Priory. Dom Antony Sutch, the then headmaster of Downside School, took charge of the service and some of the boys from the school carried the coffin to the burial ground. It was a very moving service. You can see his grave from the kitchen at the Priory, and when I go and visit him I always have a little chat, as do all the boys. It's a lovely warm feeling knowing he is nearby. It really does feel as though he is still here with us, and in so many ways he is. I'm glad he died first, because he couldn't have managed without me. I was the stronger of the two and I think he knew it. It doesn't take a moment to realise that although someone is dead it doesn't mean they don't exist.

I still think of things Ian would have enjoyed or liked or wanted to see; people die but are not forgotten. In time, grief floats above your life and drops in for short and, hopefully, bearable visits. Death doesn't kill it all. It can't destroy for you the person who witnessed so much of your life, the one person who could give first-hand evidence that you indeed had lived the way you tell it.

It's the absence of the person who knows you for better or for worse, that sharing and partnership, that's most painful. I have been a widow for many years and it has given me time to reflect. As a young woman and a wife and mother, some might say I've been very lucky, and I agree with them; but I do believe you have to give and take in life. Compromise when it is the correct thing to do and fight your corner when it's not. When Ian died, I was very fortunate to have my three sons around me and good friends who were enormously sympathetic and helpful. Still, it is not the same as having the other half. No one can share the pleasures we could as a couple, or care as much as parents about things your sons have done well, where they have behaved with honour and kindness, with friendship.

After he died, following some fifty years of marriage, and I know that he was maddeningly often absent, I was acutely lonely in a different way. I wanted somebody to share in life with the same things, but what I really wanted was my husband, so that was that.

Nobody would believe that I could be lonely, because I have a pretty lively personality. You get days when you're very down and there are so many physical manifestations, for grief is such a shock to the system. There is an erosion of your emotions, for what you go through is extraordinary and you have to be strong for everybody else. The children were grieving too. Afterwards, you feel so exhausted and dreadfully vulnerable. Bereavement is difficult for us all. But you have to get on with it. It's an inconvenience none of us can avoid. Why can't time stand still? I would like to live forever without, God forbid, getting any older, and enjoy my children and my grandchildren.

Our first Christmas after Ian died, when everybody didn't come to me, was strange. So we decided to get together at Cameron's house in Provence, where we have had such happy times, with everybody doing their little bit in the kitchen for the celebrations. It was lovely. I was glad the boys took over so completely.

I missed Ian not being with us but, in time, as the years roll along, to be totally free and not have to account for yourself can be addictive, again in a different way. I have dealt with loneliness and kept busy and happy in myself and with everything going on around me I'm luckier than most. And it's been a long time.

Life was never going to be the same again and you have to accept the door is closed. I'm lucky to be alive. I have three lovely sons and beautiful and talented (already!) grandchildren; they're all part of Ian, so it's not the end of him by a long chalk. I am now well settled in my new life, with plenty of friends and some very special ones. I travel about four or five times a year and have quite an exciting life. I'm always included in all the social events, and of course am shared amongst the boys' own family holidays. My calendar looks like a travel agency itinerary. And I'm very fortunate to enjoy good health, so I'm able to enjoy the fun.

I have come to accept that once you've done your best there are certain events and situations you cannot do anything about. It is silly to get warmed up about them and you have to let go and move on; you can waste so much energy being fixated on something that is happening in your personal life. I've learned it's important to focus your energy on the positive rather than the negative.

I never think time is catching up with me except when I go to look at Ian's grave and have a chat. I do know that one day my place will be beside him. I shall be very familiar with my surroundings and maybe later on I can do a bit of haunting with the other lady who, I am told, appears on the upstairs landing of Cameron's house from time to time.

They won't be allowed to forget me.

For the moment, I can do that in person.

Following Ian Mackintosh's death, his sons staged what was called 'the greatest jazz wake in British history' at the Pizza on the Park in London.

Robert Mackintosh: Of course, we were all in a bit of a daze through this time. Dad, who we always knew couldn't keep going at 110 miles per hour at his age, was suddenly gone. The 'event' was a way of keeping busy making arrangements and getting the word out for anyone who knew Dad, to attend. He was fondly remembered by Peter Boizot, owner of Pizza on the Park, where Dad had often played with his jazz buddies. He immediately offered his venue as the place for the appropriate send-off and celebration. On the night, we arrived, expecting maybe 150 or 200 people. The shock was that it was absolutely packed with over four hundred guests – and half the people we had never met. As we said 'hello' to some of these folk, they just responded, 'Oh yes, we've known your dad for years. Spent many a night at the so-and-so pub.' One after the other, people would refer to him as their bosom buddy. Thank God the night was filmed and recorded for posterity, because none of us really remember much in detail. It was a night of mixed emotions, filled with some of the best jazz music played anywhere in London.

The next year, a group of his closest 'Codgers' got in touch to say they wanted to have a reunion in honour of their friend Spike. We were delighted and that has continued as a pre-Christmas event ever since. It is now known as 'The Codgers Annual Luncheon – in celebration of the life of Spike Mackintosh', and in 2016 Diana Mackintosh was a guest of honour at the twentieth anniversary gathering of surviving Codgers and jazz greats. As ever, there was an endless supply of refreshment with which to repeatedly toast the memory of 'Spike'. Women were rarely seen at these occasions, so to everyone there, Diana's presence made it seem as if the often-talked-about (with slight trepidation), but never-seen, goddess Diana had made a spiritual appearance!

I always try to attend this event every year, as do my brothers, as we feel it is such a great tribute that these musicians thought so much of him, they would take the time, year after year, to celebrate his life. Of course, what I have noticed is that each year, one or two of the 'old boys' have slipped away to the waiting room above! And just last year, I think there were only two people at the lunch that had actually met Dad. So we can only think that the younger and newer additions to the Codgers Club have simply wanted to join in the celebration of the myth of 'Spike' – the original and founder Codger.

With Dad being such a huge and loving character, his sudden departure was a massive hole in all our lives. But with so many things that still go on around us in his name, he never feels that far away.

13

THE HIGH ROAD

'Please, sir, I want some more.'
CHARLES DICKENS,
OLIVER TWIST (1838)

I have continually told my sons I want a toy boy, but I've had to make do with people like Hugh Jackman and Russell Crowe and David Hasselhoff, Michael Ball, Michael Crawford, Ian McShane, various Henry Higgins and, I must say, some rather charming Fagins, as well as Stephen Sondheim, Plácido Domingo and, one of my favourites, the Duke of Edinburgh. I should be thankful, like Miss Jean Brodie, that I have been honoured by the crème de la crème. Of course, I met many heroes at the start of my life, but you don't require war to create men and women of stature. I've encountered plenty of everyday heroes. It can be as much of a struggle to do good, to circumvent the barriers of red tape and competing interests, during war or peace. I am so proud of Cameron, who has set up his own foundation that supports charities and people who need that extra bit of emotional or financial encouragement and, naturally enough, theatrical projects. He's endowed a theatrical professorship at St Catherine's College, Oxford. The theatre's done so much for him it seems only fair to return the favour. Yes, I am indeed a very proud mother, of Cameron and all my sons.

We all need someone to help, to talk to. After Ian died, it was my most lonely period, yet I was surrounded by loving friends and family. The irony is, you are cocooned by all these people and then you go back to your house and are watching television and thinking: 'Am I completely alone?' It's a very strange phenomenon. However, I did, and do, say to myself: 'Get up, get going and pull yourself together.'

I'm tough, but it was a difficult process to find your own identity after being part of a couple for nearly fifty years. It's not difficult to live alone when you have got over the loss and grief, and you can be totally selfish.

It works in many ways. Not cooking just because someone else wants to eat, and also having individual friends rather than couple friends, which is different. Over the years since Ian left, I've rekindled friendships from decades ago. Life does go on – challenging, but it goes on; I think I have reaped the fruit of that type of thinking because my children have been very supportive and close, which wouldn't have been the case if I decided to disrupt everybody's lives. I have to think of the consequences, think of all of them. They are friends as well as brothers. Robert and Nicky were at the same boarding school and were very close. Robert, being the elder brother, looked after Nick, when Cameron had left the nest. They all ended up as their own, different characters. It can be a disadvantage having a celebrity brother, but they were all individual enough for that not to count. They have all built separate careers, but always see a lot of each other. There's never been a time when they aren't in regular contact – and I can't imagine it ever happening. That makes me happy, that they enjoy each other's company. Probably got a lot of that from Ian too. I like being with them all, but not all the time.

We all must have our own time and that I know is vital. When you catch up with those you love it should be a celebration, not a chore. I am very happy now, probably happier than I have ever been. I am not looking for romance. I have had enough of that, it's too much bother. Besides, I have such a good time without it. Flirting is a different matter. I do like to flirt. 'The Hoff' (David Hasselhoff) likes to come to tea. He spends a lot of time in London. He makes me laugh. I have fun with a lot of my children's celebrity friends. The boys have obviously told them things about me, as they seem to know far too much. But what can I do, I am outnumbered! As a family, we're always smiling and laughing.

In the past, I've been an ambassador for many of Cameron's productions and I still get gifts from producers in Japan and China, reminders of my visits. In 2016, I don't think I sat still. I was all over the place, from Somerset to Florence, from Malta to Scotland, visiting Nicky's home in France, and attending many concerts and first nights. I saw *Aladdin* again, and then there was Chichester and the West End for Cameron's revival of *Half a Sixpence*, and Robert had the 20th Anniversary production of *Rent* at his St James Theatre. That was quite a night. Robert had laid on the

VIP area upstairs, with a quiet table for his mother – so I could have my whisky in peace! But he was downstairs with Cameron, the boys mixing with the people they like, the theatregoers and the singers and dancers and actors where, of course, it is much more fun. Anyhow, someone else got me my second whisky.

I find the young people of the theatre give me energy. They move quickly and with ease and when I see them on or off stage, it nags me to continue with my exercises. I like to be supple and my house has many sets of stairs, so I'm up and down them a lot. I do my stretching routines. Forgetting my spectacles on the top floor is an incentive to exercise. But I don't need them when I'm jet-skiing!

I do take staying fit seriously. I eat what I want, but I still eat carefully and with some restrictions (having found out late in life that I am a coeliac), so have had to eat in a gluten-free world – but that's no real sacrifice. Marks & Spencer's do plenty of gluten-free walnut cake; I have honey in my tea and coffee.

I suppose the only thing a little wrong is my hearing. The boys got me a hearing aid device, some tiny modern miracle. I put it in the wrong way round sometimes, but that's just to keep them on their toes. They get quite irritated about it, but I tell them I'm getting on a bit.

I keep busy with my painting and socialising. I started painting when I was eighty, so I've been doing it for a long time now. I am always giving the boys paintings – they love them. I drive to the shops when I need anything. The boys, though, were a little worried that I may not be up to it. Well, I recently went for an AA 'check-up' just to see that I still had all my faculties to continue driving. No problem there. The man said I had the eyes of a hawk. But the boys, believing that it's best to quit whilst you're ahead, now insist that my long-time housekeeping companion, Mary, drives me about for shopping and the boys take me to Somerset or I go by train. I like having my little house there, for I can see everyone or just be by myself and independent. People who go on about age irritate me. If I can go swimming or scuba diving, I don't see any reason not to. Very occasionally, I go on trips with people who want to sit around and eat all day. That's just not me. I need to be moving. I was very young when I knew life was a treasure. I saw too much death and destruction not to appreciate it.

Of course, readers who have got this far into my story will, in turn, be wondering how I have actually got this far. Well, it seems, from a recent telephone call from one of my sons, that, having passed the one hundred landmark, I am in good company, a couple of years behind Vera Lynn and three behind Olivia de Havilland [who both sadly passed away just as this book was going to print], and I thought she had 'Gone with the Wind'! Well done us. Although, I believe there is one important secret to a long life: You have to want to live it. And I do!

AFTERWORD: APPROACHING D-DAY

SURVIVING IS VICTORY

Nicky Mackintosh: I was wandering down to the seafront in Valletta, Malta, when an acquaintance called over to me: 'I see your mother's on the front page this morning.' That would appeal to her vanity, I smiled to myself. Sure enough, there was my mother posed next to a bronze bust of Mabel Strickland in the front offices of *The Times of Malta*, which was displaying her on page one that day. Gleefully smiling towards her was the award-winning actor John Rhys-Davies.

The photograph was taken after an interview she gave to the actor (who had appeared in the *Indiana Jones* and *Lord of the Rings* movies and much, much more) for a film documentary focusing on entertainers living on the island as the bombardment of Malta began. Which included, of course, my mother's long-ago rival in love, Christina Ratcliffe. That evening, she 'met' Christina again: she was brought to life in the play *Star of Strait Street* by two actresses.

Polly March played the older, 1970s Christina, drink in hand and crippled by her past and her loss. Also on stage was Larissa Bonaci as the vibrant, singing and-dancing 1940s Christina who had smitten the war hero Adrian Warburton. 'Warby' remains a remembered hero in Malta, 'The King of the Mediterranean', and the play presented by the Strada Stretta Concept was a sell-out. My mother sat a little subdued in the front row for the performance and there was a hint of mist about her eyes as the news of her Adrian's demise was presented on stage. Christina had given him what he wanted. It was bittersweet.

The family group who had watched the show with her, lively again now, moved on to dinner and then down to the seafront immediately across from where the *Ohio* had, all those many years before, brought – at the pivotal, do-or-die moment – food and salvation to the island.

She climbed up onto a vantage point and pointed out where the raiders had arrived from the sky, bringing destruction. Then, she walked to where the *Ohio* had docked and gave a clap of her hands.

There is a buzz in the air. But not from the Nazi Stukas.

Thirty-five family and friends have arrived in Malta from London, to join some forty Maltese family and friends in the birthday celebration of a Very Important Person. Everybody who came knew that being there with Diana was a special occasion not to be missed. As we gathered for a wonderful lunch under the tented restaurant set in the middle of Archbishop Street, Valletta, the Saturday edition of *The Times of Malta* was presented to Diana, showing a full-page feature of her and Cameron looking like theatre royalty at the opening of *Les Misérables* – with the caption: 'The Indefatigable Diana'.

There followed three nights of parties and dinners, starting that evening in the glorious ballroom of the Phoenicia Hotel. The pictures tell the story. Diana in her element – and the rest of us just holding on for dear life, trying to keep up. She spied a dance pole at the back of the ballroom and was up it like a cat – waiting for the cameras, that swooped on her in seconds! After the celebrations were over, the numerous e-mails, text and letters that followed said it all. Some who couldn't make it also sent delightful messages of love and affection – how she made them feel younger – or older, depending how you look at it!

Like the queen returning to her kingdom, Malta saluted her, in the knowledge that she was there throughout their wartime drama, doing her bit and proving that it would take more than a Nazi invasion to stop her and the Maltese nation from enjoying their freedom. Now, at the start of her hundredth year, she can look back in the knowledge that you don't necessarily have to be the star of the show – just being in the midst of it all gives you a far better view…

THE MOMENT OF TRUTH

I thought, finally, I could put my feet up for a while, after being the centre of attention for far too long. But it was not to be. In August of 2018, the whole family (again) trooped off to what was a wonderful wedding for my granddaughter Morgan and her new husband-to-be, Rahul. It was really quite a grand affair, which they both organised. Bringing two huge families and their friends together in a foreign country – Marrakesh – was quite a feat. We all stayed in an oasis of villas and spent a wonderful few days celebrating their marriage. On one of the sunny, lazy afternoons, as we were resting and having tea by the pool, the boys cornered me. 'Time to discuss the Big One'. I told them that I didn't want a fuss – maybe a few friends and family. And definitely NOT to mention any age.

> **Nicky Mackintosh**: Can you imagine hanging on to such vanity? She actually believes that no one knows (well, she probably can get away with 80+, but why should she?) and she can keep it quiet! Anyway, we were having none of it and Cameron soon started to turn it into a major production – where, when and who?

I gave in pretty quickly. What was the point, they were going to have their way anyway.

> **Robert Mackintosh**: Cameron wanted to get her a new outfit – 'I've got plenty of clothes (Per Uno at M & S – nothing wrong there!) ... and new shoes (probably 1968). We laboured on and just booked everything, taking no notice of her.
>
> Closer to the time, when the venue, guests and a few other major components of what was going to be the 2019 Ball of the Year came together, Cameron had obviously called upon his closest creative friends to bring off no small event. A visit to the Ballroom looked like the production tech week at one of his theatres.
>
> As we neared the date, Diana had been taken to Harrods to 'find a new outfit' at Cameron's final insistence. A young private shopper had been assigned to her, together with a room where she could look at and try

on the outfits. Straight away, there was an air of 'there's nothing here for me…'. This was going to be a very bumpy ride! The poor girl, who was going from floor to floor and bringing back armfuls of beautiful dresses (albeit not her exact size) was admonished, as though incompetent, even before the door was fully open, with 'No good! They don't fit.' Clearly, Diana had made her mind up. We did have a quiet word of consolation with the girl, just so she didn't run off in tears. Fortunately, though, as we were about to leave, exhausted and somewhat distraught, Diana spotted a very chic, classic electric-blue jacket on the rail. The bloody woman still has eyes like a hawk at ninety-nine! By a miracle, it was a 'small' and fitted her perfectly. 'This is nice. Let's go!' With a mixture of exasperation and relief, we left. The dress was left up to Cameron, which he organised to be made by a wonderful lady, whom Diana could 'tell' exactly what she wanted.

7 JANUARY 2019: D-DAY

Her Carriage Awaits To Take Her To The Ball...

I really didn't want much fuss for my birthday, but the boys wouldn't let me. And I have to say that on the day, I did feel very special. I had all these lovely new clothes and spent the morning being 'coiffed' by Daniel Galvin. In fact, he was there and wished me a wonderful day – then to be swept away to my suite at Claridge's, which Cameron had organised. It was lovely having my long-time companion Mary with me too. It was a beautiful room and we even had time for a cup of tea before the big event.

All dressed up like the fairy on a cake, I was escorted down the long winding staircase by one of my 'other' boys, Steve. I think Cameron had me in mind for a production of *Sunset Boulevard*! As I was walked into the Grand Ballroom of Claridge's, I wondered who on earth this roomful of people could be? One by one, I saw and was greeted by so many friends and family from present and past. It was almost too much to take in. I thought, if I've lasted this long, then I'd better give them a good show! Hopefully, someone filmed the evening, because it was a lot to take in. But I do remember the highlights (once I'd had a drink or two to calm me down!). The first dance was with the Hoff (David Hasselhoff to me); the first love song was proffered by Michael Ball; finally, the 'secret message' came onto a huge screen above the orchestra – Hugh Jackman (almost unrecognisable wearing some kind of camouflage, from his film set in Thailand) wishing me Happy Birthday. I even had my Royal Telegram delivered by 'King George III', direct from the stage musical *Hamilton*! What a night. Heaven knows what the staff at Claridges thought. Who *is* this old girl? Maybe they thought I *was* Gloria Swanson – at 120!

Well. I managed to get through it all and look back on the night, knowing that there is nothing more they can do to me. But it did make me quite emotional inside, because they were all there; my boys, the memory of Ian, his sister Sheila too, doing as well as me, and only a few years behind! But particularly having the great pleasure to see all my grandchildren – Morgan and Lauren, Angel and Max. And with my brothers' children – Philip, David and Julian, Marika and Adrian, it was the perfect family event. Truly a night to remember...

NOW LEAVE ME IN PEACE!

But actually, there'll be plenty of time for that later on!

For now, in Stephen's words – 'I'm Still Here.' And at 101, I don't plan on staying in the shade...

Diana Mackintosh, April 2020

POSTSCRIPT: LEGACY

'Women are irrational, that's all there is to that!'
ALAN JAY LERNER AND
FREDERICK LOEWE, *MY FAIR LADY* (1956)

Cameron Mackintosh:
'The greatest example I have in life is my mother.'

We were so lucky to be brought up by parents who always treated each of us the same. I think that is partly my mother, but more my father. My father could not do what he loved, which was be the great jazz player. Of course, if he could have, that is what he would have done. Whether he would have survived? Not so sure. Ian Christie, a wonderful jazzer and writer, brilliantly described him thus: 'Between drinks three and eight pm, Spike was a genius as a musician. Avoid at all other times!'

My father wasn't able to be the jazzman he wanted to be. He had to bring three kids into a different world. He was determined that we all did what we wanted. He never put anything in our way.

One of Dad's great gifts to us was taking us to see many of the jazz greats in their prime and sometimes introducing us to them after the show. Who could forget the dazzling concerts of Duke Ellington, Count Basie and Louis Armstrong? The brilliant trombone playing of Jack Teagarden, the haunting saxophone of Johnny Hodges, the dazzling piano playing of Art Tatum and Earl Hines, and going to an intimate Ronnie Scott's to see Ella Fitzgerald? Every time I hear these great artists on the radio, I go, 'Thanks Dad,' and hear him 'Zaba Doo Zatz' in his inimitable musical Satchmo growl, as he gratefully sips another pint.

The Mackintosh side of the family were the theatrical influence. His uncle had been on the horns and my grandmother's sister Floss – Auntie Floss – was a pianist for silent movies. She was about 6ft 3in tall and looked like a cross between a man and Beatrice Lillie. And she was as amusing as Beatrice Lillie.

All my father's family were natural entertainers. My grandmother's brother Bill went to America in the 1920s and was very successful. He stayed with Fred Astaire in their flat in New York. He was the first one to make some real money in a new country. He would bring back all the cast albums of the American shows.

Also, in the 1920s, he would make films, which was quite rare, of the family creating all these plays. We've still got them, all these black-and-white films. They were performed in the garden, short comedy dramas involving all the family members in costume and they were hysterically funny. Some of that must have seeped into our blood.

I think my Auntie Jean would have loved to have been an actress. She was perfect. She was naturally, terribly funny. There was always a sense of music as we grew up. My granny Minnie loved all that and encouraged her brother Bill to bring back as much music and show recordings as he could. In those days you couldn't buy the music, the albums, until the show opened in a particular country.

I was lucky to hear the American cast recordings of *Oklahoma!*, *The Sound of Music*, *My Fair Lady*, all those early, early shows that Uncle Bill would smuggle in. That's how I got to know Tom Lehrer and his stuff. All his songs and satire in the 1950s were brilliant. I didn't realise just how privileged I was to hear these shows when no one had ever heard them in Britain. I would hear them before anyone in the public, just because I had a relative in America who could bring it in with his luggage. That's the world we were brought up in. It's to do with that side of the family, and their passion for the theatre, which obviously gave me the opportunities to pursue my passion.

I went back to Malta quite young; there is a little picture of me and my Maltese granny. That was probably the first time my mother went back after the war. My mother knew everybody in those days. We went back every three to five years. We stayed in a place called the Meadowbank Hotel in Sliema, which was just around the corner from her family. I was left at home to look after Robert, who was probably about eighteen months old. I was five.

My searing memory is being left and my mother saying: 'I'm going out darling, look after your brother.' She had gone out and literally, within about half an hour, there was a knock on the door and there would be some naval officer calling: 'Diana! Diana!

'No, Mummy's not in' was all I could say!

You may think I am exaggerating (and my mother insists I am!), of course, but it seemed like half the Fleet were calling to visit her. In her defence, she was brought up in a small island atmosphere, where everyone knew everyone. So leaving your baby in a pram in the shade whilst you wandered down the street to chat to a neighbour for half an hour would not be seen as unusual. And she had a social life to consider!

Another time, she took Robert and me with her to Germany to see my Aunt Sheila, as they were still in the British Air Forces in Dusseldorf. My memory of war-torn Germany: the trains going past; the trains were running by then, but so much desolation going through the German cities. We were at one station and my mother got off to get a newspaper.

The train was pretty crammed. It was all intrigue, like one of those black-and-white wartime thrillers, *The Lady Vanishes*. I remember looking out of the window and seeing my mother flirting with one of the newsagents. What was she doing there? The steam engine was roaring. The train pulled out. Robert is in his cot, and I am bawling. All these German ladies were clucking around me. Five minutes later, she appeared; she had obviously hopped on at the end, the trains were so long and slow. These large German ladies turned on my somewhat diminutive mother: 'How could you leave him?'

My mother gave them absolute hell. Basically told them to 'eff off', probably in Maltese, so it sounded even worse! I doubt whether they would have survived the curses. She used the foulest language on earth. All with religious undertones, bringing bishops, priests and the Pope into untold blasphemy. The Maltese have a swear word for every one of the Virgin's orifices. That was my other great memory of early travelling with my mother. Her constant flirtation. To this day, one of the things that keeps her so young and so alert is that she is a consummate flirt. She flirts with everyone – young and old, but mainly young. She loves to be wanted. It keeps her young. She gets such humour out of it. Now, so do we. She does make you laugh. A lot. She and Dad were a double act. With just the right quantity of drink and she turning a little spiky. A perfect cocktail. We were so privileged to be brought up by two brilliant people. Slightly crazy, but brilliant.

The time when the money came in could not have been better for my parents. I was able to buy a farmhouse in France and things like that and it just gave them that next twenty years of actually having a life together, and doing things that they could enjoy together, which they hadn't had in previous years. That worked out brilliantly.

It is odd that the house I have in London, the Tower House in Regent's Park, is my mother's dream house, the one she talked about. My father knew a lot of arty people, and my mother also knew, through friends they met, a lot of artists. They did a great deal of painting at the Tower House, including a lovely portrait of my mother, painted by Raymond Skipp in 1953. All through the 1950s, 1960s and 1970s, I heard about this beautiful house they had been offered in Regent's Park but had given up to educate us. My school, Prior Park, was such a beautiful building and helped evolve my taste. I learned to appreciate the Palladian architecture. It was built by John Wood for Ralph Allen on the proceeds of the first Penny Post and I realised that a building is not just a place to lay your head, that there was more to a house than sleeping in a bed, and there was a difference between a flat and semi-detached and a beautiful house.

The first time I consciously can remember going to seek out this fabled house was when I was not far away. I was still commuting from Cuffley on my Honda 49cc when I was at Central School in 1964–65. I thought one day that I would pop around and find this house my mother had been talking about and, of course, I went there and thought how pretty it was. I was eighteen or nineteen, and I thought it was something special. Of course, I eventually found out the reason they didn't get it was partly because it had a tower with a winding staircase and not enough bedrooms. It is actually a lot smaller than it looks from the imposing facade.

More importantly, my father said they could have had it for £2,500, which was still a reasonable amount of money – you could have bought a house for £2,500–£3,000 in many parts of London – but it had a repairing lease, and with the repairing lease, even then, you would have to spend £10,000–£15,000 because they were jerry-built, those houses built by John Nash at the end of his life. That's why they didn't do it. None of us boys got that story. It stayed there and every few years I would pop by, and one day shortly after *Les Mis* opened, my mother came down with one of the free magazines that they shove through people's letterboxes and it had the house advertised. She said: 'My house is for sale.' I saw the information on the Saturday or Sunday and rang up my secretary on Monday and said: 'Let's go see it.' We went around that Monday lunchtime and as we stood in the door, she said: 'Cameron you've got to buy this.' I've been there ever since. It's a lovely story. It was meant to be. I acquire everything for a reason. I went to the Boat Show, decided I could afford a toy, and bought an Edwardian steamboat, which was moored at Henley and named *Salad Days*. A nice way to be reminded about how it all started.

My father enjoyed life far more than work. Therefore, if there was any excuse, he'd be off to the pub or playing the trumpet. He played until the end, and the day he died he had lunch and some nice wine with my brother Robert. He died of a stroke that night and all of us were with him. It's funny how God works, because he saw all of us within that last week and everything was good among us. My mother has dealt with sudden death, with death in its most wicked ways, and I think she developed her own armoury against it, like so many of her era have. I told her that someone she knew well had a terminal illness and knew she was going to die. She asked: 'When?'

'I can't tell you; no one knows for certain.'

'I'm not free until June.'

Her best friend Celia, the mother of my long-time friend Barry Burnett, always looked up to my mother, and thought my mother was the Queen. Celia had been to the opening night of *Miss Saigon* a few days before, so I had seen her in the last two weeks. She'd been to a wedding and Barry took her home – he lived above her in Seymour Place in London – and was going to take the lift up instead of the stairs. As he was calling the lift, Celia dropped dead. There and then. All dressed up and happy. What a wonderful way to go. She was about one or two years younger than Diana. We were all terribly upset but even Barry, who was very close to his mother, thought it was a wonderful way to go, as she had been all over the place seeing all her friends and having a marvellous time. She went having had a fabulous week, no pain or anything like that. I rang Diana up on the Saturday after Barry told me the news and I said: 'I have bad news. Celia has died. Barry is very upset, but Celia died very suddenly and without any discomfort.'

She said: 'Oh. Well it's a bit late in the day to get someone else. I was supposed to have lunch with her on Wednesday.'

That is part of why Diana is so remarkable, because she totally thinks positively. You know: if you're dead, you're dead. There is no point dwelling on it. I am convinced that is what it must have been like to have gone through those years of bombing, all the boyfriends who never came back. She has all the letters from them. She had to deal with it, deal with how someone you really adore, one or two of whom she nearly married; and maybe would have done if they had survived. She flirted with absolutely everybody. She used to say: 'It was a stupid thing, I never had anybody in my life but your father.'

My father – until very late in the day, when he was in his seventies – would never discuss what happened in the war. Never. We've only gleaned bits of it from other members of the family. We actually learned more about his wartime exploits and bravery at his wake. We met all these people from his past, who would say, 'Your father saved my life,' that he did this, and he did that. That is what his generation did. What the modern world has no idea about, being at the front. Diana was, in her own funny way, at the front, in and out of the bomb zones. When she worked for Mabel Strickland, she thought Diana was a very sweet thing to have around the office. But when a bomb went off, shattering their offices and windows, sending blades of glass everywhere, it was Diana who got them all to dive under the table. She was unscathed from it. I said to her: 'How awful.' She said: 'Yes, but the Germans were not nearly as scary as Mabel.' She had a beard (nearly); she was legendary. There's this fantastic picture which is a wonderful illustration of Mabel looking like she's Alastair Sim in the *St Trinian's* films.

Robert Mackintosh: Our aunts used to take us to shows whenever they could, particularly the Crazy Gang – we were taken to the their last night at the Victoria Palace [20 May 1962]. I remember it as though it was yesterday – it made such an impact on us. But on another occasion, I also remember the excitement of seeing for the first time a performance from the Pelham Puppet Theatre. The puppets were so real and their characters almost alive. They were made by Bob Pelham and were very, very intricate; the difference with Pelham puppets was there were many more strings to work the more detailed individual movements, and they were therefore much more lifelike. The voices were captivating as well as the expressions on their faces. Even the costumes were exotically colourful. Both Cameron and I were absolutely fascinated and soon we were asking our aunts: 'Could we, please, have some puppets?'

That was 1958, and from then on, we would be getting as many of the different characters as we could. There were always new ones coming out. Pelham puppets were made of wood, carved and quite expensive – the Rolls-Royce of puppets – but our aunts were delighted we were interested in something that was theatrical and creative. So one by one, we started a collection; there were policemen, clowns, teachers, doctors, nurses, animals – they were absolutely fantastic and worth their weight in gold to us, and probably cost nearly as much!

And if you had nimble fingers, you could work three of the puppets at a time.

Cameron had this great ability to produce and bring everything together. He'd seen *Salad Days*; we'd got the record. I was a natural pianist in that I could hear a tune and play it – and I could play all the songs from the show. We had all of these Pelham puppets, so we'd use them as characters in a sort of combined story of Julian Slade's *Salad Days* and *Follow That Girl*, so I played all the songs in between the scenes. Considering our ages, it was really quite adventurous.

I was only eight years old, but I could play pretty well – Julian created all his material at the piano, so I found it quite easy to listen, pick up and learn. And the main tunes were simple and catchy. We had a script and that kind of held the show together, I think! But probably, the audience were just enthralled that we pulled it off.

We had a programme; Cameron had insisted that it had to be professional and on it, typed up by one of our aunts, was the title and the credits – almost all of which were Cameron's. But when it came to working the puppets, I did have a natural gift, I suppose, for working their intricate mechanism of strings and pulleys. Cameron, however, will be the first to admit that in all things mechanical, he was somewhat backward in coming forward. If some strings became tangled, his frustration would be to keep pulling them until he got his way!

That never really changed. I remember teaching him to drive a car (I was around fourteen and picked it up at an early age), initially going through the basics. Cameron, he of little patience, rarely gave anything a second chance. If the gear stick didn't go where he wanted it, he'd push it until it did. But by some chance, Cameron miraculously passed his test on his first attempt (was driving instruction to be my future vocation in life?). But we all recall when he was driving one of our mother's very second, or fourth-hand cars (which Dad had got from a 'first-class chap') on his own one day. Cameron had forced the gear stick so much that he came home with it in his hand – not attached! Somehow he was able to steer the car and he marched in: 'This came off, it's obviously useless.'

And he wasn't much different with the puppets. It was a little bit jerky, and if he got into a complete tangle, I would grab it from him. The show must go on! I think I did have a little more panache with the puppets. But with the puppet theatre and a seemingly endless supply of puppets – we didn't need actors (should have kept that idea going!) – we had everything there and so were able to do lots of shows. I think our parents were quite proud of us.

The word got around family and friends nearby. The first big show we did was at our grandmother's house in Enfield, and there were usually about eleven family members at any one time. It was a great big place and there were three floors and everybody staying, so you had a captive audience. And there were lots of neighbours. People were definitely more gregarious in those days. There was a stage for us in the sitting room, which was a double-size room with a velvet curtain across it, with the puppet theatre set up in the middle. Showtime!

Everybody had to pay and Cameron hissed if they were late – he's never changed. That was the real start of Cameron's life-to-be in the theatre, for he was in charge of everything. I'd play the piano, rush over to the puppets and back again like a yo-yo; but Cameron was in charge of the proceedings.

Cameron did a bit of acting at his school. I always remember him as Julius Caesar, wearing a toga and looking the part, but he really wanted to present the shows. Darryl F. Zanuck was the big Hollywood producer at the time and all these producers had flamboyant names – so the shows' posters bore the headline 'Darryl F. Mackintosh Presents'. He wanted to be in charge. Julian Slade would visit him at Prior Park School every term and was tremendously helpful to Cameron as a professional influence.

Julian had a big hit with *Salad Days* at the Vaudeville Theatre and he provided so much encouragement – and advice about going to drama school and learning about the theatre. Cameron was about seventeen when the drama-school people said they couldn't do much more for him – he kept telling them what to do – and they suggested he take his ideas away and out of the school!

Our parents wanted me and Nicky to get proper jobs. After all, it must have cost a small fortune to educate us. Cameron was the first son and became absorbed in the theatre world from such an unusually early age that the idea of any other 'job' never really came up. And he was away at school 'plotting' his future from eleven years of age. What else did they expect? They didn't really have a chance. By the time I, followed by Nicky, came along, they, or at least our mother, had gathered her thoughts and was a bit more defiant about how we viewed our future. But I was in music bands at school and then I did a brief turn in the timber yard. Cameron did it before me – worked a season at Dad's timber office, but he went around telling them all what to do, so he was soon sent home before he started a strike! I went to Sweden to study the timber business, but after six weeks found myself touring the Swedish towns with another pop group. In a town close by was a Swedish band called The Hep Stars. Quite popular – later to find fame renamed ABBA. I should have joined that group! Nicky grew up through most of this, but he never had quite the same practical interest in the arts and music that we had found. His passion would take the form of all things edible. So hopefully none of us would starve!

Stella Richards (a theatrical agent and for many years a fellow traveller with Diana and Ian Mackintosh): There were many happy 'school outings' with Diana, and also dear Ian, to attend and celebrate the openings of Cameron's various productions overseas. To this day, I remain lost in deep admiration for Diana's gift of being one of the world's great packers: she is truly skilled (I've told her she should run a school for packing) and manages to travel with a match-box-size suitcase, out of which, magician-like, she produces fabulous evening and party wear, as well as all the usual gubbins one needs when away. I, on the other hand, am left dragging something akin to a cabin trunk – for the same trip – containing all sorts of stuff I don't really need, and probably missing much of what I do. After about forty years of shared merriment with Diana and the Macs, I have many happy memories of gorgeous trips on Cameron's boat with Diana and chums; plus visits to, and hijinks in, Malta, including crazy rides on rickety old Maltese buses, where Diana will happily burst into Maltese and woo the driver into giving us cut-price fares. I don't know if I can say too much about her doing a pole dance at the restaurant where the family threw her ninetieth birthday party – that's certainly burned in the memory, but possibly censored. I did manage to pair her off once in Sicily with her own personal Mafia henchman – well, long enough for me to take their picture. I think he was the most intimidated.

Wally Fawkes (Canadian-born, who adopted Britain when he was a ten year old – he was ninety-six in 2020 – and found fame as a political cartoonist and jazzman. A fine clarinettist, he glories in the whimsy of life while maintaining the need for characters and talent. During the Second World War, he said he spent so much time in air-raid shelters that Londoners were metamorphosing into troglodytes. He adopted the cave-dweller title for his band Wally Fawkes and The Troglodytes, which regularly featured Ian 'Spike' Mackintosh. He then took 'Trog' as his pen name for his illustrative work including the celebrated cartoon strip *Flook*. In a 2016 interview, he recalled going to see and hear Louis Armstrong in France with a host of other London-based jazz enthusiasts.):

We went to hear Louis Armstrong in the flesh and there was all sorts of socialising with fellow musicians. Spike and I hit it off rather nicely, although we were from very different backgrounds. His public school and me leaving school at fourteen to go to art school for a couple of years produced different social results, but the music brought us together, the music was what was important, the other stuff didn't matter.

Louis was his hero. Spike's understanding of the beat and the timing of Louis was terrific. There are hundreds if not thousands of musicians who could play faster than Louis, get more notes in, but like all great artists his artistry was to simplify and reduce it down to the truth, down to a residue of heartfelt music where all the fripperies he'd cut away like a sculptor.

Ian based his playing on Louis and he came very, very close. He didn't have the total freedom that Louis had, but within a certain range of Armstrong's music he was the best. He would have found it difficult to conform to being a professional musician. He had a lack of discipline which went along with his lifestyle. Turning up on time or turning up in the same town as the rest of the band had arrived at would have been a problem.

He would have been bored by the routine, by the same numbers every night. He was a romantic; he was very romantic, was Ian.

We made some records for Decca in the late 1950s and they were some of the best things I'd ever made. I was very lucky to catch Ian at just the right time when he played in my band The Troglodytes. The records caught the Mackintosh trumpet absolutely perfectly. He had a tremendous amount of warmth personally, which I detected in the boys when I met them later. I knew them as tiny tots in the 1950s when Spike lived at Cuffley. We'd be driving back from Liverpool or somewhere and we'd pop into his house and it would be 6 a.m. or 7 a.m. and the kids would be about. I remember playing cricket on the lawn with them in the early morning. He would have been very proud of his lads 'cos they're all good 'uns.

We had drinking days: it would be the middle of the afternoon with Ian and Mick Mulligan [the trumpeter and band leader] and Mick would look at his watch: 'God, I should have been at a rehearsal three hours ago. Shall we make this the last one?'

Ian would join in: 'That reminds me that I should have been at a board meeting at eleven this morning. Oh, well, another round.'

They got on to the subject of public school and I asked Ian what was the great advantage of going to a public school. He thought and offered: 'It gives one a sense of discipline.'

That was hilarious. His relationship with food was that you never eat on an empty bladder. I think if you've survived being blown up and getting out of Dunkirk, you take a different view of your chances of surviving. I can see him as a war hero who'd do crazy, daft things, which nobody else would see any sense to. Did that turn him into a drinker? I don't think so. I think that was in the contract.

He gave Diana a difficult time. After driving us back from a north of England gig, we'd get in to his house about 1 a.m. and he'd put the records on. Diana would shout down: 'Ian, turn the records down.'

He'd shout back: 'Of course, darling, of course.'

Then he'd turn it up again. One night, Diana came storming down and ripped out all the wires from the gramophone. She didn't say anything, not a word. We took that as a hint she didn't want any more loud music.

We met later and she was a wonderful woman who had happy memories of Ian too. He was a very, very friendly person, extremely warm, and that I can see in the boys very clearly.

There are several versions of one Spike Mackintosh story – from George Melly, Humphrey Lyttelton and countless others – but the jazz entrepreneur Jim Godbolt's stands the truth of time, and was endorsed by one central participant, Wally Fawkes, in the summer of 2016.

Jim Godbolt: I was with Spike at a party given by Wally, a very generous host. There was a lot of drinking. Spike slipped against a bamboo screen, bringing down various objets d'art arrayed in the ledges. The noise awakened Wally's eldest daughter, Joanna, then about six years old, and, in tears, she stood at the top of the stairs that led straight into the drawing room. Spike, wiping bits of Italian pottery and acanthus from his person, looked up through sprays of potted creepers, saw Joanna, and said, 'Wally, I know it's none of my business, but shouldn't that child be in bed?' But it was me, not Spike, who was savaged by Wally's then wife, Sandy. Not a word to Spike, who was now on his feet and looking for his glass. It was one of those occasions when the maxim 'sometimes you can't win' crossed my mind. Spike was indeed a combination of the opposites. All around he was wonderful.

Cameron Mackintosh: Jazz was Dad's life and he played with a veritable Who's Who of British jazz (Humphrey Lyttelton, Wally Fawkes, Sandy Brown to name but a few). He even played with his hero Louis Armstrong, whose style he closely mirrored, and whenever you hear a Louis track, it really does instantly remind you of Dad's very special talent.

However, Dad had to make a living as a timber merchant to feed and educate three hungry boys – especially me – as jazz simply didn't pay that much. The fact that Dad couldn't make music his sole profession had one silver lining for me and my two brothers, as he always encouraged us to do anything we wanted as a 'career'.

His other great example was that he always went through life thinking the best of people and was genuinely disappointed if they turned out to be 'a rotter'.

This was counterbalanced by our mother's far more heady approach to life. There was very little money around and my father was lucky enough to get a job in the family timber business. My father would say 'Jolly good chap' about everyone. My mother was a lot more cynical.

My mother assumed everyone was an assassin or a robber. My father just thought everyone was a good man, until it turned out they were a rotter – then he'd go completely against them. It got him into terrible trouble. He would give his last penny away. My mother was furious because she had to keep the family going. We still had rationing when we were brought up, and genuinely a chicken was something you got once a month, and if it was a decent size, it had to do at least two meals and make soup for a third meal. To this day, she still makes soup from anything – just in case! My father only cooked the Sunday roast. That was it. But he did it very well. In his day, most men would come home to a meal cooked by their wives; and he was out either working or playing.

When we first moved to Cuffley we lived in a bungalow and my brother Robert and I used to sit at the top of the stairs. We lived in the loft. We used to sit at the top of the stairs and hear them going at it hammer and tongs, because my father would have just got in from the pub or just come back from playing with Mick Mulligan and our mother would be screaming at him. She had a hard time looking after three boys, often on her own. Every few months, she'd tell us: 'We're leaving. We're leaving your father.' She would march us down the road to the railway station, and of course we knew going down that steep hill to the station, that there wouldn't be any trains to anywhere at 1 a.m. in the morning, so we'd have to be marched back up.

She'd tuck us up in bed and tell us: 'We'll leave your father tomorrow.' Of course, she never did. It was her way of venting her anger. She is not slow in letting you know what she thinks.

By the time all three of us were born, we'd moved out to the slightly posher end of Cuffley, on the outskirts, which is where we were brought up. We were around the corner from my father's brother, Uncle Bill. He had a slightly bigger, but sprawling house; it seemed to us quite a rich person's house really. Cuffley, of course, was where the timber company was. It was conveniently opposite the pub. All their houses were close by a pub or two. We lived there for many years. My father was determined to put us all through public school, even though we were way down the ranks financially. Firstly, we went to the convent, about a two-mile walk through the countryside, and then we all went to various schools. I was the only one who went to Prior Park in Bath. My father started to earn a little more money, not a lot, but a bit more, so Nicky and Robert both went to The Oratory school near Reading.

But in those early school days, at the beginning of each term, when we went to the local schools, she would give me four pennies as I was the older brother. That was to put the money in the phone. Loads of time I lost it. The system was, I would ring and if you pressed button A, the money went in and was taken, but if you pressed button B you got it back. But there was a brief moment when you could say something before button B was pressed. The whole trick was to ask the appropriate question very quickly and always get the money back. 'Is that you? I will be there in five minutes' and button B was pushed. If I pressed button A by mistake, there would be hell to pay – far more than four pennies' worth! She'd make you walk for a bit. It was like that. She was very astute because she had to be. Money-wise, there was nothing at all in jazz. They did it for pleasure.

People did drink a lot more in those days and it was quite cheap – they could easily be in the pub at 5 p.m. and career back at about 12.30–1 a.m. Of course, the excuse was that most 'business' was discussed over a pint or a glass of whisky. The problem was the 'business' seemed to go on for a long time and was probably forgotten by the 'last orders' bell!

So, the yin and the yang of them was that she would have to be very careful with money. She would often pretend at the local Marks & Spencer's that she'd got the wrong size when we'd grown out of a sweater or something, which we'd been wearing for ever; she'd kept the labels and would, with a lovely smile, tell the assistant: 'We need a bigger size, I got the wrong size.' Sometimes she would cut out the labels and sew them back into something else. Obviously, we will seek the six-year limitation act on any claims! She knew how to extend the life of everything. She obviously included herself in that exercise.

I remember going off to Spain, to resorts that were still being developed, and several hundred yards away from the sea view, alien to what had been in the holiday brochures. But they were deals. A few very hairy holidays. My parents screamed at each other and blamed each other. And we all had a wonderful time as a loving family. The rows never lingered and didn't spoil the fun.

Robert Mackintosh: We drove to Spain for a family holiday when the Costa Brava was being developed. We went in a black Morris Isis, which acted like an oven with all five of us piled into it. Dad had met someone in the pub who'd told him about this wonderful resort. Diana, though fluent in Spanish, was dubious. The clincher, of course, was that it was a great deal. The beach went on forever but our accommodation was above what looked like a canteen shop in a Spaghetti Western. There were hams hanging from the rafters, food on the counters and flies covering just about everything. The 'hotel' part was upstairs and it was hot, very hot, and ours exclusively. No one else wanted it! All around us was like a building site with construction going on – cement and dust and constant noise. 'Britain's holidays of the future', the signage advertised; the future looked bleak. Diana was not amused and hissed (in Maltese) at Dad throughout the holiday about his gullibility. It was grim, but when we got to the beach, it was actually a lot of fun and all that was forgotten.

But at the end of the day we had to go back to the 'hotel'. We were booked in for two weeks and, as it was such a bargain, there was no chance of going home early. The smell was terrible. There were pools of stagnant water and litter everywhere, and the sanitation was awful. We called it 'The Land of Pong' and 'Pooh Corner' after Winnie.

Robert Mackintosh: As brothers, we have always been pretty close. No doubt partly from the front-row seats we had, watching with fascination our parents' magnetic performance over the years, but also handed down by our many family gatherings on Dad's side – of aunts, uncles and endless cousins, with our grandmother 'Geggy' at the centre of it all. In terms of parenting, they were a sort of double act, somewhere between Morecambe and Wise and Fanny and Johnnie Cradock. After Dad died in 1996, there was a big hole to fill, but then our mother was a big personality, and she was Maltese. If she could see off Adolf Hitler, she could sort out the three of us. So our mother became the sole centre of our parental attention and the small but powerful beacon in our lives.

When I think back on our early upbringing and the influences our parents had on us, I do see them as very different people – like night and day, but adding up to an interesting whole. Dad always had a carefree approach to life, likewise to us; no doubt brought about by being pretty spoilt as a child by his own female-orientated family, who doted on him, as he did on us, to make us all feel very secure and loved. That's not to say he didn't test it as we grew up, and we understood that there was always a storm lurking in the background. Our mother took on the role of order and discipline, much needed with her eventual handful of three boys plus one – our dad. But in true Mediterranean style, she was the balance between us all, ensuring that even after the shouting, there was harmony... and pasta!

Whatever mixture of love and social tools they gave us to go out in the world on our own, undoubtedly this came from the heady cocktail of their unusual chemistry. They were very different in so many ways; and possibly, if it hadn't been for the unique wartime situation in which they met, the union of our parents might never have taken place.

For years, remembering moments of our childhood, we have teased Diana about how we were 'left' with the nuns at St Dominic's Priory convent school, where all of us boys did an early stint. We recall (now in unison) that under the guise of some infectious illness, we found ourselves being quarantined in a dormitory at the convent. However, this always seemed to coincide with a planned holiday our parents conveniently took at the same time. Looking back, they probably deserved it. But the truth is, I have the fondest memories of being at the convent, where the nuns adored us, so it was no real hardship. Cameron, at the age of eleven, in 1958, was sent to the prep school of Prior Park in Bath. In those days, with no motorways, it was a big trip to drive there, even in Dad's powerful Morris Isis car, with no speed limits or seat belts and few traffic lights to slow you down. Cameron boarded there, moving to the main school for the next six years. Nicky was only three so I, being at a day prep school, observed and became emotionally entangled in the day-to-day life of the parental home.

Unlike Dad – whose religious beliefs were based upon a simple kindness to your fellow man and hope for the best – our mother was brought up with, and passed on to us, a very Catholic upbringing. We all marched off to church every Sunday, Dad minding the Sunday lunch, with a handful of loose coins. Now vehemently denied by our mother, I clearly see a very dexterous hand over the collection plate, fishing for change – if by chance, or misfortune, she only had a silver coin to hand. She was always prepared to do her financial duty for the church, but there were limits. A shilling would need sixpence change in return. Her Maltese upbringing had a lot to answer for. But in hindsight, her thriftiness probably saved our bacon – it certainly saved Dad's.

If asked whether I had a happy childhood, I would immediately answer 'yes'. But actually, it was the result of a series of extremely brilliant times with our parents, their colourful friends and loving and fun family (Britain and Malta), balanced against some darker, troubled moments, doubtless brought about by a side of Ian and Diana's relationship that ignited from time to time. No doubt, these were fuelled by various frustrations and the fear of being unable to keep Dad's demons from getting him into irretrievable scrapes, sometimes made worse by a Latin temper and, more often than not, with good reason; but nevertheless, adding fuel to the smouldering furnace. But the good side definitely took first prize. And in the end, isn't this where character comes from?

All the family on Dad's side were musical – either playing or singing. I started getting piano lessons at the convent at three years old and seemed to have a natural love of it. I wasn't particularly good at the sight reading, or theory, but would soon pick up a catchy tune and play it by ear. We always had a piano in the house, as did all our family; Dad encouraged me always, sat and listened to me and gave me some basic chord structure, which he had picked up himself in his own musical world. Our mother was not musical in a practical way, didn't sing around the house – probably being both intimidated and overwhelmed by Dad's religious approach to jazz, Louis and of course his trumpet. I never remember Dad without his trumpet. So to some extent, for me Dad was always a walking, talking musician, and I naturally fell under his musicianship. My whole approach to music was, like Dad's, natural rather than studied. But Diana was just as pleased that I enjoyed music and that it was a real bond between Dad and me, as I grew up – with Cameron away during school terms and Nicky still quite young.

Soon, I would accompany Dad to some of the jazz gigs at pubs and clubs, and also to jazz concerts with some of the greats, as I vividly recall. Dad had instilled in me such a love of playing the piano that I was always at ease and enjoyed sitting at a piano anytime, anywhere. I recall on one special occasion, we went backstage to meet Earl Hines – probably one of the greatest jazz pianists ever – and being introduced to him by Dad, with great pride. I had listened to many of his records and really admired him and recognised him as if he was Elton John! 'So you play?' he said to me. 'Well play something!' He had this beautiful upright in the dressing room, so I happily sat down. No nerves; just played – anything. How good it actually was, I don't know, but he made me feel good. He was a real gentle person; tall, elegant, with a big smile – just like his playing. Nice memories to have. Diana probably felt, too, that Dad was more likely to come home having me with him (at eleven years old) than not! It usually worked that way. But for me, I just loved the music environment and the other players always chatted to me and, knowing I was playing the piano, encouraged me to play a bit after they had finished their set. In the Cuffley house, I spent hours in the piano room playing and starting to write bits of songs – with them watching one of the two channels available on TV in the next room!

But it was not all idyllic, and there were the other times when Dad would get into a cycle of social drinking (sounds less purposeful) with his numerous buddies – not just musicians, but so-called business friends. Nearly all of them drank, in the days when most business was discussed around pubs, clubs or at restaurants with much flowing liquid. Whether or not other business dads could deal with it better, ours definitely could not. And what angered my mother most was that these so-called 'friends' would insist he had 'one more for the road', knowing the likely outcome. Once he passed a certain point, he could spiral into another character – quite the Jekyll and Hyde. You could tell over the phone (if he rang) when certain humorous expressions were used such as 'old cock', his current status of imbibe. If he had actually arrived home at that moment, it could be quite funny and Diana would still be happy, based upon relief that he had escaped the dreaded downhill and dangerous path that lurked around the corner. But often, it was too late, and when he did arrive, with both of us looking down the dark driveway for a pair of headlights (even one would do, if he remembered at all), his mood was already the wrong side of black.

Understandably, there would be a lot of barking and growling (and we didn't have a dog), and the night would be a long one – of course, with

Louis or Ellington at full volume. I would be torn between the love I had for my dad (albeit quite the angry teenager when he finally turned up) and the support I naturally gave my mother, necessarily against his sometimes demonic behaviour. And school started at 7 a.m. the next morning. He would be as bright as a button, with maybe a couple of hours' sleep.

But with all his shortcomings, we still felt secure. All of us went off to private schools, living in a comfortable home that our mother kept in pristine order. More often than not, though, she would come down in the morning to find the odd body (fallen asleep mid-Louis at his loudest, no doubt), which she turfed out with a very beady look. Knowing her capabilities, they got off lightly! I am sure we learned most of our Maltese from those moments, because much of the one-way dialogue (from her) was carried out in her native tongue. On more recent visits to family members in Malta, when asked whether we speak any Maltese, we recite various expressions – in perfect accent – to the titters of 'Who taught you that?' Of course, we have now passed these delightful phrases on to our children. Always important to pass on the native tongue, especially when asked at a new school interview: 'and do your children speak any other languages?'

Whilst I grew into my music as a teenager, it was clear that my mother still expected me to get a proper job. They had already given up on Cameron taking to the stage, so it was their idea that I would be pushed (gently) towards working at Dad's timber firm (with the 'taking over when Dad retires' carrot). Cameron had done a similar stint at their head office in Cuffley. After four weeks, he was trying to tell them all how to run it. Echoes of the Central School of Speech and Drama, where he believed he knew more than they did, and so they suggested he practised what he preached – elsewhere!

Living at home in Cuffley, and with a teenager's thirst for the music scene, I often found myself among some of the sixties pop groups, including the Zombies, Cliff Richard and The Shadows, and later Marc Bolan's T. Rex. They all lived in the area and often frequented the Cuffley Hotel, where Dad befriended many of them, with their common interest being music – and drink! On one of those nights, when my mother was swiping a glance at the clock as it turned passed 11 p.m. and I guessed we were in for a long night, Dad appeared with a convoy of cars and out spilled a group of boys who, no doubt, were about to be given a high-decibel lesson in the art of jazz, from that genre's maestro – Satchmo. The group Unit 4 + 2 were currently number one in the charts and I recognised the lead singer, Tommy. After a couple of demands to 'turn it down' from a spitting Diana, I was summoned from my bedroom to be the 'man of the house' and explain that this was not a club. I added that their own lives might be shorter than their pop career if they didn't leave immediately, particularly if it caused the appearance of an extremely angry Maltese terrier in the form of my mother. They didn't think Dad was up to coming to their aid, so left a little embarrassed. Next day, I called by the pub and was confronted by a sheepish Tommy, who was actually charming and we chatted for ages. After a few invitations to hang out with them, Tommy and I started writing together at our house. Dad was delighted and my mother was actually quite happy too.

When one of the members decided to quit, Tommy asked me to sit in with the band, as I played keyboards, guitar and bass. I was still at school. But I intended to continue playing with them as soon as I left. However, under a little family pressure, I had agreed to give the 'family business' a trial go. Even though I knew music was my real interest, I did feel I owed it to them to make an effort. So, after leaving school, I took off to Sweden, where Dad organised for me to work at an enormous timber company run by one of his clients. The Swedes loved the Brits at that time and particularly their pop music. So within three weeks, I was asked to join a band, singing and playing around the towns of Sweden – burning several candles at both ends. After barely surviving minus 40 degrees of cold and 9ft of snow in the north of Sweden, I returned home four months later.

When they met me at the train station, my mother's first remark was how long my hair was – it was 1968! An independent eighteen or not, I was marched off to the nearest hairdresser to get it cut. She said I looked like some filthy boy in a pop group. As soon as I could, I wore it pretty long for the next fifty years! When I was back in England, Cameron was preparing for his first professional outings as probably the youngest theatre producer ever, and I immediately jumped back into my interest in music, writing and recording. I met up with Tommy again and was invited to join the band full-time. And so my professional music journey began. I played some gigs and began writing a lot; we recorded at Decca Records in West Hampstead, where we taped a new live version of Unit 4 + 2's hit 'Concrete and Clay', as well as some new songs I co-wrote with Tommy. Six weeks later, we were on the radio, in a show featuring current sixties pop bands.

Although Dad was delighted, my mother never saw it as a job. She had let one son slip through the net into show business, but with me she expected a proper job. So with one last attempt, they made a call. Aunt Kitty, Dad's sister, was a serious player in the oil business, so I was sent off for an interview at Shell Oil. Well, they were very nice to me, but it was clear they required a much higher level of academic qualifications; mine were mainly in my fingers! I had a few decent O levels from my four years at The Oratory school, but any thoughts of an academic career were overshadowed by my love of music. My mother was right, it wasn't really a job – maybe because I enjoyed it so much – but it led to a lot of things and to a path along which I met some very interesting and inspiring people. Following a couple of years of writing and touring with Unit 4 + 2, we decided to take a break, as the particular spark that was 'Concrete and Clay' eluded us. So I started working with Tommy's brother Bill and our guitarist, as a new act named... 'Bill and Buster'. The songs were influenced by Simon and Garfunkel and the first one released – 'Hold On to What You've Got' – became a big hit in Europe, and in particular France. It was being played on Radio Luxembourg as their weekly 'Powerplay' song, every hour. At home in Cuffley, I turned it on so my mother could hear it. She said, 'What is zat?' (the 'th' is not a Mediterranean sound!). I told her it was our song. 'How much do you get?' she said. 'Make sure they don't cheat you.'

A month later, I asked her to come with me to Paris for the weekend. We walked to the big record store in the Lido, Paris, which had rows of TV screens outside showing the pop music chart positions. There was a picture and name of each band and we were at the top – number one. There was a twinkle in her eye... and a glimmer of hope for my chosen path. 'Have they paid you yet?'

Three years later, I worked at Chappell Music, recording some songs, and met someone who would be a great friend, mentor and co-writer. Norman Newell was one of the most successful producers and writers of that early seventies period (and before), penning and producing most of the hits of Shirley Bassey, Petula Clark, Matt Monro and songs covered by hundreds of international artists. The worldwide performances of his song 'More' were second only to McCartney's 'Yesterday'. We hit it off and over the years I learned much from him in all aspects of the music industry. Diana and Ian also became very friendly with Norman and he and she shared their birthdays together (he was two days older) for many years at lavish parties given by Norman. When our parents left Cuffley and moved to St John's Wood, by Abbey Road studios, they were often invited to recordings, and on one occasion Norman invited them to the live recording of my first song, to be included on one of the very popular series of albums by Manuel and The Music of the Mountains. The forty-piece orchestra struck up and I think Dad was very proud to hear my song 'How Near Am I to Love' being performed and recorded; I think my mother felt that as this was not a pop group recording, but a classical orchestra, it was the nearest to a proper job. Job done!

It wasn't long after, around 1979 or 1980, that Diana started to work for me. She had done so for Cameron a while before, unpaid; but I paid her, which she has never let Cameron forget! I had a management agency and was looking after quite a few actors. I only realise now, after appreciating from her memoirs that she worked for my godfather, Nigel Patrick, during the war, that she had quite a lot of experience in booking artists and show business in general. So she took to it like a duck to water. I am sure most of our clients were secretly terrified of her, as they must have known she was my mother (I tried to keep that quiet too). She was no shrinking violet and would use that information whenever necessary to put some actor in their place. But whilst I was getting a reasonable income from all this, there was a time when the books didn't quite balance – overheads versus commission. And she was always nosey enough to keep an eye on the books. So one day she came into my office and said, 'You haven't got enough to pay the rent. So here is a cheque to ensure I still have a job next week.' My mouth hung open and I was about to give some limp explanation, but she continued, 'I did the same for your brother and I intend to do the same for all you boys if the need arises. At least you have been paying me, so I am just giving it back!' I think my mouth is still open... but I was very careful from then on.

I also found myself producing a few theatre plays. Having jumped in at the deep end, with some well-known names in the cast of my first two or three shows, I was discussing a new play with my co-producer John Newman and the possible casting of a well-known, rather notorious lady for its leading role. The fact is that she was best known in her previous off-stage life – as the sidekick of the notorious Christine Keeler: Mandy Rice-Davies.

So, the following day at the office, I mentioned to my assistant (mother) that I would be going to lunch and could she book the restaurant for 1 p.m. 'Who are you going with?' (ever nosey). I replied, 'John and an actress – Mandy Rice-Davies.'

'Who? That woman who slept with all those disgusting men?' She shot me a fearful look. 'Nobody will come to see her and I can't imagine why you would want to spend money on that woman.' I tried to explain that that was many years ago, when she was a teenager caught up in the sixties with everyone else. That she was now a fairly wealthy married woman and successfully working as an actress. She would have none of it. Once a Catholic...

Diana was a very thorough and conscientious assistant. Her only problem was that she maintained a very personal point of view and was usually vocal about it – often in earshot. However good someone might be as an actor, she had her favourites and the rest wouldn't get the same attention. Thank God she loved all us boys equally!

And over all the years to date she has known exactly what is going on with all three of us. Always encouraging, always enthusiastic. She just wants us to be happy in what we do. Our children love to show their 'Grammie' off to their friends, particularly at school. No one can believe that she is so vibrant and switched on – next to their own grandparents, who are probably forty years younger. At every gathering she becomes the centre of attention, from young and old alike. Fingers point. 'Look. It's her... Diana Mackintosh... "Divine and Heavenly".'

THE FAB 5

Nicky Mackintosh: Diana's long life may have started on a small island in the Mediterranean but it has been anything but quiet and unfulfilled. She has seen war and romance and mixed amongst the stars of stage and screen. However, in recent years she has also cruised the high seas as one of the Fab 5 on the MY *Gardenia* and what a carry on that has been!

It wasn't so much 'It Started with a Kiss' but rather with a lost earring! The birth of the Fab 5 amazingly was due to a simple wardrobe malfunction; but maybe not quite on the scale of Janet Jackson's at the Super Bowl in 2004!

It was at the opening-night party of *Mary Poppins* in New York in 2006 when Steven Downing first met Diana Mackintosh. Anyone who has had the good fortune to meet Steven knows that he is someone who is not nervous of meeting people. However, when Cameron introduced Steven to Diana and suggested that he take her for a dance, he did step onto the floor with a certain amount of apprehension. After all, he was about to dance with Cameron's eighty-seven-year-old mother! He could see it now, one over-enthusiastic turn and she would be on the floor with a broken hip! Disaster!

However, stepping onto the dance floor with Diana Mackintosh was going to change his life and most definitely ours! Steven didn't need to worry about Diana as he could barely keep up! It was during the last dance that the 'wardrobe malfunction' took place. Suddenly Diana exclaimed to Steven that her earring had just fallen off. The mention of the word 'earring' made Steven conscious of something sharp sticking into his skin under his shirt. As soon as Steven indicated where her lost earring could be found, Diana, without hesitation, plunged her hand inside his shirt and retrieved it. Steven's astonishment soon turned into laughter, swiftly joined by Diana's – and a friendship for life had been forged.

It was in 2008 when Cameron offered the *Gardenia* to Diana, and she could take anyone she wanted for a cruise around Sicily. My name came up with, of course, Cindy, plus our close friend, Andy Macgillivray, who had been escorting Diana for many years to theatrical press nights. Cameron, knowing how well they got on, suggested Steven as the fifth shipmate companion to Diana. She thought that was an excellent idea.

So it was at Gatwick in the summer of 2008 that Cindy, Andy and I first met Steven. Even though we had been warned by Cameron to be ready for a 'fun' time, we were still slightly anxious about being in the close confines of a boat with someone we hadn't met before. We needn't have worried, because I think by the time we were sitting on the plane waiting to take off for our flight to Sicily, we were firm friends ready to party. The Fab 5 had been born!

In 2019 we celebrated our tenth trip and when I look back, every one has been a blast, with Diana always at the centre, laughing, saying and doing the most outrageous things. On our first trip to Greece, we flew to Rhodes on EasyJet from Gatwick. We were all so excited that Steven thought that it called for champagne. The flight attendant, seeing our high spirits, asked what we were celebrating. One of us, I can't remember who, informed her that Diana and Steven had just got married and that we were all celebrating together, by cruising together on a yacht around the Greek islands. This revelation received warm congratulations from the cabin crew and best wishes for a long and happy marriage!

Luckily, there is a record of all our trips, as Steven and Andy haven't let a gesture, a laugh or anything that needed to be recorded, go un-photographed. After every trip Andy, our editor-in-chief, edits the best photographs and passes them to Steven, so he can make the final selection for Diana's Fab 5 photo album. Diana now has quite a number of these albums that record for posterity our incredible holidays. Even though every trip is different, they all have two things in common; firstly, a rich vein of fun and laughter, and secondly, a theme, whether film or a period in time. Over ten trips we have had many! Luckily for us, each of the trips has been recorded, so Diana and all of us can reminisce on the fun times that we have all had. Do we have favourites? I think it is better to ask which ones we remember the most. A sailor's life can be pretty thirsty at sea!

'High Seas Society' was very glamorous, starring the charismatic Andy as Dexter Haven, Steven as Mike Connor, Cindy as Grace Kelly, myself as the outrageous Uncle Willie and of course Diana as Liz Imbrie. From the glamour of Rhode Island we have the feigned debauchery of 'Romans and Greeks'. Picture Diana dressed as a goddess whipping a Roman nobleman on all fours with an apple clenched between his teeth! We couldn't stop laughing; nor could Diana, and we have photos that prove it! If memory serves me well, was it during that same trip that Diana, as Her Majesty, formally bestowed on Steven Downing a peerage? No expense was spared, from the golden sword to his bejewelled crown. Since then, he has become a true English lord, owner of one square foot of English land, with a coat of arms to be proud of! We have also had the unforgettable

Casablanca, when the lovely *Gardenia* stewardesses helped us transform the vessel's salon into Rick's Café! The costumes were fantastic, with Andy performing an unbelievable impersonation of Sydney Greenstreet as Signor Ferrari!

The most recent voyages have produced *Anything Goes*, with Diana playing the part of the American Heiress, and Andy as the gun-toting 'Moonface' Martin. It was a mixture of glamour, farce and great Cole Porter music. But how could we forget last year and the celebration of our tenth Fab 5 cruise and Diana's 100th birthday. For one night it was 1942 in the Mess at Luqa, a military airbase in war-torn Malta. The dinner was a typical Maltese wartime feast, but done with such imagination by Jonny, the *Gardenia's* genius chef, that it could have been dinner at a Michelin star restaurant. With the help of *Gardenia's* Harriet and Sophie, we recreated the Mess, with wartime posters and ration cards. We even had models of Spitfires and Bf 109s dogfighting over the *Ark Royal*, which was the centrepiece of the dining table. At each place setting was a place mat with a picture of five handsome and beautiful pilots in their fighters, all looking the spitting images of the Fab 5! The music was all wartime favourites, so it wasn't long before Diana showed us how the jitterbug should be done! If there was a single moment which had us all rolling around the table, it was at the end of dessert. Steven casually asked Diana what she thought of Jonny's pudding. Without a second's thought she replied, 'I loved his chocolate covered balls!' There was a moment's silence before we couldn't contain ourselves and we burst out in hysterical laughter! And then she added, 'They were really tasty.' The glint in her eye said it all – she was 'just being naughty', as Steven would often say! And she had yet to get stuck into her favourite tipple of Baileys! Needless to say, it was the quote of the night, if not the trip.

Our fun-filled days have never been restricted to just the *Gardenia*. They spilled out into the sea. How many ninety-year-olds like being towed at speed in a doughnut, purposefully careering into the companion ring like she was at the dodgems or jumping the speedboat's wake at 20 plus knots! Then there are the themed beach parties usually organised by Steven. It was a time when we relax with the crew and encourage them to join in the fun and the dressing up. Anything to do with the South Seas or the Caribbean has always been a very popular theme, mainly because it usually means 'it's cocktail time!!' However, there was one time when things didn't quite go to plan. The theme was *South Pacific* and we were in Mallorca. Although we couldn't have a BBQ because of a very sensible ban on fires on beaches during the very hot summer, we could still have a party. Jonny created a wonderful buffet for our early evening beach party. There was however a slight delay before the *Gardenia* crew could go ashore to set things up. The delay was due to the fact that the beach we had chosen was in fact filled with nudists and we had to wait for them to withdraw! When satisfied that the beach was empty and that nothing could possibly embarrass the ladies, the crew set up the BBQ. On this occasion, I wanted to arrive on the beach last, so my shipmates went ahead. I should have mentioned earlier that on the Fab 5's cruises it is sort of expected that I will do the unexpected. Gusty Winds, Isabella Bustellini and Raquel Welch have all been unexpected additions to the trips and such appearances have always required a uniform! On this occasion, I had decided that I should play the part of Luther Billis from *South Pacific*. Luckily, the small amount of time for a quick change didn't matter as, after all, I wasn't trying to play a glamorous blonde or redhead, which required a little more preparation!

Unfortunately, while I was still on board, an incident happened just offshore of the beach. Apparently, whilst he was paddleboarding, one of the male nudists thought a return visit, close to the beach where he had spent most of the day, would be fun. In that he was attired to the same extent as when he left the beach earlier, in other words he didn't have a stitch on, made his sudden appearance, so close to the shore, not particularly welcomed by Diana and the others enjoying the early evening views. After some remonstration by the gentlemen on the beach, the intruder reluctantly started to paddle away. The last parting words emanating from one of the Fab 5 did encourage a degree of laughter from the beach, but a scowl from the person paddling away. It was suggested, in not the best Spanish, that in future he should consider wearing bathing shorts, because his wiener was more akin to a cocktail sausage than a British Banger! With no knowledge of this incident, I arrived on the beach to cackles of laughter and so our *South Pacific* soirée began. About an hour later, the magnificent Aaron, Captain of the *Gardenia* and a man you would trust with your life in a force 10 gale, spied two Guardia Civil approaching along the beach. With one slick movement of his hand, he managed to remove any vestige of *South Pacific* dress that he was wearing, that might take away from his authority as Captain of a very impressive motor yacht. I watched as Aaron discoursed with the two officers, and I noted a certain amount of arm gestures. Diana then joined the group and started to converse with them. One of Diana's memorable talents is that she speaks about six languages, some admittedly more fluently than others, but nevertheless all with great competence. Thinking that perhaps there was a problem, I walked up to the policemen and in my best Spanish said '*Bueanas noches.*' There was an expression of surprise on their faces as they looked at this not very tall man wearing a grass skirt, a coconut bra and a very cheap-looking blonde wig, with make-up that looked as though it had been applied by a blind person! Having used up my knowledge of Spanish learned at school, I explained in English that I was Diana's son and the party was for my mother, who had just turned ninety (a blatant lie since Diana had just turned ninety-eight!), and that we hadn't had a BBQ, but merely brought cooked food to the beach. What was the problem? They explained that there had been a complaint of a *rave* taking place on the beach. I replied that Mitzi Gaynor singing 'I'm Gonna Wash That Man Right Outa My Hair' could hardly be classified as a *rave*. The two Guardia Civil obviously realised that someone had exaggerated the situation. Satisfied that all was well, they wished us a very good evening and apologised for disturbing us. However, as they turned to walk away, the senior officer stopped, looked at Diana, then turned to me and then to Diana and said, 'I am very sorry about your son!'

Reflecting on who had called the Guardia Civil, we all reckoned it was the 'Cocktail Sausage' trying to get his own back!

What is so amazing is how Diana has always been ready to party, when invited, with the response of her usual phrase 'why not'. One year we were in Malta and Steven, a man who likes occasionally to play the tables, suggested that we all pop into the casino in Valletta. In we trooped, passports in hand to prove our identity. The man at the desk looked questioningly at Diana's passport and scratched his head in disbelief. It quite categorically stated date of birth 1919, but the lady before him was dressed up to the nines and looking like someone in her seventies. What was also causing him a problem was that the computer was rejecting the date 1919. Eventually, he accepted that the passport was genuine and that Diana could enter. He still shook his head in disbelief, that someone of Diana's age would want to go gambling at 10 o'clock at night, when she should at the very least be tucked up in bed drinking her cocoa! A very similar incident happened on our last trip leaving Croatia. The immigration officer was convinced that Diana's passport was a forgery and enquired if she had any other form of identity. Perhaps some travel insurance papers? I replied that, at 100 years old, it was not possible to get travel insurance; however, as her son, I could vouch for the passport and her age. After conferring with her colleague, she said Diana could pass. I thanked the officer and remarked that Diana must be the oldest traveller to have passed through today. She replied that no she wasn't, in fact she was the youngest, because they had to put down her date of birth as 2019, since their computer system wouldn't go back to 1919!

Not all the Fab 5's holidays have been on board the *Gardenia*. One year we went to Italy, to be more precise to Florence, Siena and San Gimignano. The Agriturismo Hotel, although set beautifully in a vineyard, was not exactly up to the standards of the *Gardenia*. There was not the great luxury of being waited on hand and foot, and we certainly missed Jonny's fantastic lunches and dinners. However, the fun and laughter was by no means diminished. Diana was in her element, remembering how she used to be a tour guide in the seventies and eighties and therefore knew everything about the history.

It was a wonderful trip seeing Siena and the square where the famous Palo is run. However, the highlight of the trip was going to Florence, where Diana was married to Ian in 1946. She wanted to visit the house where the service and reception took place – but where exactly was it?

'You have to go to Bellosguardo, that is where Villa Mercedes is located.'

Now, Villa Mercedes is the actual house where Ian and Diana were married. It belonged to some Italian count who gave Diana away. Remember, this is Italy just post-war, less than a year after it had ended, so none of Diana's family could travel from Malta. We had hired a car for this trip, so we thought it would be relatively easy to find a posh suburb like Bellosguardo. The first problem was that Andy insisted on using a map of Florence, and I was taken with the idea of using the car's satnav. At no point did they seem to agree on the best route. Added to this, it appeared that the city of Florence had decided to rip up all its roads and consequently there was chaos everywhere. Eventually, we did reach our destination, at least Bellosguardo. I asked Diana if she recognised anything? An innocent question, except that it had probably been seventy years since she had last been here! There were so many little roads. Suddenly Diana shouted, 'I think it's near here.' We could see a road that certainly looked promising, as on either side were some very nice houses. At the same time as the road started to descend, it became noticeably narrower and narrower. With an incline looking like 1:5 and towering stone banks barely 6 inches either side of the wing mirrors, I was getting exceedingly nervous. It was looking increasingly likely that I would have to reverse back a steep, winding, narrow road when, like a mirage, a small drive appeared to my left. Now with enough room to open one of the car's doors, I ordered Andy out to have a look down the road and see if it looked any wider A quick look revealed that unfortunately the road was equally narrow and also appeared to have a rather tight bend in it. The thought of the hired car being physically stuck in the road ahead made me decide to turn around. But easier said than done! Twenty minutes later, and with a rather strong smell from the overheating clutch, I had managed to point the car uphill and with a certain relief retrace our route. Suddenly, a road appeared on our right, which seemed to lead to a square. Since I was anxious to give the car, but most importantly its clutch, a rest, I took a chance. I saw a space in front of a very impressive building, so parked there. Was it divine intervention or just sheer luck? Who knows, but right in front of me were the words 'Villa Mercedes'! Nearby, a middle-aged man was loading his car in front of two open doors that revealed a large courtyard. I enquired, 'Is this the entrance to Villa Mercedes?' 'Yes,' came the answer.

I quickly explained the story of my mother being married in the house in 1946, as she was a good friend of the then owner.

'Oh yes he was a Count. My father bought it from him. You must come in, as he would want to meet you.' So here Diana was, seventy years after she had been married. We spent a couple of hours with them, as they showed us around the old house. We couldn't get into the church, as it was full of their belongings, but we did take a picture of Diana standing beside the door. I recognised the balcony that looked down onto the courtyard from one of the wedding photos taken all those years ago. It was a marvellous couple of hours and as a parting gift, they gave us some jars of marmalade made from the orange orchard that was in the garden. It was the perfect way to finish our holiday.

Would the Fab 5 have come about if it weren't for that lost earring in New York all those years ago? Who knows? All that I can say is that the Fab 5, like the legendary musketeers, believe in 'All for One and One for All'. Diana certainly brings out the best in us. And I think it's fair to say, we bring out the best in her. Who will forget her showing her legs as she pole-danced on the stern deck!

We are all looking forward to our next adventure!

Robert Mackintosh: Diana may have reached the big 100, but she is certainly 100 per cent on the ball. No Michael, calm down! So it will not be a surprise to any of us that at the point, just before the life of this extraordinary woman goes to press, she will be the ruthless editor of her own truth – as she would like it read. The following few anecdotes, if they have passed her scrutiny, might help the balance of the often-pointed finger towards Dad, for the many misdemeanours in their life together.

Yes, Dad drank a great deal and smoked – both of which he did with the utmost pleasure. But then I have many distinct memories of our mother also smoking, probably more as an affectation; but she wasn't a teetotaller either. She certainly joined in the jollities when they went out to their parties. I remember I was about fourteen or fifteen when we joined their great buddies Tessa, Mac, Ray and Bea for a trip on Mac's sailing boat – an old tub of a thing moored in the Hamble river near Southampton. It was so bleak down below, almost scary. It made the *Mary Celeste* seem like a P&O cruise ship. I loved boats and was soon given instructions on the compass navigation for our trip ahead (as the newly appointed youthful 'acting' Captain), as we were to make for a party hosted by David Milford

Haven on the Isle of Wight. My prime duties on this trip seemed to revolve around the opening of wine bottles. We got there somehow, with a mixture of singing, Dad playing the trumpet against the wind and a volley of orders given by an aggressive and diminutive ex-rear-something officer, Mac. Finally, we anchored just offshore. I took them all over to the club in the little dinghy, which rocked scarily from their on-board exuberance. I sort of lurked about through the evening, popping my head into the club, where a *very* jolly time was being had by all, including my mother in full flirting flight – with Milford Haven's arm casually draped around her shoulders.

At about midnight, I shot some anxious glances towards my mother, who was certainly doing her bit in the partying stakes. When I finally managed to get them all out together, they were oblivious of the journey ahead. I don't know whether it was the extra weight of the drink that made the dinghy sit lower in the water, but I was very nervous as I set off across the quite choppy Solent towards the boat. It was very dark, with a lot of water slapping over the side of the boat – the inside! Diana was certainly no teetotaller that night. They climbed into their hammocks below decks and the snoring began. And that definitely included her. The next morning was a quiet affair. Only the sounds of Bloody Marys being poured into their tin cups. Dad got off any 'third degree' that day, and rightly so.

'Aunt' Bea (often sailing companion to Ray Skip) would come to our house for the occasional weekend. Quite a glamorous woman, I thought. She was a model, I found out, and lived and looked the part. She drove a convertible white Ford Consul, with red leather upholstery. Headscarf and left arm across the front bench seat – straight out of a fifties movie. She was great fun and we got on well together. I was in my mid-teens and she was quite a young boy's fantasy. But, whilst she did get on very well with my mother and they were good buddies at many of the parties they went to, Dad particularly enjoyed her company because she was, underneath the glamour, a good solid Irish drinker. At dinner, they would always have plenty of wine, including my mother, but then another bottle would be opened, just before the end of the meal. Diana knew this meant for a serious night of drinking and that Ian and Bea would leave her well behind. In fact, Bea left them both behind. She had an Irish degree in the art of alcohol.

To be fair, in her heart, our mother probably felt that one way to try to deal with Dad was to join him in some of his social activities, rather than criticise them. Unfortunately, he had mastered it to the degree that very few could have ever kept up. So she had no choice but to give in and try to hide the keys to the various cupboards for as long as possible. It's funny that the end result of their years of raising us and passing on their personal mantra of life is that none of us smoke and our drinking habits are healthy enough, but not to excess. But the code that Dad found hard not to live by was that corks are for taking out, not putting back. This was probably the biggest dilemma that ran through their fifty years together.

I am sure she did enjoy herself at the many parties, dinner outings and clubs they frequented in their early life together. She had done much the same as a teenager and young woman in Malta. But her strength of character, which throughout her lifetime has never been hidden, would not allow her to go too far in anything. In Dad's case, he just loved going too far all his life – and did so whenever he could get away with it.

And then there's his get-out clause, which they both signed up to – 'for better or worse…'. Take your pick! In the end though, they each had a great helping of both – as did us boys.

Cameron Mackintosh: As Diana approached her centennial, we had some DNA done as part of a family tree study. With Diana there is a big chunk of her that comes from Sweden – I am sure she was a Viking; her mother was northern Italy. There is also quite a lot of Celt in there; it seems I have a far greater proportion of Mediterranean, and there's not a huge amount of Scot in me, though I do wear the kilt well. My father was more Welsh than Scottish. Diana is much more European, Spanish, Italian, Maltese. I think, as always, it is the genetics of mongrelism that gives you the toughness. But I don't think she would like to know that she was a mongrel. That's something they would have eaten during the war!

Quite late in life she took up painting. There are one or two of her paintings that I have particularly liked. She did do one of the Scottish house. I didn't want it. I didn't think it was her best. She never let me forget it: 'People would pay me a fortune for this. Why don't you want it?' I've got probably about forty of her paintings. All of which I love and treasure, but there were one or two I just didn't think were up to snuff. That's what she remembers. The ones I didn't take. 'The others are fighting over it, why don't you want it?' I took her to the David Hockney exhibition a few years ago, when he had huge paintings, massive ones on show. She really wanted to go. She went in to see it and said: 'I paint like that. I do a lot of things like that.'

She didn't take any notice of the Hockneys at all. She just used it as an excuse to bring everyone into her conversation about how well she painted. 'Everyone wants to see them. Everyone wants to buy my paintings. They offered me £50! I don't know why I didn't do this earlier!' She started at eighty. Some of them are really very good, and she has put them in the little house in Somerset. A recent one has appeared which she has signed. But it's a copy of a famous painting! She hand-paints her own version of a famous picture, which is fair enough, but some are photocopies of the original to which she then adds her signature at the bottom. It's not worth making a fuss with her; but when visitors come by (Stephen Sondheim quite recently), she shows them off as her recent paintings! Despite some furtive looks, it does keep her mind going. That's the worst thing about getting old. You have less people to share your time with, so you become inventive.

It's like this house in Somerset. Michael and I have been here for more than twenty-four years now and, hopefully, I'll be here another twenty years; maybe we'll make fifty years, if I follow my mother's example. It's timing. In some of the farm buildings which we acquired some years back, I store many of the sets and costumes from my productions. I have a full-time historian to keep them in order and catalogued. Many of my shows appeal to new generations of audiences and hopefully for the next twenty years these productions are going to have another life.

I think my mother has had the great fortune to have had several lives, and I'm so grateful I was able to enable her to do so much after our father died. But she can drive us all up the walls, although we're all laughing as we climb them. Her health is truly remarkable and more important than that, her spirit. The only real problem she has now is the old hearing apparatus is not quite what it should be. Of course, there are the usual aids to combat that, as we are aware that important information seems to remain in the distance, but what often stands in the way of the obvious solution is the degree of vanity that exists. In Diana's case it is no small amount. Nothing must be seen to even suggest that she hasn't perfect pitch, so to speak. Finally, through much delving into the problem via our friend Paul (who works with deaf musicians), a solution became available through one of the smallest hearing aids I have ever seen. The main problem is that it needs tiny batteries, which, as well as being very fiddly, have a life of only two to three days. Sometimes that appears longer than we can cope! Of course, when the batteries are dead, it is as though her ears were completely stuffed with a plastic plug. No sound. But as she is a person who never throws anything away, the dud batteries often find their way back into the box, to add to the confusion. Whilst Diana is by no means colour blind, sometimes the red hearing aid does not always find its way into the right ear and so on. And how do you manage to flush one down the loo?! So there are days of constant smiling at what anyone says, or moments, in the middle of a deep discussion at table with a neighbour, when she simply cuts through with a totally different statement or observation. But we also think that she uses it partly as a weapon to get the conversation back to her, because she manages to pick up every nuance if it's about her.

We're trying to get an implant that you change every three months, which would change her life. That's the thing we would love to get done, so she can enjoy her remaining years – with sound!

But if that's our only gripe, then I think we are all extremely lucky, for the joy she brings into this world. When my father was alive, I bought them a house, because I wanted them to use the money they had in their old house, as well as the support I continued to give them to enjoy themselves. Probably about twenty years ago she started talking about giving things to us, to the children, the nephews and nieces, and wanting to help, making sure that everyone else in the family was alright. They would say: 'I don't want anything.'

I told her: 'And I don't need anything, as you know very well.'

She said: 'You don't understand. I have to treat you all equally. What you do with it is another matter.'

That is one of the reasons, I think, that we have stuck together as a family so well. My mother and father treated us all the same, however successful or not that we were at any particular time in our lives.

She has her little house on the estate. She said to me: 'You know I have a nice house on the estate?'

'Yes, Ma, I do know, I built it for you.'

'Oh, it's a nice house in the country, not the estate.'

On the basis that all of us are only around for a visit, she has made the most of her time. She has certainly taught us to do the same; that's her legacy. I'm certainly doing my best to leave things in good order. Wealth is only relative to what you do or achieve with it. All parameters, like conclusions, are inconclusive. For a start, I'm only worth a billion or so (they say) if I want to sell all my shows and theatres, which I don't propose to do. But I've known sufficiently hard times not to be affected by wealth. I'm a war baby – I was brought up with rationing and my parents always had to struggle. There was a newspaper article that described me as 'the man with the Midas touch'. Then someone said to me, 'Cameron, it's a very nice article, but just remember one thing: Midas choked on the golden apple.' I'm not afraid I'll do that – and anyway, if I do, I'll deserve it.

I survived because I never took on big responsibilities in my private life. In the early days I lived on two or three pounds a week and learned to cook – and I'm a good cook – because I had to. Even when I went on holiday, I stayed in other people's houses. Now I enjoy using some of my success to enjoy time with friends and family on holiday. But, and I'm sure I inherited this from my mother, if I'm taking a short flight to Scotland or the Continent, I travel economy. I go on EasyJet all the time and I've got my travel pass for the Underground, which I use whenever I'm dashing between different rehearsal rooms.

I probably couldn't tell you my week's grocery bill, but I use public transport for two reasons. It's often the most practical way to get around London and it's important for me to know what it means to someone to fork out £50 or £60 for one of my shows. I realise that the people who've helped make my fortune are those who have to budget carefully and who believe their hard-earned money will be well spent at any of my shows. I know this sounds silly, but I've never been interested in money other than having enough to enjoy myself. Obviously, I don't have to worry about balancing the grocery bill these days – but I did, and learned how to do that from her. She brought us up to value everything and everyone. My mother is probably my biggest critic and influence to this day.

Cameron, Robert, Nicky and Friends
April 2020